DATE DUE

BRODART, CO.   Cat. No. 23-221-003

RACE COURSE

RACE COURSE

AGAINST WHITE SUPREMACY

Bill Ayers
Bernardine Dohrn

Third World Press
Chicago

Third World Press
Publishers since 1967
Chicago

First Edition
Printed in the United States of America

Front Cover Image by Stephen Alcorn
Photograph of Authors by Mary Ellen Mark

Library of Congress Cataloging-in-Publication Data

Ayers, William, 1944–
Race course against white supremacy/Bill Ayers, Bernardine Dohrn. — 1st ed.
p. cm.
ISBN 0-88378-310-x (cloth: alk. paper)
ISBN 0-88378-291-x (paper: alk. paper)
1. Racism—United States. 2. Whites—United States—Attitudes. 3. United States—Race relations. 4. White supremacy movements—United States. I. Dohrn, Bernardine. II. Title.
E184.A1A94 2008
305.809'073—dc22
2008004391

Ayers, Bill
Dohrn, Bernardine

ISBN-13 978-0-88378-310-8 (cloth)
ISBN-13 978-0-88378-291-0 (paper)

12 11 10 09   6 5 4 3 2 1

*To the two baby
women
—the granddaughters—
who
keep us futuring*

...the white man. He's an enemy to all of us. I know some of you think that some of them aren't enemies. Time will tell.

—Malcolm X

One wishes that Americans, white Americans, would read, for their own sakes, this record and stop defending themselves against it. Only then will they be able to change their lives.

—James Baldwin

CONTENTS

PUBLISHER'S STATEMENT

Early in 2007 my wife, Dr. Safisha Madhubuti (Carol D. Lee), I, Dr. Bill Ayers and Bernardine Dohrn sat down for dinner in their home on the South side of Chicago. We had known of each others' work and unique contributions for decades but because of our cultural doubts, histories and schedules never took time to break bread together. This dinner confirmed our friendship and led to the book that you are reading.

I am primarily a poet and educator. I founded Third World Press in 1967 in the middle of the political, social and cultural upheaval that will forever define that time. Out of the hundreds of books we've published this is my first (and hopefully last) statement justifying one of our books. Just a little background, my wife is one of the leading scholars/activist/educators in the world. She has served on the faculty at Northwestern School of Education and Social Policy for over seventeen years. Bill Ayers is the Distinguished Professor in the College of Education at the University of Illinois at Chicago and has published over fifteen books and is highly respected in his field as an educator, activist and scholar. Bernardine Dohrn is an Adjunct Professor of Law at Northwestern University School of Law, and is respected internationally for her legal mind and her work worldwide on behalf of the left-out, pushed-out and under-served populations. My wife and I founded four schools in Chicago – a pre-school (private), two elementary schools and a high school (all charter). Bill, Bernadine, Safisha and I remain political and cultural activist; this is partially why we met to eat, talk and design ways in which we could improve upon our relationship and work more effectively for our respective communities and the country. We all came of age in the deadly, volatile, dangerous, misrepresented and misunderstood sixties and seventies. We all cut our young teeth on the streets of this nation.

We were all motivated by injustice at all levels of human activity where the Black and women Human Rights struggles and the Viet Nam War were the centerpieces. My wife and I are products of deep poverty, both educated in the apartheid schools of urban America. As a result of exhaustive self and formal study, political/cultural work and struggle, and familyhood, we excelled and escaped victimhood and the common end-point of America's seasoning – niggerlization, in effect, functioning 24/7 as a self hating idiot unaware of and disbelieving in logic, facts and accurate history.

PUBLISHER'S STATEMENT

In the early 1970s, my wife and I worked primarily, if not exclusively, in the Black community. The 1980s, more specifically, the campaign and election of Chicago's Mayor Harold Washington, placed us in continuous contact with activists of all cultures. And it was during this period that we engaged on the political and educational front with Bill and Bernardine.

Bill and Bernardine's journey is what this book is about. However, it must be clearly understood that we are all products of this country's history. We cannot escape it. Yet this history – especially over the last fifty years, has largely at the popular culture level been distorted, revised and dumbed down creating among a very large portion of the nation a people with collective amnesia. We know that ideas have consequences and that the Republicans, most certainly from Ronald Reagan on, have moved efficiently and effectively in controlling the means in which ideas are disseminated: newspapers, magazines, film, television, radio, education (at all levels), books and journal publishing, and the many conferences, retreats and gatherings at universities, colleges, think-tanks and institutions of worship in the country (see Tentacles of Rage: The Republican Propaganda Mill, A Brief History by Lewis H. Lapham in the September, 2004 issue of Harpers Magazine).

The liberating work of young people of the 1960s and 1970s has, for the most part especially in popular culture been reduced by media to negative hippie sound bites, "riotous" images of the 1968 Democratic Convention in Chicago, angry pronouncements of Black Nationalist, The Black Panthers with weapons at the ready, women burning bras and anti-war protesters destroying draft cards. The enlightening statements and actions of Malcolm X, Martin Luther King Jr., Fannie Lou Hamer, Rosa Parks and others are quoted and reported out of context and used to discredit them and progressive movements. Corporate media, as it is today, has not been fair or "objective" to our generation. However, it must be stated in no uncertain language that our actions – that is, the political, social and cultural work of tens of millions of young people of that generation changed America and the world for the better.

That evening in Hyde Park we dug deep into our collective soul and agreed that our stories had not been fully told. We understood that racism, i.e., white world supremacy is not only alive and well but is a growth industry that continues to devalue, make small of, race bait, under-mind, negate, and often imprison (COINTELPRO*) or kill (Emmett Till and others) those who actively oppose it and offer liberating alternatives (see Charles W. Mills The Racial Contract for an excellent analysis of this political reality). White Supremacy as "state terrorism" is quite evident at a world level in the wars our country chooses to fight from Viet Nam to Iraq and the economic policy practiced worldwide. The sub-prime debacle is the canary in the coal shaft. The death of the canary and the escalated war against workers will emerge after the 2008 elections when hedge funds, credit default swaps and derivatives finally expose the hidden tipping points beyond the sweet music of lies told to Congress and the American people by the so-called "best and brightest" led by their arrogant lying leader, Alan Greenspan.

Our work, the work of Ayers and Dohrn and tens of millions of others made it possible for Hillary Clinton and Barack Obama to run for the Presidency. And President Obama's successful campaign started on the streets of Chicago. This is not at all to minimize the critical influence of his parents, grandparents, extended family, international travels and a first-class education at the best universities in the country. However, it is imperative to note that the generation that preceded his must not be "whited-out" as if the lives lost and destroyed on the streets of America or the fields of Viet Nam and elsewhere had no positive influence or impact on today's political, economic, social and cultural realities. No greater lie could be told or believed.

Race Course was completed and scheduled to be published in April of 2008. We made a collective decision to delay publication until after the election. We did not want this book crushed or lost in the disinformation frenzy that characterized so much of this campaign. That this was the correct decision is confirmed by the tens of thousands of times that the McCain/Palin campaign attempted to join at the hip Obama and the "terrorist" Bill Ayers. We need not replay these cowardly acts by the "straight talk" McCain, the right-wing sludge machine and corporate media. Clearly, as incorrectly reported, Race Course was not conceived, written, or published to benefit or profit from the possible presidency of Barack Obama. In fact, the profits from the sales of Race Course will be donated to help stop the death penalty and aid in providing literacy programs and activities among incarcerated men and women in the nation's prisons.

Robo-call this to a country that has lost over 125,000 jobs from Wall Street, millions of jobs from Main Street, the bankruptcy of investment houses, banks and millions of common folks. As the automobile, airline, building and construction industries, insurance companies, retail and more remind us of the "third world countries" that the right so righteously mocks and criticizes, we finally see the lies in the small print in the contracts, as the fried chickens are really coming home to roost. Yet, this is only the beginning of our collective misery: the deflation of our industrial capacity and the looming credit card meltdown as major U.S. cities and states seek critical aid from Washington.

I commend Dr. Ayers and Attorney Dohrn for this brave and revealing book. As you read this I am sure you would agree that children and young people remain at the center of their enlarged hearts. Their unending challenge is against intellectual apathy, the ill-defined and ever forecasted fear, corruption and greed endemic to corporate America, debilitating poverty, ignorance and negative information passing as fact.

Race Course in its unique way contributes to highlighting a corporate consumer culture fueled by cheap products from the sweat shops of the world, where people are exploited to keep the myth of "free market international capitalism" alive. Race Course is the finely written, detailed, introspective and moving memoir of two the nation's most committed patriots. With the aid of their biological and cultural families, brothers and sisters in the movement, they continue to fight in the tradition of John Brown and Frederick Douglass to make this world a more livable and loveable place for all. As Barack Obama states, "This is our time our defining moment." This historical document clarifies a brief passage that, indeed, aided in making the election of the first Black president possible.

Haki R. Madhubuti, poet
Founder and Publisher of Third World Press
University Distinguished Professor and
Director of the MFA Program in Creative Writing at

Chicago State University

INTRODUCTION

Before our children were born, before that dizzying and redefining experience opened a new world of learning and changed our lives forever, Malcolm X famously noted that while Black people had an abundance of Washingtons and Jeffersons and Lincolns in their families, white people didn't seem inclined to call their kids Nat Turner or Cinque or Frederick Douglass or Harriet Tubman. Why? he asked rhetorically and pointedly. Why the discrepancy and why the color line—even here?

Later, when we decided to have children, we thought about Malcolm's question, and we chose to take it as a challenge. By then we were veterans of anti-war campaigns and the Black Freedom Movement, and we'd fought on the side of the Student Nonviolent Coordinating Committee and the Black Panther Party. We'd come to think of racism as the defining sickness in the country's soul, white supremacy and the myth of white superiority as the theoretical and practical evil we were born into, born to resist. We'd come to think of ourselves, then, as aspiring "race traitors" or, as someone called us disparagingly, "Uncle Toms of the white race." We took it as a compliment.

We named our first-born Zayd Osceola, both to remember Zayd Shakur, a Panther killed by the police, and to raise up the name of Osceola, a Seminole leader who never surrendered to the U.S. policy of relocation and extermination of Native peoples. Next came Malik Cochise, named in honor of Malcolm himself as well as a renowned indigenous American, the great Apache guerrilla fighter, Cochise. Our third child, Chesa Jackson, adopted when he was fourteen months old, came to us with his name already attached, but he fit right in—his first name a Swahili word for dancing feet, his second taken from George Jackson, the Soledad Brother murdered by guards at San Quentin prison. Zayd Osceola, Malik Cochise, Chesa Jackson—to love and to remember, to honor and, in a modest way, to cross the color line.

Our children were born as outlaws and grew up on stories of freedom fighters: We see in Zayd's baby album his changing table adorned with postcards of Ho Chi Minh and a framed photo of Zayd Shakur; above Malik's bed stands Malcolm X as well as Nelson Mandela and Walter Sisulu, revolutionaries long imprisoned on Robben Island; Chesa's T-shirt from his kindergarten portrait is a silk-screen of Rosa Parks in dignified resistance. They had their youthful list of heroes: Robin Hood, Amilcar Cabral, Stuart Little, Jackie Robinson, Che Guevara, Harriet Tubman, Peter Rabbit. They liked outlaws.

INTRODUCTION

Zayd is a playwright and papa now, Malik a bilingual math and science teacher and athletic coach, and Chesa a writer and activist and law student focused on justice and liberation in Latin America. Like every family, we have our special stories, our shared experiences and common memory, our language, family myths, and unique family lore.

The culture in our household was shot through from the start with politics and activism and resistance—the kids grew up on picket lines and in demonstrations, our little apartment abuzz with visitors, meetings, organizing plans, along with the more mundane daily dialogue. Because we never had a TV, conversation was the dominant current in the room. Our kids' earliest words included "dog" and "ball" and "moon," of course, but also "No Nukes" and "Fight Racism." Even without a literal understanding of every detail or cause, there was a pervasive sense that we, all five of us, stood somehow for "peace" and "justice"—"against racism"—and for "fairness." Chesa would often say, "That's not fair," in the same indignant tone whether referring to the smallest injustice in his daycare center—someone failing to take turns, perhaps—or to some, monstrous outrage: a police murder of a child on the streets of Brooklyn, the war in El Salvador. The kids knew that we were trying to live our lives as fully as possible, and sometimes that meant living them in public and concrete opposition. We wanted them to experience in the details of each day a kind of loving, child-friendly, and happy resistance.

One day, when Zayd was a toddler, we emerged from his swim class at the Y and were swept accidentally into a militant feminist march surging toward Times Square to protest pornography and the commodification of women's bodies. Without a thought we impulsively joined in and swirled along, chanting for a few blocks—NO MORE PORN! NO MORE PORN!—and then dropped out when Zayd saw a pizza sign and realized he was hungry. As we settled into our booth, Zayd asked lightly, "That was great—why were we saying, 'No More Corn'?"

And some years later driving outside the city, all of us together, the road becoming long and boring, Malik, catching a fragment of family lore from some random place in his memory, said, "Poppy, tell us about the time you burned your credit card." "Whoa, Malik, slow down—Pops had indeed burned his *draft* card, it's true, several times," but, "we joked, he's not that radical."

We were leaders of the Weather Underground on the run from the FBI in those years—for over a decade, in fact—and our first two children were born in walk-up flats in anonymous parts of town with the help of midwives. Chesa, the child of friends and comrades, joined us when his mother and father were arrested alongside members of the Black Liberation Army and sent to prison for an armed bank robbery that went wrong. Each of our kids started life with an invented identity—of course, every identity is invented and then reinvented, but each of them was actually outfitted with a false birth certificate and an assumed name along with the standard-issue Oshkosh B'Gosh overalls and tie-dyed T-shirts. Born on the run.

***

This book is the result of a provocation and an invitation. Our neighbor, the poet Haki Madhubuti, said to us over dinner one evening, "As people who've worried and wondered about racism most of your lives, you really ought to write it up and write it down." Write it up, write it down—that sounded almost perfect. Our imperfect understanding of racism and the structure of white supremacy, of oppression and exploitation, of resistance and liberation has been a roller-coaster affair, off-road and cross-country, a race course and demanding endurance. We've experienced moments of clarity as well as long patches of uncertainty, folly, and ignorance. We've encountered obstacles, made choices—not always good ones—and been knocked off course more than once. And we are, like most everyone else, entangled and beleaguered, filled with messy contradictions, powered by both selflessness and opportunism, wisdom and stupidity, courage and cowardice. Our teachers have been many and various, and the following pages are an interpretation of the path so far—an homage to some, a cautionary tale for others, an expression of hope. But the race isn't nearly done, the journey necessarily mid-course.

In part because Haki asked, we agreed at once. His poetry and essays have always been a part of our traveling bookshelves, and Third World Press is a forty-one-year-old treasure-trove of art and analysis by African American thinkers. The invitation enticed us to take a risky turn at co-writing—a certain challenge even to our sparkling and sturdy thirty-six year partnership and love affair. In these pages we alternate between writing as individuals and speaking in tandem, and this mirrors the way we've actually lived and the way we tend to think—together and apart, oneness and separateness. The word "we" has multiple meanings here—Bernardine and Bill, our family, citizens of the U.S., white people, people in the Movement, folks in a particular political formation—and we (Bill and Bernardine) try to keep it clear as we go along.

In the front line of our teachers today are young people, including our own children, and so we write here to a bright new wave of artists and activists and organizers and educators struggling toward consciousness and humanization. Their learning and growth has been different from our own, and they live in a more complex, globalizing world whose dynamic contours and shifting dimensions are sometimes incomprehensible to us. We rush to keep up, to comprehend knowing that our perspectives are necessarily partial and contingent and time-bound. We've always had elders who joined us in solidarity along the way, and now we try to live like them.

INTRODUCTION

We write in part to learn, to keep this discussion alive, a talk between the two of us as well as with others. As in any authentic dialogue, we speak with the hope of being heard, but we also listen with the possibility of being changed. Gaps, misinterpretations, lapses, unintentional hurt sometimes—it all necessarily goes with the dialogic territory. This book, then, is not a solid and completed thing. It provides a few hints perhaps, a catalog of our own aspirations and transgressions, our understandings and misunderstandings so far, but it needs a reader to make it whole. This is but a draft of a draft, incomplete notes from a conversation, an active but contingent race course so far.

We write to raise questions about how we live and what might be required of us all moving forward. The road is always twisty and tangled, and we intend to live and write into—not run away from—the contradictions. Race, class, and gender, for example—so interwoven, intertwined, and yet distinct—seem impossible to get right in one leaflet, one breath, or one lifetime. We acknowledge the clarity of the prison abolitionists and reparations organizers, the ethical actions of the anti-globalization and anti-war movements, the courage of the new immigrant/labor activists and women insistently rising up, the breakthroughs of environmental justice actors and of queer militants as critical to our own ability to grow and make change. Because we want to stand up for social justice and human emancipation—to oppose unnecessary suffering and undeserved pain—because the circumstances are urgent yet again, we feel a palpable pull to find one another, to fight through the walls that separate us, to nourish the points of overlap and convergence.

There will certainly be new claims to land and resources and new questions concerning the fair distribution of wealth, emerging movements for freedom and peace, new threats of genocide and ecocide, exploitation and human displacement, militarism and materialism. As always, the struggles and the resolutions will turn on our evolving understandings of justice and our capacity to stir ourselves to action. We seek, then—for ourselves and others—a fuller recognition of the humanity of all, a deeper commitment to human solidarity and planetary survival. This commitment will necessarily gesture toward radical transformations inside each one of us no less than in our relationships with one another and the wider world. None of us can be safe standing idly in the middle of a race course. We must all keep moving.

We write, finally, against a willful and disingenuous ignorance, to inflame the debate about white power and privilege, to note that the crimes in our national history have, at this late date, been neither adequately faced nor addressed, and to participate in a flash course about some of the ways in which every one of our current crises feeds on and intersects with racism. We write to name and oppose the entire edifice of white supremacy—the uniquely Made-in-America phenomenon as well as the beast gone global—a structure that has never been popularly analyzed, understood or widely debated or defeated and at last throttled and killed.

FREEDOM NOW!

Bill Ayers

I am invisible, understand, because people refuse to see me.
—Ralph Ellison

Riding an early morning bus in New York City with our son Zayd, bright-eyed and chirpy, five years old and just beginning to read, the bus packed with commuters, the mood a resigned grumpiness as we groan down the avenue toward school and work: "Poppy," Zayd says suddenly in his large outside voice, turning to me expectantly. "What's a kike?"

A sudden silence falls as dozens of eyes lift and, in my mind at least, begin to sizzle, laser-like, into my head. "What?"

"A kike. What's a kike?"

I freeze. "Where did you hear that word, Zayd?"

"I read it," he replies proudly. "See?" He points to a stab of red graffiti slashed across a rear window. "*I HATE KIKES*," it reads—all uppercase—and it's punctuated with a swastika. He'd sounded it out.

"A kike—a kike—"

I don't want to be here, don't want to be called upon to explain this part of our world to him, not yet, but here I am. Miraculously, I imagine the crowd receding, until there is only me and Zayd, his basic trust intact, his childish hope undiminished, and his deeply human sense-making engine firing on all cylinders. I'm his guardian and his guide at this point—I have to respond.

"Kike," I begin in as calm a voice as I can muster, "is a word full of hatred. It's a word full of violence, a word used by people who want to hurt Jews, like hateful words meant to hurt Black people." I'm into it now. "It's a lying word, because it says that some people are more human than others, that some groups are superior to others, that some are less than human. People who are filled up with hate might call you a 'kike.' It's the kind of word we should never use, the kind of word we always object to and oppose."

A little too didactic, for sure, too sermonizing, but I'm relieved to have been able to spit it out at all. Zayd's face never loses its open and intent concentration. "OK," he replies simply. "What are you going to do about it?"

"Damn!" I feel like shouting. "Haven't I done enough?" But I dutifully dig for a magic marker in my backpack and obliterate the stain.

"OK," he says again simply.

A child's question: Why is that man sleeping in the street? Why is that woman bleeding? Why is he acting that way? The ground shifts and we adults are forced (or invited) to make sense again, to dig deeper, to discover something truer, and more complex. Children's questions can be disruptive and disquieting, which may explain the knee-jerk answers we hear ourselves repeating: I'll tell you later, or When you're older, or When I have more time. Don't ask. Don't look. Don't stare.

Our avoidance reveals our incomprehension, our personal dogmas and our easy beliefs, our own uninterrogated and insistent common sense. And it brings us face to face with our own fears—do we really want to open every door, to doubt every truth, to wonder again at every mystery? It's a lot easier to simply live within the walls of our own self-constructed blindness: "I'll tell you later"—the door slams shut and we sigh with relief within the illusion of safety.

What is racism? What is race? Prejudice? A scapegoat? Genocide? An ethnic group? One childish question leaps to another and another, and each asks us to reconsider the world, to confront our own gaps and ignorances, to rethink our taken-for-granteds. If we're strong enough, or just lucky, we push tentatively through the cotton wool of our shackled consciousness, the pseudo-language of clichés and slogans, and we take the question as a guide and a conversation.

If we think of children's questions in this way, they may become occasions to notice the obstacles blocking our own paths, and if the questioning child tugs hard enough, we may even be stirred to action. I might have left the gruesome graffiti alone (as did hundreds of fellow travelers) had I not been prodded by my fresh-faced five-year-old who, without any drama or theatrics, simply assumed that I could be counted on to explain the world to him and then do the right thing.

What is racism?

Each of us could write a book. Mine begins with a privileged white child's question: "Why is Celeste brown?" Celeste cleaned our house, and I'd just noticed something: color. "Shush," mother scolded. "We don't talk that way." Why was this childish observation, of all the things we could choose to talk about, unspeakable?

I was raised on the idea that every person was worthy of empathy, each to be respected, none superior to any other. This lesson was a steady mantra throughout my childhood:

Both my mom and the Declaration of Independence heralded the self-evident truth of equality among. As I grew, this explicit, articulated value seemed more and more at odds with the world as it was, and it presented itself as a contradiction: Do I say that the values my parents taught me were no more than fairy tales and hypocritical mind-candy offered to a credulous child? Do I note that the foundational documents of U.S. history include and embrace a cruel joke? Or do I try to enact and live by those values and thereby put myself in escalating conflict with my family, my community, my church, and my country?

I was also taught to stand up for what I believed, but again the contradiction: If what I believed was pretty much what everyone else believed, no standing up was needed; if my beliefs ran against the grain, on the other hand, no one really wanted me to stand up. Clearly, the road of life would be bumpy.

There was, years later, another moment of muteness when our three kids came home from junior high school one day with a story of a fistfight in the cafeteria. "Paul called Tony a 'po**ck,' and then Tony called Paul a 'ni**er,'" Zayd reported, "and then they really got into it." After describing the fight and noting that both boys were suspended from school, our kids wanted to know, "Which is worse, 'po**ck' or 'ni**er'?"

They had studied the Indian wars, the enslavement of Africans, and the Holocaust in Europe, and so we had a lengthy, engaged talk about the historical weight of words, the ways in which meaning can link to power and control, why calling a Jew a name in Germany, for example, might resonate with unique intensity and power. This led to an involved discussion of both the cooptation and sometimes the internalization of hateful language. Our friend Pat can call herself a dyke—but you better not.

When we went to school the next day, delighted to urge a broader discussion so that all the kids could benefit from reflection on these difficult and complex issues—issues already abuzz in the informal curriculum of the cafeteria—we were told that that talk would be troublesome. "We don't have a race problem here," the principal assured us, "and this might stir something up. Besides," she continued, playing to other fears, "math exams are coming up." A teachable moment discarded and lost. And in that screaming silence a lens of distorted images, fears, misunderstandings, and cool calculatedness slips neatly into place. We are, each of us, born into race and place, and all the early lessons are about knowing something of each. But we are—I was—instructed in speechlessness.

Growing up in our constructed racialized surroundings, a cultural context that so few of us white people can even acknowledge, means that we draw a common-sense experience of race into ourselves with every breath, that we drink it in, beginning with our mother's milk. A society founded on the attempted genocide of the original indigenous people, built on the labor of African slaves, Latino serfs and Asian and white indentured servants, made fabulously wealthy through conquest and exploitation, manipulation and mystification, a society like this one, is a society built on a solid—and shaking—foundation of racial subjugation. But we can never really understand what we can't name, and we can't ever solve what we can't discuss. And race remains unspeakable: "We don't talk that way."

***

In the mid-1960s, I became an organizer for the East Side Community Union in the Lakeview section of Cleveland, Ohio. The Community Union was an extension of the Southern Civil Rights Movement into the North—a grass-roots effort to organize disenfranchised and marginalized citizens of the ghetto into a powerful force capable of effectively fighting for their own needs and aspirations. I was drawn to the work as a self-imposed exile from what I found mind-numbing and soul-stunting in the prison of my privilege; I came in search of my own humanity as much as to be of use. Our creed and our theory was that legitimate and just social change would necessarily be led by those who had been pushed down and locked out, that struggling in the interest of the most oppressed people in society held the key to fundamental transformations—internal and personal as well as social and collective—that would ultimately benefit everyone. We saw our political and educational work as ethical work—organizing as righteousness. Our first job was to make ourselves part of our new community, to listen hard to what people told us, to be respectful neighbors. I was twenty years old.

As Alex Witherspoon pushed his dog-eared paperback copy of *Invisible Man* across the table toward me, he lowered his voice: "Here's a present from me to you," he said. "The whole damned American story in a nutshell." The presentation felt oddly formal, uncharacteristically solemn, some kind of street-level awards ceremony. Thanks, I said, reaching out and taking his hand a bit awkwardly.

Alex and I had been cooking our meals together for months by then, haunting the barbecue joints and local dives together, walking the streets of Cleveland's east side, rapping to the people and knocking on doors in order to "build an interracial movement of the poor." We were mapping the need, but we were also exploring the hope. "Let the people decide," we said, a mantra boiled down from our faith in participatory democracy. Were we friends? We were thrust together by our work, our intimacy almost entirely circumstantial, the stuff of shared risk and common experience. We sang together at community gatherings and prayed together at rallies. We picketed and demonstrated and inevitably, I suppose, found ourselves talking about our hopes and our fears, embraced by the quiet and the dark of night.

Alex was an avid reader—a small pile of books grew and morphed and shrunk like a living thing near his bed, and his back pocket always bulged with a read-in-progress. He'd suggested books to me before, but this exchange, hand to hand, was a first. Alex cared about me enough to want to teach me something—about America to be sure, but possibly about himself as well. The whole American story, he'd said. To me *Invisible Man* was a gesture of friendship.

Within a couple of years the East Side Community Union had become a vital part of the neighborhood. There was a large, dynamic welfare rights project affiliated with an emerging national organization; a housing and rent strike committee organized building by building, demanding fair rents and reasonable upkeep and repairs; a community health project led by two young doctors; a store-front office where people dropped in for coffee and conversation; and a preschool operated out of a church basement. All of these projects were built on the energy and intelligence of the people of Lakeview—energy, people, and intelligence that the larger society had ignored and beaten down.

Alex moved along the street with long, purposeful strides—tall, rail-thin, prominent Afro perched atop a deeply lined face; I, a kind of fresh-faced, white sidekick, wide-eyed and credulous, hurried to keep up. He was thirty-three-years old, a veteran of the Movement in the South with a proud record of arrests from the important campaigns; I was twenty and a college dropout, recently arrived from Ann Arbor intent on participating in the freedom struggle. We shared an apartment with other community organizers, all of us young, idealistic, and filled with the spirit of the Civil Rights Movement in full eruption—we took miracles to be our birthright. Justice was in reach, we imagined, and racism would soon be swept away—a revolution in consciousness, and then a revolution in fact, was just beyond the horizon. We felt blessed—sanctified— to be living in this time, of all times, to be present at the awakening: That year I became a volunteer in the army that would take on the American monster, end the American nightmare, and at long last heal the deep, deep American wound.

We were seeding then what we thought could blossom into a "beloved community," because, as Alex said again and again, "The ghetto's got the richest soil in America to grow a world of peace and freedom." He'd laugh his deep, sly laugh, his eyes twinkling, and he'd take a hard pull on his Camel. "America's stark-staring mad," he said, "and her best hope is right here in this clarifying wreckage. We're going to make some American magic."

The magic began with Alex's wild, unruly way of thinking—*clarifying* wreckage, he'd said—a mind-blowing twist on what had been a one-dimensional gray assumption of need and need alone. In our apartments and in our project houses we shared everything—food and clothes, resources and dreams—and the magic grew. For us the personal was political and the political personal—we ached to live in a world that could be, but was not yet, and so with one eye on that partially-mapped territory of our imaginations, and one eye fixed on the evident east side landscape of hard edges and serious struggle, we soldiered on.

Alex had been a militant with SNCC, the Student Nonviolent Coordinating Committee, in the South and preceded me in Cleveland by a year, home to care for his mother and to help set up the Community Union. I'd left behind a map of my life already drawn, a territory of privilege and access that felt to me not only predictable but, by now, uninteresting, flat, and pointless. I yearned for something more vital, more purposeful, and I arrived in Cleveland as an exile.

The Movement was shifting away from attacks on the *legal* barriers to integration, and we organized, instead, around *de facto* segregation and issues of economic justice; we intended to build an unstoppable force of poor people in the big cities of the North, who, we thought, would not only improve their own lives, but would along the way turn the planet upside down. We borrowed inspiration and songs from the humanizing energy of the Southern Movement, but we were drawing new lines and plowing new ground in these concrete ghetto streets: "Oh Freedom, Oh Freedom."

***

Alex knew *Invisible Man* almost by heart, and we talked about it off and on for days, laughing at some scenes, practically crying at others. I'd read Richard Wright and James Baldwin, but Ellison opened another window onto a wider field.

"I am an invisible man," the narrator begins. He is alive but flailing unseen in a void, the frightful struggle against powerful forces actively determined to erase his humanity and subjectivity, to look through him and to turn him into an object, a thing: "[T]hey see only my surroundings, themselves, or figments of their imagination—indeed, everything and anything except me." That anguished and very personal cry that refuses to be swallowed up in the vacuum—it outlined a universal horror so clearly that it felt like a description of a part of my own life as well. And yet it perfectly fit the madness of racism.

One morning as we sipped coffee and munched eggs and toast at a diner, still talking about Ellison, Alex surprised me. "We haven't even mentioned yet the most important line in the book," he said in what seems in retrospect like a running tutorial. "And it's right up-front in the prologue." I didn't know what he meant. "Remember the part where the preacher takes as his text the 'Blackness of Blackness,'" he said. "And he chants out 'black is…an' black ain't'? When I first read that I practically stopped breathing." He looked at me hard for a moment. "Why?" I asked. "I mean, that's it: Black is ... an' Black ain't. The whole thing—race itself, man—it's a joke, but you can't laugh ... It's a fantastic joke, and it's killing us—all of us in America." *Invisible Man* was an atlas, and Alex, my geography teacher.

***

Our apartment was a third-floor walk-up in an anonymous brick building on Lakeview Avenue, one of a long line of shabby buildings slouching toward the street as far as the eye could see. The poverty struck me at first like a fist—I'd never seen anything like it, even though I'd read about it in books by then and seen many, many pictures of poor people in hauntingly beautiful photographs. But those anesthetizing images conveyed nothing of the smell of hardship or the taste of want, the enveloping feel of lack and loss and need. In Cleveland I saw for the first time what it was to be broke, not waiting for a check, and what it was to be hungry, not just ready for lunch.

The organizers—eight of us—read and studied together, and sometimes Alex would lead a more formal session of political education. Books were part of our lives, and the books we sought were those that might be wielded as weapons in the struggle—*The Fire Next Time, The Wretched of the Earth*, the poetry of Nikki Giovanni and Sonia Sanchez and Don L. Lee. We were hungry for affirmation and for any formulation that might clarify, amplify, or point us toward effective action. We wanted charts and maps. I remember Alex reading aloud from Kenneth Clark one evening about the dark ghetto and its invisible walls that had been erected by white society to confine the powerless and perpetuate their powerlessness.

"Lakeview and Hough didn't just happen," Alex said, referring to our community. "This neighborhood's an actual colony, its colonial status enforced with all the power of law and money, and with violence or the threat of violence when peaceful means fail." A colony—it seemed to describe all that we surveyed there, and a light bulb went on for me. Alex argued that racism as bigotry was built upon the ground of race as a convenient invention for colonization and exploitation. My own learning landscape was opening and widening.

Knots of men collected on corners and in the vacant lot next to our building, smoking, passing a bottle or a skinny joint. They were unemployed or underemployed, always waiting it seemed, inmates in some abandoned outpost or camp. "The colonized," Alex would say. Ordinary folks—they paid their taxes, loved their children, and put their pants on one leg at a time just like you and me—assigned to this artificial city-within-a-city, this colony, and why? "They hold no currency," Alex said. "They lack funds, influence, access to power, and for that, they're trapped." The immense panorama of waste and cruelty was overwhelming; our everyday work organizing rent strikes or community speak-outs, petition campaigns or political rallies was designed at root to help our neighbors collectively resist the casual disregard of their humanity.

On our corner a group of street characters, all fixtures on our block, well known, reliable, and oddly reassuring, gathered for early morning parleys—part news bulletin, part scandal sheet, part debate, part bull session, part ongoing dominoes tournament. Eddie Robinson was called Thunderbird, James Thompson was Lil Bit, Willie Jones was now Ismael Akbar, father of three little girls with their own recent name changes—they were now Mali, Kenya, and Ghana. Alex, of course, saw this as prime organizing turf, and soon the men allowed me in a bit, too; I hung out there, paying for my admission by being the first schoolteacher any of them knew who lived right there on the block with them, and because Akbar, who believed that all white people are devils, said that I was a good teacher for his girls.

I was a bit too eager to please, and exhilarated to be an exception to the white-people-are-devils construct. I read a deflating essay by Amiri Baraka around this time defending the white-people-as-devils thesis, pointing out all the ways whites are willfully, defensively ignorant even as they concretely benefit from the hierarchy of race. Working himself into a lather on the subject, Baraka busts out with, "I mean *all* white people are devils, even Dave De Buscher." If, according to Baraka, the great Knicks forward is a devil, I thought, how much could I hope for myself?

Inside myself a rift already well underway was deepening: Skeptical of religious appeals, suspicious of most universals, I nonetheless thought that most white people were indeed devils, or that they were at least devilish in a thousand little ways, as well as a few fundamental ways not so little. Appraising America through that looking glass—through the lens of the ghetto, the colony—it didn't take long for my world to flip on its head. Yes, I concluded, white people are devilish because they allow themselves to be blinded to the unjust system that buys their consent with a few gold coins. And I benefited, too, so who was I kidding?

There was a whole education to be had on the corner:

"You hear Henry Allen beating up on that gal's been staying with him?"

"Yeah, it got plenty loud about midnight."

"And when she was shrieking there at the end, and he threw her out the window?"

"Man, I saw her fall. Don't know how she lived."

"Yeah, and the cops was here in thirty minutes, ambulance took a hour, she could've died."

"Black people don't mean a thing to them, man. Whenever you want them, you can't get them for a prayer, but then when you don't want them, man, they're *everywhere*."

The buzz was sometimes complaining, sometimes boasting, sometimes bitter, always shot through with a quick line of laughter. The subject of white folks was never far away:

"I like all the reading going on at your school, Bill, Akbar began one morning turning to me. But you should weed out some of those books. Some are silly, some absolutely racist."

"Racist?"

"That Dr. Seuss," he spit out. "He travels around the world collecting specimens for a zoo, and you see how he treats all the Brothers?"

"Or *Curious George*," Alex chimed in. "The man in the yellow hat goes to Africa and kidnaps a cute little monkey, brings him back in a cage on a ship, and they live happily ever after."

"Exactly!" said Akbar. "Racist to the bone!"
"Man," Akbar said on another day. "You see what they doing now? They talking about making kayaking and synchronized swimming Olympic events. Everybody knows Black people don't like water. Just another racist scheme to keep us from those medals."

"Yeah, man," replied Lil Bit. "You right. Why don't those white people make double-dutch jump rope an Olympic event?"

"Exactly, and I'll tell you why." Akbar again. "Because Mali and Kenya and Ghana'd be up there on that stand, little Black angels giving a black fist to the festival of whiteness."

Pride and rebellion, excess and illusion, always laughter.

Alex was a public character and a street philosopher like the others, plus a smart organizer to boot. The people with the problems, he often said, are also the ones with the solutions. He had an extensive knowledge of the history of race science, the eugenics movement, the slave trade, and the Holocaust in Europe. "It's all a fantastic joke," he insisted again, "in the service of inequality. If you're in favor of justice, you've got to be against race, period."

"I'm not so sure," Akbar said now. "I've been Black all my life, and I'm finally 'Black and Proud,' so don't snatch that from me just yet."
"OK," Alex allowed. "Be 'Black and Proud' for now, but let's change this monster system so we can all just be human and happy."

***

"What color am I?" Alex asked me once as he and I walked down the street.

"You're Black," I said, surprised.

"Why so insistent?"

"I'm not insistent. I'm just assuming."

"So you assume I'm Black, and society confirms your assumption with a whole catalog of assumptions of its own, and so it becomes, what? A fact, like the 'fact' that you're white ... but you know, you've got a matriarch from Ethiopia way back somewhere. And look at me—I'm dark, but I'm not black."

"True, you're brown."

"I have a white grandmother and a white great-grandfather. How much white I got to have to qualify?"

"To qualify for what?"

"For membership in the country club of the fully human."

Before I knew Alex, race was securely fixed for me—the received wisdom of American common sense. I might have come to oppose racism, but race was a fact. By the time Alex was through, race had been queered up in my head. It was real—I could *see* it, could benefit or suffer from it—and it was false—the perverse invention of some mad genius. "Man," he would say some days before bed. "Another hard day in the war to make white Americans better people." We laughed together, but I held onto an impossible hope: that his comment was somehow aimed at others, and never at me.

***

We worked hard to become part of our community in order to resist its reduction to a colony. We projected possibility. I listened to what people said, and was as respectful as I knew how to be to my new neighbors. We all wanted to become good citizens of our block. "Don't make a big fuss," Alex said to me one morning. "But pick up the litter on your way to the bus stop."

We knocked on doors, talked around kitchen tables, hung out on stoops, and went to picnics in the park. I was an identifiable outsider, of course, living here by choice, not necessity, but I went earnestly door to door, trying to engage people in conversations that might reveal the obstacles they faced in their lives, and in the naming of those barriers, creating the possibility of coming together with others to chart a struggle for repair. I'm sure some people were suspicious or mistrustful, and why shouldn't they be? Who were these outsiders, these agitators? Who was this white boy? And where will he be next year? But what struck me was how many folks readily embraced me, took me into their homes, their families, their lives. While my motives and ambitions might never be fully sorted out (how much was guilt, how much ego or idealism or hopefulness, how much juvenile rebellion or pride?) no one questioned my humanity, no one doubted the humanizing potential of the Movement, and most people greeted me with abundant faith and extraordinary goodwill.

Our agenda meant nothing to us unless it could be realized in light of the particular agendas of the people of Lakeview. We didn't want a "career" here—the point of our work was to somehow, as we said at the time, "organize ourselves out of a job." We could be catalysts for change, but we could never substitute for indigenous leadership. We could be community educators, but we had to be mindful of the fact that authentic teaching is always at its heart listening and learning. We wanted to help create organizations of, by, and for the poor.

When we first knocked on Dorothea Hill's door she opened with a big, welcoming smile. "Oh, you're the civil rights kids from down the block," she'd said. "I've been waiting for you. Come on in." We talked long into the night about children, welfare, schools, and crime, all the problems of life in the neighborhood. Later when I asked Mrs. Hill why she'd told Alex she'd been waiting for us, she laughed and said, "I saw the Movement on television for years fighting for justice; as poor as I am, I figured after a while it would have to reach my house."

Dorothea Hill had grown up on the block and was now raising her own children here. She was active in her church and PTA, and she was the person others looked to for guidance and help. She was a born teacher, perceptive and respected, active and generous. When a child was hit by a car on Lakeview Avenue, it was Mrs. Hill who called a meeting in her living room to press the city to install a stoplight; when a back-to-school welfare allowance was cut, Mrs. Hill organized the protest; when a rat bit a youngster while she slept in her apartment, Dorothea thought up the dramatic tactic of taking dead rats with us downtown to the demonstration and piling them on the front steps. "Get the rats out of Lakeview and City Hall," Mrs. Hill chanted. She was the first president of the Community Union.

Mrs. Hill opened meetings with devotions that were part prayer, part politics. "Thank you, Lord, for Your many blessings, for Your mercy, and please, Lord, help us out on this demonstration next week." Then we sang songs—"May the Circle Be Unbroken," "This Little Light of Mine"—to bring us together as a group, reminding us of our common purpose and making us all feel a little stronger. When she began to set the agenda, Mrs. Hill would always interject her own words of wisdom: "Tonight we'll be talking about welfare rights and the Welfare Work Book we'll be publishing soon. Now remember, just because you're poor and on welfare doesn't mean you're not a citizen, and citizens have rights;" or, "Now we'll move on to figuring out about starting up this Children's Community School. Our children are poor, true, but that doesn't mean they don't have fine minds. We have to think about how to stimulate those fine minds." Dorothea Hill never missed an opportunity to underline that point: "I'm poor because I haven't got any money. I'm not mentally ill! I'm not culturally deprived! I'm not lazy and I'm not stupid!"

In the midst of our efforts and in (some would say, cynical) response to the massive upheaval among African Americans for civil and human rights, agents of the government-sponsored poverty programs began to appear. Their first efforts involved a "community needs assessment," in which they surveyed neighborhood people in order, they said, to "define problems" and "craft solutions." They used a "scientifically" developed instrument, a questionnaire that could be easily quantified and ranked. Instead of searching for the strengths and capacities in the community, they looked only at deficiencies; instead of focusing on problems as shared and social, they probed individual deficits that stopped short of collective action; instead of uncovering root causes and targeting specific enemies, they avoided structural analysis. In brief, while they applied the rhetoric of the Civil Rights Movement, they shared none of its spirit nor its larger educational, ethical, or political purposes.

Dorothea Hill, in the eyes of the poverty program workers, was a vast collection of ills. She had dropped out of high school, become pregnant at nineteen, and was a single mother with three young children, one of whom needed expensive glasses. She had been arrested once as a teenager for shoplifting, and had hung out at that time with a group of Lakeview Avenue youngsters who called themselves the Street Demons. Now she was on welfare, and she occasionally worked cleaning white people's houses while her oldest boy watched the little ones. She also took cash from the children's father, a long-distance truck driver who sometimes spent the night at her apartment. In other words, Mrs. Hill, by their account, represented the whole litany of behaviors that add up to a "culture of poverty," or a "prison of deprivations," or a "tangle of pathologies": welfare cheat, gang member, criminal, unwed teen mother, neglectful parent, high school dropout, and on and on. The government-people were fairly drooling over Dorothea.

This kind of portrait was easily sketched of many people in Lakeview. It is, of course, a false picture—incomplete, negative, pretentious, self-fulfilling. It highlights certain isolated incidents in a life without considering others. It attributes explanatory power to things that would never be applied to white or wealthy people. I (and many others I have known) could be tagged with at least three of these labels depending on where and how and when the observer took the snapshot, and yet I would never be tarred as representing a "culture of poverty"—the privilege of whiteness and background and wealth that accrued to me by accident and chance. And, predictably, the labels conveniently lump a few selected incidents together to fit a preconceived, stereotyped view of poor African Americans. Embraced by conservatives and liberals alike, this facile view holds that the social system and structure of white power is either fundamentally fine or, at any rate, beyond scrutiny, that any problems related to race or class are relics of the past and that anyone should be able to do well now unless plagued by some complex, difficult to change, *internal* psychocultural effects. In other words, we've done too much already (conservatives) or as much as we can (liberals) and we'll all hope for *those people* to get it together or somehow disappear.

Not surprisingly, the programs proposed as a result of this kind of shoddy, suspect thinking—backed up by "research"—tended to be unhelpful, debilitating, and even harmful. They offered services; we opted for solidarity. They turned people into clients; we believed in people becoming their own agents. They perpetuated dangerous generalities and degrading stereotypes about individuals, and failed to identify or challenge any systemic problems that generated the problems in the first place. Everything "bad" from the point of view of the experts was a trait within poor people of color themselves.

***

Outside of Cleveland, the world was in flames—Viet Nam, Santo Domingo,

Sharpesville—it reeled in agony and despair, and still most Americans seemed to be sleepwalking through the whole thing, unaware, uninvolved, disengaged. And then in the middle of that summer we were swept along by something red and loud and violent and in our own backyard—an urban uprising to some, a rebellion, and to others, black anarchy and a ghetto riot.

Stories rushed up the street faster than fire: Cops on Superior Street beat a woman on her way to church, and on St. Clair a cop shot a boy point-blank and called him "ni**er." But on Euclid two cop cars were burned to a crisp, a bank was trashed, and money was blowing in great gusts down the street. True or not, each story was embraced and passed along because it was believable and then believed.

The strange thing was to live in an atmosphere simultaneously terrifying and deeply energizing. The mood was festive one minute, like a giant community picnic with everyone laughing and sharing and handing things around, and the next minute the sound of shots fired from somewhere—or the sight of flames leapt suddenly to life—and everyone was wheeling around, scattering. One afternoon I saw thirty or forty people—young and old, men and women, the respectable as well as the neighborhood characters—pulling together to tear a grate off the large plate-glass window of the supermarket. No one urged caution, and no one objected. That night Donald Hall, a kid who worked with the Community Union but would, in a year, join a black nationalist group and change his name to Jamal Daoud, showed up at our apartment, singed and smoky, took a shower, and left with fresh clothes from Alex. "People are fed up," Alex said to me flatly. "We've been dispossessed so long, maybe taking back isn't so bad." Night after night, day after day, each majestic scene was so terrible and so unexpected that no built environment would ever again stand innocently fixed in my mind—every human topography became temporary.

The project house was our command post and community center—Dorothea and half a dozen others took turns distributing food and coffee and medicine to a large crowd every morning, and I ran a regular ambulance service to the emergency room in my beat-up Oldsmobile. Returning from the hospital one night after curfew, Alex and I were surprised at a checkpoint on Lakeview Avenue, stopped at gunpoint, spread-eagled on the pavement, searched and released, but not before a whole rash of questions about what a white guy was doing with a Black guy on Lakeview Avenue in the middle of all this. The mindless bond of white solidarity was at least momentarily smashed on the pavement: I wanted to be with Alex, not with them. The baby-faced Ohio National Guardsman, a white boy who'd probably been pumping gas in Akron the day before, searched me, sweating and breathing heavily, looking wide-eyed and terrified. I was terrified, too, and I felt unhinged. Alex and I didn't dwell on it—we weren't actually hurt, and things were bad everywhere.

***

Stokely Carmichael, who with Willie Ricks had raised the banner of Black Power on a march in Mississippi that summer, spoke to hundreds of people at a church down the street from the Community Union a few weeks later. "We can't wait for white people to decide whether we're worthy of our freedom," he said. "We must *take* our freedom. We can't allow others to do for us, we must *do* for ourselves. We can't accept white standards of beauty or intelligence, we must *rid* ourselves of self-hatred." "This much is crystal clear," he said. "We're one hundred percent human, and like other humans we need the power to run our own lives." We're Black; and we want power. Black; power. Black Power.

The church vibrated with the excited chant, and I remember a boy of fourteen or fifteen with a huge smile racing up and down the aisles with his fist pumping, inciting us to get louder. I was one of maybe a half dozen whites sprinkled through the jammed and pulsing crowd, and I chanted enthusiastically along with the rest.

When Stokely declared during a trial later that year, "There isn't a white man I can trust," a young white Movement activist who'd worked closely with him, cried out, "Not a single one, Stokely?" Carmichael stared at his friend and responded, "No, not a single one." If the young activist had taken offense, then Stokely was clearly right. But if the young man wanted to live in serious solidarity, he would have to find a way to keep on loving, keep on moving, keep on fighting. He would necessarily put it aside and find his way to a deeper commitment. As Malcolm said, "Time will tell."

Stokely's words were interpreted by Movement people again and again over the next months to mean that I needed to get out of the way, and that I needed to organize "my own people." It felt both necessary and false. Necessary because I knew by then that the problem of racism was in fact a problem of white people primarily. False because whites didn't feel in any way like "my own people" by then.

My allegiances and non-allegiances deepened and settled—I would try to stand with Dorothea or Alex against the complacent or the mighty, or both at once. With privilege and oppression organized along a strict hierarchy of race, I wanted to claim my allegiance to humanity, to somehow become an enemy and an exile—not to deny the racial reality, but to refuse its seductions. I wanted to interrupt the common sense of race, to side with the people of the world against the small but powerful group of dangerous men determined to dominate. Easier said than done.

***

Freedom Now!

The Community Union lived for only a few years. It was founded in 1965 shortly after Reverend Bruce Klinger was run over by an earthmover and killed during a Movement sit-in at the Lakeview Avenue construction site of what would become another segregated school. It was gone by the time Ahmed Evans and a group of young nationalists engaged in a deadly shootout with the Cleveland police in a Lakeview Avenue apartment in 1968. In between there was struggle, hope, possibility, occasional heroism, and one of the most loving attempts to change all that is glaringly wrong in our society.

Before that summer we had begun each meeting with a song, but after all that had happened, whenever we opened our mouths to sing, it seemed we could only scream. The apocalypse was soon upon us, the serial assassination of Black leaders in America linked somehow in our minds to Lumumba's death in the Congo and to the thousands of Made-in-America murders in Viet Nam every day. The air was acrid in our throats, and we felt the steady approach of a police state. We steeled ourselves. Alex began to spend more and more time away from the project, to sleep away from our apartment, and to keep his own counsel. I mostly missed his radiance, but I was consumed with my own changes then, and with the more serious demands of a more intense time. There was less and less talk of our beloved community, and more and more talk of self-determination, anti-colonial struggle, and revolution. Alex had a foot in both territories for a time, but then he slipped away, a man without a country. He gave up the hope of igniting any American magic at all and set off for West Africa. I remembered James Baldwin's assertion that a Black man's attitude is designed to "rob the white man of the jewel of his naiveté, or else to make it cost him dear." Alex had tried the former, and now, I thought, he'd act out the latter. Alex had become a revolutionary, and the tide was rising.

The Black Panthers, the Black Liberation Army, the Detroit Revolutionary Union Movement, and the Republic of New Africa exploded onto the scene, and then George Jackson and several Attica Brothers and Fred Hampton were assassinated, and soon after that I set off on the run for over a decade, charged with conspiracy to cross state lines to incite riots and attack government property. Alex had been a good man and generous teacher in my "race course"—he established a standard of honesty, integrity, and courage for me to aspire to. He also set a pattern that has lasted my whole life, and to this day I seek out a mentor or a tutor wherever I am. When it's my turn to be the teacher, I remember Alex on the corner: "You have to be willing to listen and learn because people are always the experts on their own lives," he'd say. "But at the same time you have to be willing to tell the whole truth however you see it, whoever it upends."

Ralph Ellison writes, "My world has become one of infinite possibilities. What a phrase—still it's a good phrase and a good view of life, and a man shouldn't accept any other; that much I've learned underground. Until some gang succeeds in putting the world in a straitjacket, its definition is possibility. Step outside the narrow borders of what men call reality and you step into chaos ... or imagination."

Stepping outside the narrow borders of received reality, I imagined that another world was possible.

AWAKE!

Bernardine Dohrn

The world is white no longer and it will never be white again.
— James Baldwin

I only hope that before too long the people of my race in my country will wake up to the fact that they are endangering the peace of the world.

— Eleanor Roosevelt

Our son Zayd chased down a baseball one spring afternoon and trotted it back to me with a question: "Have all the freedom fighters we love been killed?" I reeled, thinking frantically of the posters and photos in our apartment: Osceola, Lumumba, Malcolm, Che, Martin Luther King, Fred Hampton, Zayd Shakur, George Jackson. "No, of course not." We were in Peacock Park because it was then the only playground in New York City that was free of broken glass and dog poop, so children could run around safely. "No"—triumphantly—"there's Rosa Parks! She refused to stand up when a mean white man told her she couldn't sit on the bus, and she changed the world. In fact, she works in Detroit. We could call her up and see if she could come visit our day care center." (She did.)

Questions from a four-year-old jar the normative world, pierce the subtext beneath the taken-for-granted. Did I almost assume that the most courageous would be assassinated, shot down, cut off at the height of their powers? Who did we celebrate and who did we leave out? Was there no way to plan for a long life of resistance?

***

I was fifteen years old, the same as her, the day I saw Elizabeth Eckford on TV. She was wearing a checkered, flounced skirt that went down to mid-calf, a crisp white blouse, open at the throat, and sunglasses; it looked as if she had a crinoline slip underneath. It was a September back-to-school day and Elizabeth was carefully dressed in first-day-of-school clothes, the kind of outfits I too sewed for school, except that she walked alongside a mob of hundreds of jeering people opposing her admission to Central High School in Little Rock. She was alone that morning because plans had changed about where to meet up with the other eight Black students and her family had no telephone. She clasped her books tightly to her chest and climbed up the imposing steps to face the National Guard troops, armed with fixed bayonets attached to their rifles. The troops—children themselves—refused to open their line on orders of the governor, who predicted that "blood will flow in the streets" if Black students tried to enter Central High. They raised their weapons toward Elizabeth, pointed at her. At the same time, a small group of white students went past the Guard and entered the school. She turned back, walking slowly past the yelling crowd again, toward a bus stop a block away. She kept her head up.

I watched her from an all-white suburb in Milwaukee in 1957. I was preoccupied with being popular, with Elvis Presley, the Milwaukee Braves, and modern dance, but Elizabeth cut into my adolescence. She was like a little dart that burrowed into my ignorance.

Not that she threw me into action. I didn't talk about her to my parents or friends; she only occupied some secret space. It didn't occur to me to write about Little Rock as an editor at the high school newspaper or in civics class. I didn't yet identify my own segregated high school, or the equivalent apartheid that characterized Milwaukee schools, as problematic. We were singing "Hail! Hail! Rock n' Roll" with Chuck Berry, and my idols were young Henry Aaron and "Go-Go Billy Bruton." But Elizabeth, by her courage and with her dignity, schooled me that day—something of great import was happening out there, and Elizabeth Eckford interrupted the record. She nudged me a little off course.

Along with Elizabeth, I gazed at Hazel Bryan in that menacing mob dominated by women outside Central High. Her name was not publicized, but Hazel was the most prominent face in the white throng of five hundred. Elizabeth walked by in her shades, staring straight ahead, deliberate in pretending that the racist mob wasn't there. I know now that they were shouting, "Get a rope and drag her over to this tree!!" and "Lynch her!" and that they followed her, swarming around her at the bus stop, one spitting at her. It was white women who were implicated with the act of terrorizing Elizabeth, of fearing her. Their faces were contorted with rage; they hated her and threatened her, these women who shouted at her. I had no tools to analyze why it was white women hating Black youngsters. Not just white women but ordinary white women, not rich or fancy women. Surely they weren't like my parents, who taught me that everyone is created equal. Back then, I couldn't hear Hazel, and I didn't know anyone like Elizabeth. They pointed to a world that I couldn't yet see.

Daisy Bates, who was state president of the NAACP and ran the *Arkansas State Press* with her husband, worked with the nine teenagers and with their parents to prepare them for the insults, the tension, and the pressures that their attendance at a school that didn't want them would entail. A rock was thrown through her living room picture window with a note tied to it, just a week before Elizabeth walked to Central High. The hand-printed note said: "Stone this time, Dynamite next." Bates later wrote *The Long Shadow of Little Rock* about the effort by Black parents and the NAACP to enroll nine Black students at Central High School two years after it had become the law of the land via *Brown v. Board of Education.* Yet the most experienced and realistic anti-racist organizers did not predict the level of white resistance and violence that the children would face. Today, when I use the stories of Daisy Bates, Ernest Green, and Elizabeth in a class on children's rights, I still wonder at the decision of the parents who agreed to send their children into that epicenter of white supremacy, triggering a backlash of firebombs, death threats, armed soldiers, mobilized mobs. They weren't naïve: Every family of the Little Rock Nine knew about the murder of Emmett Till just two years before; all the parents recalled the last lynching in Little Rock, in 1927. They must have been driven by their passionate, unreasonable hopes for their children, their wakefulness to their moment, and perhaps their own thwarted ambitions and rage.

Emmett Till was the same age as Elizabeth in 1955, same as me. I saw his tortured and distorted face in the satin-lined casket in Chicago. The *Jet* photograph must have been reprinted in *Life* magazine, which, along with *The Saturday Evening Post* and the *Reader's Digest*, came to our house every week. Emmett Till had traveled down from Chicago to Money, Mississippi, to stay with his uncle where he would be safe; the train took me each summer from Chicago down to Clinton, Illinois, to stay with my great-aunt Agnes and great-uncle Ted, who was a mechanic for the Illinois Central Railroad. I helped pack Uncle Ted's lunch pail each morning and sometimes walked to the railroad yard to meet him coming off shift, his damaged hands covered in grease and oil, his blue coveralls sweaty and soiled.

But for Emmett, in Mississippi, the quiet pleasures and apparent safety of small-town and rural life—the wooden water tower above town, the haunting howl of the train whistle at night, the fresh corn, fragrant tomatoes, and fireflies, the walks around the square on a Saturday evening—turned lethal. He was seized, disappeared, tortured and murdered. Allegedly, he whistled at Carolyn Bryant, a white woman whose husband owned the grocery store. Emmett's waterlogged body was found in the Tallahatchie River, one eye gouged out, his crushed-in head with a bullet in it. His mother, in Chicago, was able to have his body returned on the promise that she would not open the casket. Defiantly, Mamie Bradley opened it for the world to view, *Jet* magazine published the photos of Till, and the line of 50,000 Black people who came to bear witness stretched around blocks on the South Side. Poet Audre Lourde describes "the avid insistence of detail ... the severed lips, how many burns/his gouged out eyes / sewed shut upon the screaming covers / louder than life / all over / the veiled warning, the secret relish/of a black child's mutilated body." Mamie Bradley demanded and provided the opportunity to see, to discern.

In Mississippi, the all-white jury had taken one hour to acquit the grocery store owner and his brother-in-law after defense counsel argued: "I'm sure that every last Anglo-Saxon one of you has the courage to free these men in the face of that [outside] pressure." Although I looked from a distance, puzzled and disturbed, it's obvious today that Elizabeth and the African American Little Rock students surely experienced Emmett Till's death more intimately, the veiled warning, something like an undertow of terror that agitated their childhoods.

I look back at that girl I was with some dread, disquiet, and wonder. My white students today express a similar unsettling astonishment about their ignorance. But Elizabeth and Emmett didn't catapult me into immediate action. Instead, they slipped into some file category: "Remember to get back to that later." I have vivid memories of the flowered wallpaper in our living room and the sweet smell of my father's pipe tobacco, but I can recall only vaguely the deep unease caused by these children who were my peers, the ways they disturbed my slumber, flashed into my girlish, fearful dreams, disarranged the security of the ground beneath.

Now these episodes are history, and I worry that they combine to make us feel sanguine that impunity and violence against Black youth is ancient history. The stories can be heroic in retrospect, or they may call on us to feel nothing except relief that we are far more advanced in "race relations" today. They don't require us to ask what we might have done ourselves back in Little Rock, and they fail to ask us to see today's everyday episodes of hatred and cruelty directed against Black children: in the harsh charging of the Jena 6 in Louisiana; in the death of Diamonte Driver, who died of a brain infection in February 2007 in Maryland after his mom could not find a dentist willing to perform an $80 tooth extraction causing his abscessed infection; in the beating death of fourteen-year-old Martin Lee Anderson in a Florida boot camp; in the three million students suspended and expelled from elementary schools (52 percent of whom are youth of color); in disparate rates of survival and health outcomes, in confinement, in persistent poverty.

These two crimes against Black adolescents festered, troubled, burrowed in, and insistently reappeared. There was violence and murder, assault and anger, but also more courage than I knew could exist. They bothered my departure from high school, first-generation college off to a state university in southern Ohio. In curious ways, Elizabeth and Emmett stayed with me, guided my next steps, and the puzzle of the white women who harmed them stayed with me, too, vexing my search for a bigger world filled with meaning.

Martin Luther King, Jr, came to town in the fall of 1965, just weeks after the Watts rebellions left thirty people dead and the Black community of Los Angeles devastated. When I had considered the possibility of volunteering to go South for Mississippi Freedom Summer the year before, my boyfriend talked me out of it—and I let him. Now Dr. King and the Southern Christian Leadership Conference (SCLC), committed to illustrate that entrenched and systemic racism was not the sole province of the deep South and that nonviolent initiatives were relevant in the North, selected Chicago as the first Northern city of the Civil Rights campaign. He arrived with fourteen "lieutenants" for three days of demonstrations and meetings about school and housing segregation, what SCLC would call "a system of internal colonialism." It was only eight years since I had watched Elizabeth Eckford on TV. I was determined: This time I was not going to miss it.

I was beginning my second year of law school, one of six women in an all-white and almost all-male class at the University of Chicago. Just that summer I worked as a legal intern at the brand-new Legal Services for the Poor offices in New York City, meeting with community groups in Brooklyn, the Bronx, and the Lower East Side to give meaning to the mandate "maximum feasible participation of the poor." These words were inserted into the statute authorizing the Poverty Program, or "OEO"—a signature policy initiative claimed by President Lyndon Johnson but long fought for by the Black Freedom Movement, organized labor, and community activists. Back at school I was the local chair of the Law Students' Civil Rights Research Council and working with Eleanor Jackson and a group of welfare mothers at the Chicago Welfare Rights Organization in a storefront on Roosevelt Road. So I was beginning to know a little, but not much.

I pushed away from the university, from law school, to try to shift location, to reposition. It was a left turn, but it felt more like a blind lunge toward changing my frame of reference. It required a tiny, insistent first step to show up at the Warren Avenue Church in Garfield Park on Chicago's west side. A deliberate move to dance nearer to the whirlwind and see if I could be of use—in this case by reaching out to the lawyers who represented Dr. King in Chicago.

What I was single-minded about discovering was both obvious and mysterious. There was some rumbling, elusive, fragmentary knowledge that there were events that were shaking the world, and they were being forged by students and sharecroppers in the South, farmworkers in Delano, Lorraine Hansberry on Broadway, and Malcolm X a few doors down the block on Greenwood Avenue at Muhammad's Temple No. 2. I had a growing notion that being a good girl from the Midwest, even getting good grades, was not enough. It had something to do with pursuing freedom—related to an adolescent fantasy of going to New York or Paris or Rio, but much better because it might be deeper and more substantive than romance. The world just outside the university circle was spinning and churning; I imagined, with a strong and growing certainty, that liberation, mine as well as others', was on the agenda, and the Black Freedom Movement was coming to town. I didn't yet know it involved gender or class consciousness or imperialism, but I was poised to be somehow changed, to be humanized, to be lit up. And the risk was appealing.

King was invited to Chicago's rigidly racially segregated landscape through the efforts of Al Raby and the Coordinating Council of Community Organizations. Raby and Black parents across the city built a movement to educate Black children, challenging inequality and routine failure in the Chicago Public Schools. Two massive school boycotts by Black parents, the first involving two hundred thousand students who stayed home, demonstrated the depth of support in the Black community. Ultimately this century-long struggle to educate Black children was coalescing in the fight to shut down the infamous Willis Wagons, flimsy aluminum trailers drawn up at overcrowded schools in the Black neighborhoods to facilitate a double, shift program, where two sets of students attended classes each day, rather than moving Black students to underused white schools. The trailers were named for school superintendent Benjamin Willis and served as mobile classrooms to maintain the educational structure of white supremacy and strict segregation.

I showed up with a handful of law students at a crowded, somewhat chaotic downtown law firm, unsure of what we might be getting into in the autumn of 1965. We were assigned to research and identify the largest slum owners in the city. Two of Dr. King's Chicago lawyers, Gil Cornfield and Gil Feldman—the two Gils, delegated our tiny volunteer cohort to this corner fragment of the larger Chicago Open Housing Campaign. We were invited into early SCLC strategy meetings with the veterans of the Southern Civil Rights struggles who accompanied King: James Bevel (field director), Bernard LaFayette (working at the American Friends Service Committee), Mary Lou Finley, Bernard Lee, and Jesse Jackson (starting up Operation Breadbasket to obtain more jobs for Black workers)—all about my age but with scores of arrests and beating scars, confident with strategizing experience.

Within weeks, our group of law students returned to the SCLC field workers chagrined. In the middle of an intense debate about Chicago strategy and focus, Bernard LaFayette asked about our research, and all eyes turned toward us. Although we secretly imagined becoming heroes, in fact we were unable to untangle the blind trusts and complex legal ownership using public records to identify large slumlords, and to the SCLC leadership I had to admit defeat. We tried to explain all the work we had done, the thwarted searches, the clerk's records. Without missing a beat, Dr. King escalated: "All right, we'll call a citywide rent strike."

The heart of this fair housing strategy combined grassroots organizing to achieve concrete improvements in living conditions with a challenge to the whole system of segregation by open housing marches into white-only residential neighborhoods. Chicago was, after all, the most segregated big city in America: 95 percent of the Black population lived in neighborhoods that were predominately Black and poor, with average family incomes of $3,200 per year; 41 percent of the "ghetto" dwellings were rated as uninhabitable, compared to 18 percent for whites. Housing segregation was a form of economic apartheid, an enforced isolation from economic resources, good schools, access to jobs transportation, and a living income, and countless other advantages. So the idea of a network of organizing tenant unions to conduct rent strikes, residents using their own skills and energy to name their conditions and transform them—in combination with massive marches to break segregation—was rather magnificent. Brilliant, I thought.

SCLC staff and the younger leaders they were training went door-to-door in Lawndale and West Garfield Park, armed with leaflets asking residents if they wanted to meet in the evening to discuss conditions in their buildings. They let me come along, wearing a dubious armband that said: "Legal." Children, babies, grandmothers, and parents crowded into a tenant's living room with family from the adjoining apartments. Standing in the back were SCLC veterans and young Chicago organizers like Margaret Sloan-Hunter and Prexy Nesbitt, who was returning home to Lawndale from a year abroad at the University of Dar es Salaam in Tanzania, the first African American to study there—eyes wide open.

First, the tenants described their living conditions and made lists of what was wrong with their decaying buildings: no hot water, leaking roofs, no heat in winter, rotting stairs and window frames, no front-door locks, rodents and vermin. The residents vividly described efforts to get the landlord to make repairs or to do essential work themselves. Women with babies on their laps, slouching adolescents smoking and chewing gum, animated men with suppressed anger—all grew the list of wrongs. The talk turned to what to do.

One possibility, Bernard LaFayette softly suggested each evening, was to put their rents into an escrow account every month and use the funds to bring the building up to code. A vigorous debate broke out about how to decide how to repair the roof, the broken boilers and windows, the lack of hot water, the rats and roaches, the unlocked front doors. They, the people with the problems, were being transformed through their own activity into the people with the solutions. They had to decide whether to do the repairs themselves or hire contractors; they would prioritize the order of repair. It was our job to prevent them from being evicted if they followed the rules. I was transfixed watching the curve of the meeting, the animated discussions by mothers with infants on their hips, old men with missing teeth chiming in, people in their work clothes thinking through the consequences of withholding their rent. Suddenly, terrifyingly, after a vote to go forward, Bernard pointed to me to explain how we would protect them from retaliation—I was a second-year law student, out of my league as both lawyer and organizer. But I was eager, enthusiastic and ready to learn. "We'll begin by creating a list of residents of this building, and opening an escrow account ..." I said that night. I was patently naive. Despite my efforts at sophistication and exotic worldliness, it was apparent that I was a twenty-three-year-old, ill-informed, overeager Midwestern white gal. As to the white part, I was clearly there on probation—probably long-term probation. The unspoken assumption was that SCLC was a Black-led organization, and white people had to be awake and prove themselves over a long period to stay as participants. SCLC organizers were talking about Black Power as a growing force, and the role of whites in civil rights organizations was no longer assumed. And being female was both entrée and danger; I knew just enough to be cautious. I most wanted to learn from James Bevel because he knocked my socks off with his eloquence and radical clarity, and he was willing to teach. Bevel wore an embroidered skullcap, jeans, and a jean jacket whether he was in the neighborhood, speaking in churches, or meeting with the Chicago Real Estate Board downtown. His kinetic energy, dynamic speaking presence, and strategic militancy were legendary, as was the celebrated brilliance of his wife, Diane Nash. I tried to watch him at the Warren Avenue church headquarters or talking to people in the neighborhood on corners or in parks. He began showing up with his comrades at my Hyde Park apartment, shared with two other women students, one from Swaziland. Late at night, I would make pasta or chicken cacciatore and listen to them unwind by debating among themselves, turning over the question of the focus on segregated housing, worrying about confronting the growing white resistance and escalating violence with mass nonviolent demonstrations, trying to integrate the war in Viet Nam with Chicago organizing.

Dr. King flamboyantly moved into a third-floor walk-up tenement apartment in Lawndale, called Slumdale by its one hundred thirty thousand African American residents. Lawndale was occupied by the National Guard during the time of the Watts rebellion in Los Angeles just months before; it was near the SCLC Warren Avenue Church headquarters in adjoining Garfield Park. King brought photographers and news media with him as he moved into his freshly painted flat on Homan Street on a cold January day in 1966; his wife Coretta Scott King joined him there for one highly visible day before she returned to Birmingham. Tongue-in-cheek, a daily newspaper suggested that Dr. King moving from building to building might be the best way to improve slum conditions in Chicago.

The *Chicago Tribune* consistently editorialized against Dr. King's presence in the most starkly patronizing and superior tones: "The doctrine he enunciates, if universally applied by all citizens, would lead to anarchy"; "He now assumes to vest himself with control over the property of others in an open challenge to the law"; "He has also met with the national head of the Black Muslims, who proclaim their racial superiority, and has said that his movement will cooperate with the Muslims in fighting 'an evil system' which produces slums."

By March, the *Tribune* was promoting itself as a leader in the fight against slums, "long before the arrival of the Rev. Mr. King," citing its promotion of legislation that led to "slum clearance": "The *Tribune* takes satisfaction in having taken part in many battles in this war ... " they wrote. "Legal procedures have been worked out," the editors lectured, "and the prospect is good that all slums will be eliminated in a few years, unless there is another big surge in the migration from the southern states." Their conclusion: "Illegal procedures such as those of the Rev. Mr. King will not help Chicago."

In April, the *Tribune* fulminated: "His disrespect for property rights has been well advertised, and may have given encouragement to such persons as the pillagers and arsonists in the Watts area of Los Angeles...The question is the fundamental one of law and order."

The new End the Slums Campaign further escalated when SCLC told the media that four of the tenants from a six-flat building were withholding their rents from the slumlord to use the funds to repair the building—a trusteeship. The press and real-estate interests seized on this as the coming revolution, accusing King of "seizing the building," invading the property rights of others, and "ordaining himself with powers above the law." I was on fire as our group of students shifted into high gear.

Frank Soracco, another SCLC Southern veteran, let me quiz him endlessly and was gently tolerant in teaching me. High-strung and low-key at the same time, Frank told stories about the South and hospital organizing, and had an easy way with people on the west side. He was fine with being silent, standing at the back of the room, and he modeled in a calm way how a white Italian person might be present in a Black neighborhood in a historic moment, as it was coming apart in a cataclysmic storm. I could sit next to Frank, whisper questions as tensions developed during long meetings and watch him for clues. What happens when the sheriffs start to evict rent-strikers? How can we take marchers into Gage Park and rely on the white Chicago Police Department for protection? Did SCLC anticipate the level of Klan violence and rage among white Chicago residents? Prexy Nesbitt urged me to read Langston Hughes and Amiri Baraka, to check out Nina Simone, pointed me to C.L.R. James, and challenged my loose liberal assumptions that all could be easily made well for the poor who were not part of the American dream. They were too good to make me feel like the student or to act like the teacher, but both knew that I was on a crash course.

I stayed up all night coordinating plans for teams of lawyers and law students to appear with stacks of motions and briefs in Landlord/Tenant Court in downtown Chicago, where the city's only African American judge, Judge Edith Sampson, presided. She was rumored to evict someone every thirty-eight seconds, and she was not happy to see us representing tenants who were withholding their rents. Judge Sampson was known to order us out of the courtroom, but we regularly filed our huge piles of motions and briefs, slowed down the works, and forced the city inspectors to start feebly enforcing the building code by issuing citations for the broken roofs and lack of adequate plumbing in the neighborhoods of Lawndale and Garfield Park. I found the legal work of preventing evictions hugely exciting and challenging in a different way than door-to-door organizing—it was the first time I saw up close the law as a tool in an organizing strategy for justice. It was part of King's notion of creating a situation of "creative tension," which regularly edged up to confrontation.

Awake!

As we catapulted into the steamy Chicago summer, the sidewalks sizzled, the fire hydrants were being turned on by local residents, and the tension and pressures intensified.

One blistering hot June day, Louella Washington's family was evicted from their Garfield Park apartment, despite our frantic legal efforts. The sheriff's men were carrying Mrs. Washington's furniture, dishes, and clothing down three flights of stairs and piling it up on the sidewalk when I joined the crowd that was growing around the now-homeless family. Four children held on to their mother's dress, the youngest watching and fearful, the eldest shimmering with anger but silent. A large and powerful man walked up next to me and took off his light blue, seersucker suit jacket because of the heat. When the SCLC organizers arrived, they invited him to speak. Muhammad Ali passed me his jacket to hold and walked up to the front to give encouragement to the evicted family and their neighbors. "People have a right to live in dignity," he said. "Louella Washington has a clear right to withhold her rent until this building is repaired. Black people who are trying to improve their circumstances must be supported."

Ali, in the midst of defending his heavyweight title nine times, had just been reclassified 1A by his draft board and had made public his intention to refuse to fight in Viet Nam. "I ain't got no quarrel with them *Viet Cong* ... They never called me *ni**er*." After his talk, as the sheriffs were readying to drive off, the SCLC team quietly began lifting the furniture and walking it back up three flights of stairs and into the vacated apartment. I joined in and carried boxes, made light by our righteousness, up the several flights of stairs, and felt a part of something glorious. By the time we left, the Washington family was back in their apartment. It was a silent and nonviolent response to law and order, to our legal failure to prevent the eviction, so peacefully executed, so deeply satisfying. Direct action, indeed.

The numbers of tenants asking for support to conduct rent strikes and to organize tenant unions accelerated across the city and spread like wildfire into the new south suburbs—far exceeding our legal ability to react, and outstripping the Movement's ability to respond. But it was a popular Movement, and it rode its own wave. The young Black women organizing the rent strikes and the open housing marches managed to cut their teeth with SCLC during the Chicago Freedom Movement, and several showed me how to resist the seductions of male leadership by forging their own paths. Margaret Sloan-Hunter was nineteen years old that spring of 1966; while still in high school she had founded the Junior Catholic Interracial Council to work on issues of racism. With SCLC in Garfield Park, she organized tenants' unions and campaigned against the lead-paint poisoning of Black children. We weren't friends, I didn't know how to try, but I took notes and watched this focused and persistent young woman.

Margaret later worked as coordinator of the Hunger Taskforce of Operation Breadbasket, also founded that heady season. She went on to be one of the early editors of *Ms.* magazine, a poet, and a founder of the National Black Feminist Organization. In her being and her practice, she refused to separate the threads of her identity concerns: "I'm not Black Monday, Tuesday and Wednesday and a woman Thursday, Friday, and Saturday." When Margaret spoke up in a meeting or drew out the tenants' concerns by asking more questions and then actively listening, I metaphorically took notes. It was that way every day.

Gradually evident to me was a larger mosaic of the Chicago Black Freedom Movement that included the Nation of Islam. In fact, within the first weeks of Dr. King's arrival in Chicago, he had met with the Honorable Elijah Muhammad, leader of the Nation of Islam, and they agreed to work together in a "common front" on the campaign against slums. As Freedom Summer swelled, even I could see the involvement of parts of the labor movement such as the Packinghouse Workers, of the Urban League and forces who had integrated Southside Rainbow Beach, and of the Black women's clubs and organizations who raised funds, wrote articles, and did the work of preparing meetings and keeping organizations running. There was the Congress of Racial Equality, the Woodlawn Organization, and the Black ministers who allied with King, allowed him to use their churches, and defied the powerful Reverend Joseph H. Jackson, president of the National Baptist Convention, who famously claimed that King's civil disobedience tactics were "not far removed from open crime."

Eleanor Jackson was one of the feisty Chicago women organizing for welfare rights, for adequate income and job training, and for their children's futures, simultaneously building a parallel movement that became a political force for and by poor women. I met Mrs. Jackson and her circle of mobilized welfare mothers and organizers because previously I had worked for a year as a caseworker for the Cook County Department of Public Aid just before going to law school. When I left the job, I had the manuals, the guidelines, and knowledge of how things worked inside, and I took them to Eleanor who knew how to make practical use of my experiences. Watching her run a meeting was more illuminating than law school lectures: The women's humor spiced their burdens, directed always against the powerful. And their determination to make life better for their children kept them moving forward. These women, called "Welfare Warriors" by scholar/activist Premilla Nadasen, began organizing against the diminished amount provided by welfare checks that could sustain no one, and to protest humiliating "raids" to look for "illegal" men as proof of the double stereotype of Black women's sexual immorality. The tidal wave of the Chicago Freedom Movement year contributed to founding the National Welfare Rights Organization based on the demands for an adequate income for mothers of young children, access to education and job training, and good day care. As in the arena of fair housing, Eleanor Jackson and these welfare activists were connecting the dots and dazzling me with their tireless energy. Seeds were sprouting in all directions.

Meanwhile, as summer simmered to humid ninety-eight degree weather, Dr. King spoke to a rally of thirty thousand people at Soldier Field (only 10 percent white) proclaiming, "So let us all, white and Black alike, see that we are tied in a single garment of destiny. We need each other." The other King, blues legend B.B. King, played. Dr. King led a march of some five thousand wilted rally survivors downtown to tape a paper with fourteen Open City demands for integrated housing and employment on the locked door of City Hall. On the West Side, James Bevel and Bernard LaFayette were preparing waves of nonviolent volunteers to implement King's call for open housing marches into the white neighborhoods of Marquette Park, Gage Park, and Chicago Lawn, a strategy designed to reveal "the depth and the dimensions of the problem." It was to be a frontal challenge to residential segregation by using nonviolent direct action.

The next July day, police waded into an open fire hydrant scene on the near west side, arrested a group of youngsters, and provoked a confrontation that escalated into a sustained riot of street anger and cries of Black Power. At a meeting at Shiloh Baptist Church, Dr. King and Mahalia Jackson arrived having negotiated the release of the six arrested teenagers; the youth spoke of police brutality and the absence of swimming pools or playgrounds. Dr. King's pleas for nonviolence met with the first church heckling I ever heard, and hundreds of young people walked out. Fires, looting, vandalism, and sniper shots spread throughout the week. Some Blackstone Rangers, Vice Lords, Cobras, and Roman Saints spread out with SCLC organizers to calm the rage; other gang members surrounded occupants of cars driving home through the west side, shattering car windows and terrifying the unsuspecting. I was urged by SCLC colleagues to return home and stay there; Frank Soracco insisted I leave immediately, reminding me that my presence would require that others look after me; reluctantly I drove past fires, barricaded streets, and shattering glass in Garfield Park and Lawndale, back to the relative cocoon of Hyde Park.

Two people were killed in the riots, eighty people seriously injured (including two police officers who were shot), and five hundred arrested. Mayor Richard Daley called for and got four thousand National Guard troops who again rolled in with tanks across the west side; he publicly blamed SCLC: "People that came in here have been talking for the last year of violence, and showing pictures and instructing people in how to conduct violence." Dr. King and Archbishop Cody met with the mayor. The result was ten portable swimming pools and hydrants refitted with sprays. "*Hot town / Summer in the City*," sang the Lovin' Spoonful, as the sirens screamed, and resident anger exploded.

But beginning that very Sunday and every weekend, I joined the massive SCLC marches into all-white Gage Park, Belmont Cragin, and Marquette Park, designed to challenge entrenched patterns of residential segregation and the powerful economic forces that benefited from the status quo. The marches stretched for blocks, filling the width of the street; at the front of the line (invisible to us in back), Black and white clergy locked arms. Sometimes we raced blocks ahead to the front of the march, where I witnessed the collared white clergy become the particular target of enraged white mobs who threw rocks, bottles, and cherry bombs over the police deployed to "escort" us marchers. I passed growing crowds of jeering teenagers and young men who sported swastikas and held up KKK signs. Sometimes their shouted accusations were aimed at me and other young white women. Residents stood at the edges of their carefully tended lawns or on bungalow porches, fearful and hostile, mostly of Lithuanian, Polish, and Italian origin. "All of the other groups learn that one of the quickest ways to demonstrate one's kinship with a white supremacist order is by sharing racist assumptions," bell hooks would write. We marched past rows of tidy houses, helicopters overhead, the world media converging. It was exhilarating and ominous, in part because our presence was revealing the very violence that enforced ordinary white privilege but was rarely so visible to so many (white) Americans.

Bevel and LaFayette coordinated a new wave of vigils and demonstrations outside F.H. Halvorsen Realty at the corner of Kedzie and 63rd Street in the heart of Marquette Park. The point was to highlight that the real-estate industry not only discriminated against African Americans but spent large amounts of money to challenge the constitutionality of Chicago's tepid anti-discrimination housing ordinance. The crowd of opponents to open housing rapidly ballooned to ten times the number of nonviolent volunteers, so that Bevel chose to shepherd us out of the area in police vans. Two days later, a march of two hundred fifty left New Friendship Baptist Church on Saturday morning, walking several miles west along 71st Street into Marquette Park to reach Halvorsen Realty. Again, police protection could not restrain the larger crowd of angry white residents who threw bottles and rocks, forcing us to retreat in some disarray. The internal SCLC debates raged all afternoon and evening about whether to demand police protection or to risk harm to demonstrators in order to dramatize the violence of the Northern color line. I was unsure how to balance the scope of moral responsibility to protect our own activists with my clear preference for continuing the momentum of the demonstrations. Each side of the argument was persuasive in turn.

The next afternoon, we came back to Marquette Park, with returning cars and vans parked under police protection. We were again attacked and overwhelmed by several thousand furious defenders of segregation. The racist chants, the attacks on nuns, the rage at Daley's police for protecting the marchers seemed only to feed their fury, and a teenage mob sent forty marchers and two policemen to the hospital before they attacked our vans, slashing tires, pushing cars into the golf course lake, and firing them with Molotov cocktails. We sang freedom songs and retreated to Ashland Avenue and the safety of the Black neighborhood. It was shocking and turbulent, a bit invigorating, an echo of Little Rock's mob fear and aggression. The images of that Sunday were flashed around the world, and remain emblematic of Chicago's violent stand in support of white power, the symbols of white supremacy, and segregation.

On Friday, August 5, 1965, Dr. King was struck in the head by a thrown brick and knocked down. Cars and buses of the marchers that were parked in Marquette Park were again trashed and burned. Almost a thousand Chicago police were deployed in riot helmets along our line of march, but the white racist crowd of five thousand had signs calling for extermination of Blacks, and they went after the priests and rabbis with a frenzy normally reserved for Dr. King, Al Raby, and SCLC leaders. Demonstrators were pulled from cars and beaten. We climbed into transit buses gathered to get us out, and the buses were surrounded, their gas tanks filled with sugar and windows smashed. After police lines moved us out, we learned that the mob turned its frenzy on the police and on Mayor Daley, stoning police cars until midnight. Dr. King spoke to a packed crowd at New Friendship Church that night, vowing to march in twenty neighborhoods like Gage Park. "I have never in my life seen such hate. Not in Mississippi or Alabama. This is a terrible thing."

James Bevel and Jesse Jackson roused the next mass meeting at Warren Avenue Church with a pledge to continue the marches and to take them into Cicero, the all-white near suburb where teenager Jerome Huey was beaten to death when his job interview had left him on Cicero streets at dusk in May. The marches grew larger and the threat of escalating violence was throbbing. For many of the young activists, including Prexy Nesbitt and Bernard LaFayette, the challenges would lead to a lifetime affiliation with nonviolent resistance. Yet the words of Malcolm X, assassinated just the year before, also haunted the escalating drama with the concept of self-defense: "I don't mean go out and get violent; but at the same time you should never be nonviolent unless you run into some nonviolence. I'm nonviolent with those who are nonviolent with me."

Every weekday night throughout the summer, Black churches overflowed, paper fans moved the hot air while the audiences waited for Dr. King. It was the assignment of the young preachers who followed the rollicking gospel singers to warm up the crowd and keep everyone engaged until King arrived. Often, that took hours. This was the rhetorical finishing school for Jesse Jackson, James Bevel, Bernard LaFayette and others who toiled to improvise, entertain, and agitate the throngs without peaking until the entrance of Dr. King. Between them, they provided an analysis of where we were, what brought us here, and what was needed to move forward. There was not discussion and debate, but there was rhetoric as high art form, and these nighttime rallies spread encouragement, comfort and hope.

The emerging Latino movement appeared to join forces with the SCLC's direct action in Chicago; Puerto Rican organizations like the Spanish Action Committee of Chicago and the East Harlem Tenants Council in New York came to show solidarity and build their own forces. In Uptown, Chicago's poor white neighborhood of Appalachian migrants, community organizers from Jobs or Income Now (JOIN) were adapting the rent strike strategy to their own neighborhood. Chicago seemed to me like an epicenter of global turmoil, a bellwether of where the polarized country might be headed.

Meanwhile, the *Tribune* continued to denounce King as an outlaw: "Causing violence to achieve political ends is criminal syndicalism." Catholic Archbishop Cody withdrew his support for further demonstrations, noting that continuations would "very likely result in serious injury to many persons and perhaps even loss of life." *The New York Times* editorialized that "the Chicago demonstrations run the risk of major violence...A moratorium on these open-housing marches is essential..."

As the climate of crisis deepened and as death threats poured in, we now know the FBI was secretly wiretapping and spying on Dr. King as part of COINTELPRO. The contradictions within the Black Freedom Movement were accelerating, and Black Power, resistance and militancy were growing forces, as white power dug in to defend the status quo. I listened at an SCLC retreat as Bevel, Jackson, LaFayette and Raby argued to escalate, while others in SCLC counseled negotiation and settlement. Dr. King's national allies and supporters flew in to lobby him daily, themselves cajoled or persuaded to intervene to convince him to leave Chicago: United Auto Workers official Walter Reuther, financial supporters like Harry Wachtel, close advisors like Stanley Levison, and members of his own SCLC national staff such as Andrew Young. Archbishop Cody called for a moratorium on demonstrations, "with a heavy heart." The mayor sent out feelers for settlement talks. The marches continued into Bogan, and then into three new neighborhoods led by Raby, Bevel and Jackson. The vigils continued at real estate offices and savings and loan association sites in the Chicago Loop.

The open housing marches became the lightning rod that made the color line visible outside the South, at least to sleeping whites, to the media, to politicians. As historian Taylor Branch concludes, Chicago "nationalized" race. It illustrated what racism looks like in waves similar to the Southern Civil Rights Movement: tear gas, broken bones, inequality, racial apartheid, and virulent white resistance. Chicago was the visible secret violent underbelly of urban life, the defense of white power and privilege; everyone could see that the moderate cry for equality, fair housing, and access was being resisted with force and fury.

Simultaneously, even I could see that the dynamism and drama of mass mobilizations was overwhelming and submerging community organizing strategies. This pattern of sacrificing local work that developed grassroots leaders in favor of mass mobilizations and confrontation, well-documented and criticized by Ms. Ella Baker and SNCC activists in the South, was apparent to all in Chicago. Ella Baker, a behind-the-scenes genius and guiding force in SNCC, insisted that the people with the least be at the center of strategizing and decision making. The detailed organizing of tenants, building by building, continued in Chicago but was diminished. Although the interconnected economic, social, and political forces that result in rampant inequality were no less powerful and entrenched in Chicago than in Mississippi, in the North the complex system of white supremacy standing invisibly in the doorway was in some respects less apparent, more difficult to personify. The powerful real estate industry was largely unseen, obscured, not the focus of attention. Banking and lending institutions, and decades of federal policies that promoted segregated housing, were disguised or murky. The mayor was deploying his police to protect the marchers. It seemed as if the primary opponents of open housing were the residents of white neighborhoods, fiercely protecting their homes and lawns. Mayor Daley was determined to resist the call for open housing but equally resolute about not being perceived like menacing police commissioner Bull Conner while preserving "Chicago's image."

The Viet Nam War continued to escalate; as a law student, I was increasingly asked to do community-based draft counseling at the Warren Avenue Church headquarters. This consisted of holding clinics to prepare lay volunteers to be draft counselors, to teach about exemptions to the draft, alternative ways of resisting, and to recruit panels of "experts" (such as clergy, psychiatrists, doctors, and employers) who were willing to write letters to draft boards, urging them to reclassify a particular youth to exempt them from military service. Over the following seven months, King would wrestle more and more with the moral imperative of the U.S. invasion of Viet Nam, and the massive deployment of African American youngsters in the front lines of that occupation. His heavy-hearted conclusion rolled forth in his speech at Riverside Church in New York on April 4, 1967, where he denounced the war, against all advice from his financial supporters and most Civil Rights allies: "I knew that I could never again raise my voice against the violence of the oppressed in the ghettos," he said, "without having first spoken clearly to the greatest purveyor of violence in the world today: my own government. For the sake of those boys, for the sake of this government, for the sake of the hundreds of thousands trembling under our violence, I cannot be silent." The same month, Muhammad Ali was indicted by the U.S. government for refusing to join the military to fight in Viet Nam; he was stripped of his boxing title and his license to fight.

By the time SCLC was seated at the summit negotiating table with the mayor and Chicago's economic leaders—including the Chicago Real Estate Board, which had spent millions fighting Civil Rights legislation and was at that very moment continuing to challenge Chicago's fair housing ordinance in court—the die was cast. Under continuous pressure from ongoing demonstrations at a hundred real estate offices, Daley went to court and secured an injunction limiting the number of marchers and of future marches to one per day. King rejected proposals from Bevel and Jackson within his own ranks and from other Chicago militants to march into the tinderbox of Cicero, site of a brutal "race riot" in 1951 and noted for not having a single Black resident. Following a large march into the far southeast side near the steelworks, which again resulted in violent opposition, and the appearance of the American Nazi commander George Lincoln Rockwell and his cronies in Marquette Park, Dr. King hesitated, announcing plans to take three thousand demonstrators into Cicero the next Sunday. The National Guard was dispatched in preparation. But the pressure on King to retreat was intense; the pressure on Daley to obtain a settlement was enormous: "We've got commies, we've got Nazis, and everybody else you can name showing up. I wish they'd go home!" Dr. King announced a moratorium on marches. Once the Black Freedom Movement was out of the streets at the end of August, there was no bargaining leverage left. King called the face-saving summit agreement "far reaching and creative," but it had no teeth. He left town.

The Chicago Freedom Movement morphed and changed as social struggles do. Welfare rights went national and—for a while—grew in strength. Housing organizing continued on the ground and in the courts, and Chicago CORE led the elusive march into Cicero, but the weekly galvanizing marches for justice were over. Segregation both changed shape and was reinforced. The war in Viet Nam loomed as a vast shadow over Chicago's west side and the poor neighborhoods, devouring young men, skewing priorities. But thousands of people, including me, were transformed by the Chicago Freedom Movement's campaign to address racial injustice in the Northern ghettos, and the young Black organizers who were there would become leaders and activists during the next decades.

Since his death and subsequent canonization, the vibrant and real Martin Luther King, Jr., the thirty-seven-year-old activist who was constantly attacked by the powerful and was continually growing, radicalizing, and deepening his critique of the "three dangers" (militarism, racism and consumerism) has been erased from memory. The gloss of history makes it seem that Dr. King's 1963 "I Have a Dream" speech melted the hearts of mistaken and privileged white folk, who saw the light and instantly embraced justice, or at least became nice. But he was not welcomed in Chicago by the powerful, and I learned something about virulent racism and structural white supremacy when King came to town, and began to realize other lessons when he left. I was unlearning white supremacist attitudes and values in street seminars. A student of the depth and shape of institutional racism. Schooled and instructed, I was moving further away from the Socratic world of law school.

***

New organizing worlds opened up to me simultaneously – even as I nominally returned to third year law classes. Under the "El" tracks on Wilson Avenue, Hank Williams blaring from bars, the Goodfellows — slicked hair, cigarette packs rolled into the t-shirt taut across biceps — patrolled the community documenting police abuse...In the Uptown neighborhood of Chicago, I first saw white radicals working in a poor white Appalachian community, supporting local leaders and challenging racism by building coalitions with Black, Chicano, and Puerto Rican organizations across Chicago. JOIN was created by former SDS student activists who had left their universities to work as community organizers in the neighborhoods of the dispossessed, and by local leaders like Peggy Terry, Junebug Boykin, and (surprisingly) Mrs. Dovie Coleman, part Black/part Indian, raised in Mississippi, who organized welfare recipients (mainly white) in Uptown. "The problem is that we've been fighting each other and never got to see the real cause. The real cause has been that the poor white thinks he's better than the n....., while the big shot guy is sittin up there laughing at both of em."

SNCC had challenged white students to leave the Black community and to confront the task of organizing white people. Hearing me speak about the rent strike strategy as invented by SCLC on the West Side at some meeting, JOIN invited me to talk with them about their organizing efforts for habitable housing in Uptown, where poverty among whites was the defining issue. They had just launched three rent strikes, high profile actions with mixed results when the landlords just refused to comply with court-orders.

Welfare mothers were a feisty and energized force here, as on the West Side, and Uptown women, the majority on welfare and fresh from Kentucky or West Virginia, appeared fearless. Their decisions were communal and by consensus rather than dominated by a single charismatic speaker/leader; children were, of course, present during lengthy meetings, as were elderly relatives and the disabled. They gave me *The Dollmaker* to read, and Tillie Olsen stories. Neighborhood safety, productive youth activities, adolescent protection from violent police retaliation, and the demand for jobs with a living wage were part of their issue-oriented work. These women were used to sustained coal-miner labor struggles and brutal poverty in Appalachia, which they were translating into the mean Chicago streets. JOIN was established in the wake of *The Other America* by Michael Harrington, which exposed the face of one-quarter of the U.S. population living in extreme poverty—the majority white. In Uptown, community leaders sometimes called themselves "hillbillies" or "white trash" as a badge of pride and, like poor African Americans on the west side of Chicago, these families actively continued their connections to the rural part of the country from which they migrated: in this case, the mountain hollows and mines of Appalachia. Their military had its own lengthy tradition and was simultaneously and re-energized by insurgencies in the Black community.

Uptown community organizers were interested in my new connections to volunteer lawyers and legal services for the poor. Akin to my experience on the west side, I was increasingly asked to provide draft counseling and advise young men about how to resist going to fight in Viet Nam. These were the fertile recruiting fields for the draft and the military—no jobs, no likelihood of college, easy picking. Teenagers like Robert, with severe asthma, would have obtained an easy deferment had he been a middle-class college student. When he and his mom came to our draft counseling clinic, we had a network of volunteer doctors, one of whom examined Robert, gathered his medical records, and provided a file for his draft board. He obtained the medical deferment to which he was entitled and was not drafted. We organized a network across Chicago to expand community draft counseling and to recruit and train law students, doctors, and psychologists to volunteer their time one night a week in the poorest neighborhoods.

We met with our picket signs in the freezing, 5 A.M. mornings outside the ancient red brick armory near Lake Michigan, where the biting wind raced up the valley like streets: "The hawk is on the wing," Chicagoans say. I arrived before the buses that carried eighteen- and nineteen-year-old draftees from across the region, who were to be inducted into the U.S. military by taking a step forward once inside the armory. There was a slight window of forty-five arctic seconds between the moment the young guys got off the bus and when they entered the armory; we leafleted them, urged them to resist, and offered them both legal support and the pleasure of making a moral choice to oppose conscription in an immoral and unjust war. I don't recall a single successful recruit at that final frigid moment. We tried to make them think about the consequences of what they were doing; we thought we were at least planting seeds. But we found them again at military bases around the country and at the new coffeehouses opening just outside bases where anti-war and anti-racist literature and talk were available and, increasingly, these GIs found themselves. Contrary to lore about the Viet Nam anti-war movement, it was not only the relatively privileged students and middle-class youth who resisted the draft and opposed the war against Viet Nam. The militancy of former soldiers would be aroused by the end of the decade, and returning GIs opened a decisive new front of credible anti-war rebellion and defiance.

That same link to JOIN—through former student leaders Paul Booth and Michael James— brought me to my first national Students for a Democratic Society (SDS) meeting that fall in Berkeley, and to the SDS national office on West Madison Street in Chicago. I was in new territory listening to the SDS debate in Berkeley, even more chaotic than the SCLC debates on the west side where ultimately Dr. King made the decisions after listening to a range of passionate opinions. Here it appeared that whoever was present voted. The deliberation was about a proposal called "From Reform to Resistance," and the SDS National Council adopted the first resolution that counseled resistance to the draft—a position that advocated breaking the law. The fury of the debate, the verbal dancing and fencing, what we would later come to call the "male nitwit-know-it-alls" swept me away. I can only recall the arguments that favored resisting the draft, which seemed entirely persuasive. As Michael's new girlfriend at the SDS meeting, I had a certain cache; I also experienced a piercing anxiety and insecurity around women who were clearly his former or concurrent girlfriends but were themselves experienced activists, thinkers, and debaters. It would be months before I began to make a bit of sense of women's oppression, the perils of identification with men, and the structured competition with other women.

Returning to Chicago in the fall of 1966, I moved in with Jane Adams, the first feminist I ever met, who worked with SNCC in the South and was now an SDS national officer. Our apartment became a place where organizers from the Southern Civil Rights Movement crashed on their R & R breaks, or came to raise Northern money, or stopped as part of burnout and stress. Jane was a homegrown prairie radical; she grew up in Carbondale in the hills of Southern Illinois, daughter of rural activists and heir to the leftwing of the populist and agrarian movements of the heartland. Jane's mom was an avowed feminist, so Jane taught me to rethink how I thought of myself and the ways I viewed other women. In my initial enthusiasm for women's rights, I talked the five other women in my law school class into going downtown to meet with the Women's Bar Association members. It was a disastrous encounter; the women lawyers who had tea with us were all either law librarians or legal secretaries in their husbands' law firms. My sister law students were enraged at that vision of women and the law, and not sympathetic to the barriers faced by these older women attorneys. As it turned out, each of the six of us faced enormous gender barriers to getting our first jobs and one, who later became the first woman president of the American Bar Association, often told the story of being unable to get a job as a lawyer after graduating from the University of Chicago Law School. Because of changes in the draft law ending law student exemptions just two years later, women suddenly broke into law schools in equal numbers.

That next year, as a law graduate and National Lawyers Guild organizer, I finally made it to Appalachia. I traveled to Hazard, Kentucky, with Hamish Sinclair, who was an organizer with the National Committee for Miners. He met with coal miners, their wives, and their families, traveling through the hollows of coal country. We stayed with strike leaders, and the depression and loneliness of the women was apparent after a single night in their cabins. It was a revelation to see poor white poverty in such stark terms. The women grew and canned their food, supplemented by huge government-subsidized bags or cans of cornmeal, rice, green beans and mayonnaise. I recognized the pink pills on the medicine cabinet shelf as the same antidepressants and sleeping pills that women were prescribed in the suburb where I went to high school.

In these isolated and lush hollows, the women and children were home alone; the men went to work in the coal mines or enforced the strike. Asbestosis and Brown Lung were not yet recognized, but the rate of injuries and physical harm from the treacherous work was evident and being documented by the committee. No one there was surprised by the fierce level of organized resistance of the miners to the coal companies, their sustained opposition to the official goons, and their high level of armed militancy. And the women's eyes: knowing, harmed, trapped, determined.

On this same trip through West Virginia and Eastern Kentucky coal towns, we journeyed on to stay with Anne and Carl Braden in Louisville, just at the time when the sedition law under which they had been indicted a decade earlier was declared unconstitutional. At their home, I was a new unknown girlfriend, but privy to heated political discussions. Legendary by this time as militant anti-racist organizers in the South, the Bradens had spoken up and spoken out, braving jail, isolation, and retaliation. In 1950, three young men were seriously injured in a car crash two hours south of Louisville; the nearby hospital refused to treat African Americans, so one young man died on the hospital floor and the other two survived only after transport back to a segregated hospital in Louisville. Anne Braden responded, first by organizing the Interracial Hospital Movement and later the Civil Rights Congress and then the Southern Conference Educational Fund (SCEF). I was getting the picture: The women who made a life of resistance to racism and poverty had file drawers filled with numerous organizations and coalitions they forged and then watched disappear— sometimes with successes, often with failures. Anne Braden forged a determined life as a white Southern woman who rejected white supremacy—and it looked to be lonely as well as lively. She lost friends to controversy and government intimidation. She sent her children to be raised by her racist parents so she could organize for Carl's freedom when he was arrested and jailed for treason.

The Bradens had "fronted" as the white purchasers of a suburban home in a white segregated neighborhood for African Americans Andrew and Charlotte Wade in 1954. As soon as the Wade family moved in, shotguns were fired into their new home, and a dynamite blast exploded under their young daughter's bedroom. In response to the racist uproar over their role, Carl, Anne, and four other white activists of the Wade Defense Committee were indicted on charges of sedition and, incredibly, of dynamiting the Wade's house. The McCarthy-era anti-communist witchhunts merged with white segregationist backlash and Carl was convicted and sentenced to fifteen years. Anne, alone with two young children, began a public defense campaign that led to Carl's release after seven months and the dropping of further prosecutions. Seven years later, Carl would serve another prison sentence, this time for contempt of Congress for refusing to testify before the 1958 House Un-American Activities Committee (HUAC) hearings on "communist party propaganda influence in the South," relying on First

Amendment rights of speech and assembly. His case had been argued in the Supreme Court by Leonard Boudin, my friend, mentor, and colleague among New York anti-war lawyers, and later our son Chesa's grandfather.

Anne wrote for and edited *The Southern Patriot* newpaper and interrogated us about the situation of the miners in the eastern part of the state. She was aggressive and sharp, intimidating to me but clearly fearless. She wanted to know how anti-war organizing was addressing racism. She was interested in GI organizing and class consciousness. At this 1967 moment—a rising tide of resistance—Anne was operating full tilt, with colleagues, allies, and partners. As a white Southern woman dedicated to organizing white supporters to end segregation, Anne Braden cut a special path across the South—writing, mobilizing, resisting, and refusing to be isolated. She, like Ella Baker, Fannie Lou Hamer, Peggy Terry, and Annie Stein, wrote the syllabus for me and for successive generations of young women students and activists.

BORN INTO WAR

If the law is of such a nature that it requires you to be an agent of injustice... then, I say, break the law.
—Henry David Thoreau

War is a racket. It always has been. It is possibly the oldest, easily the most profitable, surely the most vicious... It is the only one in which the profits are reckoned in dollars and the losses in lives.
—Major General Smedley D. Butler

In America, every mother's child is born into race—it awaits us, it abides, catches us at first breath. We can't possibly know the ways it will define us, the wages it will extract, not in those first moments, so that can't be why we cry out. But even disguised or invisible, uninvited or unwelcomed, race marks us from the very start—it's in our mother's milk, as we said, in the North American air we breathe. Race is inescapable, and it's a life sentence, with no parole in sight.

When our eldest child was only a month old we three boarded a bus near Chinatown heading toward Golden Gate Park for a picnic to welcome Zayd and to show him off to our friends. A white-haired, pink-cheeked couple sat smiling and nodding across from us, and in what had become a familiar ritual to us as new parents, began cooing and cooching. We smiled and nodded, too, until, as the cheery couple gathered their belongings and prepared to depart, the man leaned toward us, smiled a yellow-toothed smile and proclaimed in a loud whisper, "It's so nice to see a beautiful white baby for a change—too many colored."

"Go away!" Bernardine erupted forcefully. Pow! The scene turned sour, the couple fled, and several people turned away uncomfortably. Turning to Zayd she whispered, "Don't listen to that racist man, honey." We wanted our baby to feel beautiful and loved, of course, but not beautiful or desirable because of whiteness. By then we knew that whiteness was an obstacle he'd have to learn to overcome if he would live in a fully human world. Zayd simply blinked and smiled his infant smile into his mother's face.

Race is shifting and capricious and unstable, and because the delusion of white supremacy is both entrenched and precarious, it has always required a large army to police its borders—it's a fool's errand, ultimately, but the U.S. has never wanted for race patriots willing to muster up and volunteer for the job. It's tempting for the privileged to imagine the racial border guards as old buffoons or delusional bigots or, more typically, screaming mobs and night-riders, the Klan and the Minutemen, hooded rednecks in full eruption—comforting but untrue. Liberals might add a conscious conspiracy by a powerful elite, but that, too, is an insufficient explanation. The truth is more difficult to face: The border guards set up their little stations inside the heads and hearts of every white person, as well as in the core of capitalism; the line between good and evil is a thin one, and it runs down the middle of every soul. Racism is inscribed in our shared historical experiences, entangled in our culture, embedded in our economy, enacted in the everyday patterns of our lives. It's structural; it's personal.

David Malouf, in his novel *Remembering Babylon*, imagines the unraveling of a settler community on the Queensland coast of Australia in the nineteenth century when a man stumbles from the outback who looks and talks like a native but is, unmistakably, an Englishman who had been raised by Aboriginals from boyhood. Without the illusion of normal borders, the neat and handy division of "us" and "other," the town spins irrevocably out of control. Those barbarians were (and are) as Constantine Cavafy points out, "a kind of solution." Without "them," "we" can so easily become uncertain and then unhinged.

The active troops patrolling the border of race in the U.S. have always included the "good people"—judges and lawyers, doctors and social workers, clergy and artists, merchants and industrialists, scientists and teachers—surely those who claim *not* to see the horrors around them, those who are sleepwalking through their lives, those who seek refuge in a reassuring racial innocence and a privileged ignorance. As James Baldwin persistently argued, the insistent claims of innocence lie at the very heart of the nation's crimes.

Zayd's welcoming picnic in Golden Gate Park was lovely. People filled the meadow and brought blankets for the ground, cake and fruit, beer and barbecue, and little presents for our new baby. Three elderly Black women, co-workers of Bill's on the waterfront and sisters from Belize, held Zayd, cuddled and tickled him, passed him around for close examination, and offered Bernardine a quiet word of wisdom: "Nurse him as long as he wants," they said. "He knows when it's time to stop." One of them added, "You must have three children, because one will die, and then the two will have one another." That advice unsettled us, for it threw into relief our own privileges and a contrasting life experience far, far from our own.

***

We were both born into war, launched into life under the leaden shadow of Pearl Harbor, the Holocaust, Dresden, Stalingrad, the Blitz, Hiroshima and Nagasaki. While World War II can never be reduced to a single narrative nor even a series of famous events—too much slaughter and genocide, too much mass murder, too much fierce contention over colonies—it was also, on another level and importantly, a war of ideas. Like the War for Independence and the Civil War, this war involved huge ideas about the nature of humanity and the question of freedom. The bloody consequences were sprawled across the globe for all to see.

On one side stood a range of ideas about hierarchy and control, superiority and order, "the science of race" and the desire for "racial purity"; arrayed against that, an unlikely coalition embracing diverging insurgent ideas about human rights and dignity, socialism, resistance to fascism, equality and enlightenment, democracy and liberation. The war fueled or ignited an unprecedented wave of anti-colonial struggle in Africa,

Latin America, and Asia, and provided force and impetus to the Black Freedom Movement and the fight against white supremacy in the U.S. There had always been resistance to the myth of white superiority and its logic of genocide, of course, and the survival against all odds of an African American people or nation—based in part in the South but with a far-flung diaspora—was eloquent testimony to an ongoing effort characterized by loss and endurance and, ultimately, one of the great human triumphs in history. But in the 1940s, with the wars of ideas, and battles and resistances on the ground in every continent, everything heated up.

On December 10, 1948, the General Assembly of the United Nations adopted and proclaimed the "Universal Declaration of Human Rights," establishing and codifying moral norms and standards for every person and guaranteeing basic rights for all. This document bears the scars and the bloody footprints—as well as the profound and enduring hopes—generated out of the human slaughter, genocide, and aerial bombing of civilians that was World War II.

Universal Declaration of Human Rights
PREAMBLE

Whereas recognition of the inherent dignity and of the equal and inalienable rights of all members of the human family is the foundation of freedom, justice and peace in the world,

Whereas disregard and contempt for human rights have resulted in barbarous acts which have outraged the conscience of mankind, and the advent of a world in which human beings shall enjoy freedom of speech and belief and freedom from fear and want has been proclaimed as the highest aspiration of the common people,

Whereas it is essential, if a man is not to be compelled to have recourse, as a last resort, to rebellion against tyranny and oppression, that human rights should be protected by the rule of law,

Whereas it is essential to promote the development of friendly relations between nations,

Whereas the people of the United Nations have in the Charter reaffirmed their faith in fundamental human rights, in the dignity and worth of the human person and in the equal rights of men and women and have determined to promote social progress and better standards of life and larger freedom,

Whereas Member States have pledged themselves to achieve, in co-operation with the United Nations, the promotion of universal respect for and observance of human rights and fundamental freedoms, Whereas a common understanding of these rights and freedoms is of the greatest importance for the full realization of this pledge,

Now Therefore, **The General Assembly** Proclaims **This Universal Declaration of Human Rights** as a common standard of achievement for all peoples and all nations, to the end that every individual and every organ of society, keeping this Declaration constantly in mind, shall strive by teaching and education to promote respect for these rights and freedoms and by progressive measures, national and international, to secure their universal and effective recognition and observance, both among the peoples of Member States themselves and among peoples of territories under their jurisdiction.

Article 1
All human beings are born free and equal in dignity and rights. They are endowed with reason and conscience and should act toward one another in a spirit of brotherhood.

Article 2
Everyone is entitled to all the rights and freedoms set forth in this Declaration, without distinction of any kind, such as race, color, sex, language, religion, political or other opinion, national or social origin, property, birth or other status. Furthermore, no distinction shall be made on the basis of the political, jurisdictional or international status of the country or territory to which a person belongs, whether it be independent, trust, non-self-governing or under any other limitation of sovereignty.

Article 3
Everyone has the right to life, liberty and security of person.

Article 4
No one shall be held in slavery or servitude; slavery and the slave trade shall be prohibited in all their forms.

Article 5
No one shall be subjected to torture or to cruel, inhuman or degrading treatment or punishment.

Article 6
Everyone has the right to recognition everywhere as a person before the law.

Article 7
All are equal before the law and are entitled without any discrimination to equal protection of the law. All are entitled to equal protection against any discrimination in violation of this Declaration and against any incitement to such discrimination.

On and on in the idealistic spirit of emancipation and enlightenment, in the service of humanity:

Article 26
*(1)Everyone has the right to education. Education shall be free, at least in the elementary and fundamental stages. Elementary education shall be compulsory. Technical and
professional education shall be made generally available and higher education shall be equally accessible to all on the basis of merit.*

*(2) Education shall be directed to the full development of the human personality and to the strengthening of respect for human rights and fundamental freedoms. It shall promote
understanding, tolerance and friendship among all nations, racial or religious groups, and shall further the activities of the United Nations for the maintenance of peace.*

(3) Parents have a prior right to choose the kind of education that shall be given to their children.

Elegant stuff. Exhilarating. Liberating. And none of its content lost on African Americans struggling for justice in a segregated, Jim Crow society. The power of the people. Ideas to unleash the energy of the whirlwind and the volcano. And they did.

Mary McLeod Bethune drafted a Ten-Point Program adopted by the National Council of Negro Women after World War II that called for removing all restrictions on voting in elections and primaries, ending restrictive covenants that maintain segregation in housing, making lynching a federal crime, providing increased federal funding for education on a nondiscriminatory basis, outlawing discrimination in employment on the basis of race, creed, color, or national origin, supporting the efforts of the United Nations to maintain world order and peace, participating in food distribution programs to peoples and countries in need, amending the Social Security Act in order to extend benefits to domestic and agricultural workers, and establishing programs to prevent and control juvenile delinquency.

On December 17, 1951, William Patterson and Paul Robeson delivered to the United Nations a petition entitled, "We Charge Genocide: The Crime of Government Against the Negro People," an indictment of lynching as genocide. Robeson was accompanied by several signatories when he presented the document to a UN official in New York City; Patterson, executive director of the Civil Rights Congress (CRC), which had drafted the petition, delivered copies to UN delegates meeting in Paris.

"Out of the inhuman Black ghettos of American cities," the introduction read, "out of the cotton plantations of the South, comes this record of mass slayings on the basis of race, of lives deliberately warped and distorted by the willful creation of conditions making for premature death, poverty and disease." The federal government claimed it had nothing to do with the lynchings, but this petition said, "you knew about it and you did nothing. You knew about the super-exploitation and inhuman hardships inflicted upon the Black people and you did nothing. Your inaction, your indifference in the face of oppression means that it was policy."

Among the signers were the eminent African American historian and freedom fighter Dr. W.E.B. DuBois, George Crockett, Jr., later a distinguished judge in Detroit who went on to serve many terms in the U.S. Congress, New York City Communist councilman Benjamin J. Davis, Jr., Ferdinand Smith, labor and civil rights lawyer, and Claudia Jones, a Communist leader in Harlem later deported under the witch-hunt Walter-McCarran Act. Also signing were family members of the victims of legal lynching: Rosalee McGee, mother of Willie McGee, framed up on rape charges, and Josephine Grayson, whose husband, Francis Grayson, was one of the Martinsville Seven, framed and executed on false rape charges in Virginia. The section entitled "Evidence" documented hundreds of cases of lynching drawing on decades of research, reporting, and activism led by Ida B. Wells-Barnett. The petition charged that since the abolition of slavery ten thousand Black people had been lynched. The full number, it stated, will never be known because the murders often went unreported.

Legal battles in concert with grassroots efforts and partial victories lurched forward: the election of Adam Clayton Powell, Jr. to the U.S. Congress in 1944; *Brown v. Board of Education* in 1954; Rosa Parks and the Montgomery Bus Boycott; the Little Rock

Nine and the Civil Rights Act of 1957; the U.S. Commission on Civil Rights (USCCR) recommending the suspension of federal funds for colleges and universities with discriminatory admission practices in 1959; the Freedom Riders and the sit-in movements in 1960; the desegregation of the University of Georgia with the admission of Charlayne Hunter and Hamilton Holmes in 1961, and the struggle to admit James Meredith to the University of Mississippi in 1962; the Battle of Birmingham and protest marches of 1963; Mississippi Summer and the murders of James Chaney, Andrew Goodman, and Micky Schwerner and the Civil Rights Act of 1964; the Selma to Montgomery March and the Voting Rights Act of 1965; Watts in 1965; and Chicago Freedom Summer in 1966. The beat carried on.

***

Let's look at the Universal Declaration of Human Rights for a moment in light of the reality of our own times, through the lens of racism in the U.S. today.

On June 13, 2005, the U.S. Senate passed by voice vote a "non-binding resolution" read: symbolic and toothless expressing "the deepest sympathies and solemn regrets ... to the descendants of victims of lynching, the ancestors of whom were deprived of life, human dignity and the constitutional protections accorded all citizens of the United States." Seven Senators dissented—imagine that; not that the other ninety-three were being fully authentic, but still, seven couldn't even pull themselves toward a muffled "sorry." On that day, according to the nonbinding resolution, "the Senate remembers the history of lynching to ensure that these tragedies will be neither forgotten nor repeated." The action came in the context of a string of convictions against aging white segregationists—Byron De La Beckwith, Bobby Frank Cherry, Edgar Ray Killen—for previously unresolved murders from the Civil Rights era.

Who can object? On the other hand, what does any of it mean? Is it legitimate atonement for anti-Black violence? Is it superficial and cosmetic and self-congratulatory?

From 1882–1968 white terrorist mobs lynched over five thousand African American men, women, and children—mostly young men—in the United States. This number, while smaller than the "We Charge Genocide" figure, represents fully documented cases by today's historical standards. Anti-lynching legislation was introduced into Congress hundreds of times over those years, and on those occasions when a bill passed the House, it was always killed in the Senate. Most white people—even those who opposed the lawlessness—tacitly accepted the underlying demonization of African Americans, especially African American men, as dangerous and potentially out of control, and had developed a "fixed notion," abstracted from data, context, and complexity, assuming that the Black lynching victims were, after all, likely guilty. It's true that some few whites supported Ida B. Wells-Barnett's masterful campaigns against lynching, and there's some ray of hope in that historical fact, but it's also true that active white opponents of lynching were a teeny, tiny company—apart from a small but significant group of radicals associated with the Communist Party and a few smaller socialist bodies, almost no white people took any overt action against lynching whatsoever—and it's easy in retrospect to valorize those few as representative of all of us. They weren't.

The lynchings in the post-Reconstruction South were a key part of a campaign of terror with the goal of preventing free Black people from owning land and developing economic or political power. A minority of hard-core killers—some prominent officials in the light of day—actually donned the white robes, lit the fires, set the bombs, and threw the heavy ropes over the branches. But many more white people were called upon to inflame the fear, promote the allegations, witness and celebrate the events, identify with the vigilante murderers, and to link their privileged status and favored fates to those deadly deeds. The message to Black people: At any moment and for any reason whatsoever your life or the lives of your loved ones can be randomly snuffed out. And the corollary to whites: Celebrate or shut up, but enjoy your privileges. The intention—and the consequence—was systemic social control through random intimidation and unpredictable mayhem and murder. Prejudice was a partner and an outgrowth.

Every year since 1989, Representative John Conyers (D–Michigan) introduces H.R. 40, a bill that would create a commission to analyze the impact of slavery and to review whether "any form of compensation to the descendents of African slaves is warranted." Every year, H.R. 40 quietly disappears.

In 2007, Representative Steve Cohen (D–Tenn.) introduced a bill—which now has over fifty co-sponsors—apologizing to African Americans for the "fundamental injustice, cruelty, brutality and inhumanity of slavery and Jim Crow," and calling for a "commitment to rectify the lingering consequences of the misdeeds committed against African Americans..."

The same year the Virginia state assembly voted unanimously expressing "profound regret" for the state's part in "the most horrendous of all depredations of human rights and violations of our founding ideals in our nation's history."

It's a good thing to note the wrongs of the past certainly, but a much better thing to identify them forcefully, right the wrongs, and work to repair the wounds. But failing to examine the deeper issues—in this case the system of white supremacy, the multiple mechanisms that attempt social control of an entire population, blatant racial disparities and economic injustice and targeted brutality—and then using the apology exercise to illuminate today's injustices and today's challenges empties the gesture. Of course the era of slavery and actual lynchings should never be repeated, but are there any contemporary echoes, any current-day sites of racial inequality and oppression? Could we start with infant mortality? Life expectancy? Could we collectively choose to repay the debt? What should be done?

A Black telephone company employee discovered a doll on her desk with a noose around its neck and a note saying she didn't deserve her recent promotion; a Black high school principal received a noose in the mail; a Black professor at Teachers College found a noose suspended from her office door.

The history of race has always been a history of violence and resistance. Just as racial attacks and mob violence accelerated during previous economic dislocations—notorious white riots in Detroit and Chicago during and after both World Wars, the Zoot Suit riots in Los Angeles in 1943—reported hate crimes in the U.S. stand at close to two hundred thousand a year, and the number of hate groups has risen 40 percent in the past few years.

In the "golden age of lynching," the tortured Black body surrounded by grinning whites was the face of white supremacy. In 1955 Emmett Tills's mutilated and broken body—displayed in an open casket because of his mother's grief and rage and courage showed the world what white supremacy could do and at the same time sparked the innovations of Little Rock, the freedom rides, sit-ins, and voter registration drives. James Byrd was dragged from a pick—up truck in Jasper, Texas, in June 1998, his body ripped apart and dismembering along the way, but still alive and suffering up to the point that he was decapitated, and no pictures of the body were ever made public. Perhaps the motive was respect for the family, perhaps denial, but there is vicious evidence here of agendas unfinished and work to do.

Facing history, acknowledging the truth, opening our eyes to the enduring inequalities between Black people and so-called whites, acting on what the known demands of us this is a necessary part of putting an end to slavery's lengthening legacy. In fact, it may be the only way forward, the only path to ending our racial sorrows and overcoming white obliviousness and what Randall Robinson has called "the time-release social debilitations of American slavery"—crippling poverty, rotten schools, mass incarceration, poor health, dilapidated neighborhoods, stunted life expectancy.

THE MODERN SLAVE SHIP

Bernardine Dohrn

Neither slavery nor involuntary servitude, except as a punishment for crime whereof the party shall have been duly convicted, shall exist within the United States, or any place subject to their jurisdiction.

—Thirteenth Amendment
U.S. Constitution

Even though the Thirteenth Amendment to the U.S. Constitution outlawed involuntary servitude, white supremacy continued to be embraced by vast numbers of people and became deeply inscribed in new institutions.

—Angela Y. Davis

Every other day we received a telephone call from deep in the bowels of the prison industrial complex during the twenty years when our children were growing up. It came in the form of an automated voice message: "This is a collect call from a New York State Correctional Facility. ...If you will accept the charges, please press 3." The frequent calls were from Kathy Boudin, our adopted son Chesa's other mother, and they came from the women's maximum-security prison in Bedford Hills, outside New York City. Less often, the calls were from Attica, or Dannemora, or Auburn, or Great Meadow and they came from David Gilbert, Chesa's other father. Both were serving life sentences and both have remained engaged and devoted parents to Chesa, adored by him. They became family to Malik and Zayd as well.

Our relationship to the gulag—the modern slave ship that sprang forth and was multiplying across the land—was intimate and ongoing. Of course it was also wildly privileged: The collect calls were paid for by parents and grandparents, and frequent and regular visits by Chesa, and bi annually by all of us, were subsidized as well.

During the first week of each school year, beginning in first grade, Chesa would matter-of-factly announce to a startled teacher and his small classmates that he had a mother and father in prison. Predictably, concerned parents would call me the following evening, wanting to know if it was true and careful to note that they were seeking advice about how to respond to their own child's questions about prison. To a person, throughout elementary school, they assured us that they were fully supportive of Chesa, and they were. It became a rolling seminar for us and them, a set of judgments about honesty and openness, information—but not more than could be handled. It was Chesa's brilliant way of announcing himself and integrating his families. He taught a cohort each year about an often invisible aspect of millions of children's lives, pre-empting potential name-calling or stigma. Everyone followed his lead onto the high road....

The boys grew up visiting prisons. Chesa was an experienced pro, recognizable and even treated affectionately by the most miserable of prison guards. He taught Zayd and Malik the ropes: Don't bring anything into prison from the car that is contraband—food, chewing gum, keys, magic markers, puzzles, papers, books, toys—empty your pockets, take off your shoes, don't get annoyed, be prepared to wait. Visiting Kathy was easier because she was just outside New York City. After the Attica rebellion, momentum from women prisoners, and legal efforts to improve conditions of confinement, legislation was passed to get mothers in prison on an equal legal footing

54

with parents on the outside who had children in foster care. Efforts by the crusading Sister Elaine Roulet, with support from the warden, led to the creation of a children's center for the 80 percent of women prisoners who had children. The sunlit visiting room at Bedford has a well-stocked children's playroom at one end and an outdoor patio for summer play alongside. The Parenting Program at Bedford has been standard-setting: group work with mothers, programs for children, for adolescents, for home families where the children currently live, the summer visiting program, a newborn center, and transition centers for women paroled.

Over two decades of visiting Kathy taught the boys a great deal about gender/race/class and society. Few white women are in prison; 89 percent of the women in prison in the U.S. are women of color. Today's fastest growing prison populations are women and immigrants. Women particularly women of color, women who are poor, immigrant women, lesbian and transgender women, disabled women, teen mothers, and sex workers—women who are marginalized and stigmatized, are both disproportionately survivors of extreme domestic and sexual violence, and driven down the path to prison and criminalization. This process is what Beth Richie calls "gender entrapment": That complex context of economic and social relationships involving interpersonal violence, sexual assault, and state violence in the form of economic assault (such as welfare reform, low-wage work, immigration raids, deportation, child welfare practices) that together constitute gender violence, particularly for women of color. Yet gender and sexuality are rarely synthesized with the crossroads of race and class, or represented in ways that reflect their composite identities or intersectionality.

Incarceration is only partly about crime. Violent crime rates for both males and females declined sharply since 1994, but the number of adults convicted of felonies in state courts increased and two-thirds of those convicted were sentenced to prison or jail. The number of women in jails almost tripled between 1990 and 2006, and doubled in correctional institutions (1986–1997), increasing faster than the rate for men. There is little evidence that women were committing more crimes; rather, changes in law enforcement and sentencing practices ensnared more young females in the system. These were the women that Chesa and his brothers met at Bedford Hills.

The African American and Latina women and girls, who are disproportionally incarcerated in jails and prisons, have come from urban neighborhoods impoverished by structural racism and neglect: those parts of the cities where extreme poverty, violence, lack of jobs, and health services are chronic. Imprisoned women and girls have experienced extraordinary levels of sexual assaults, intimate partner battering, and violence before jail or prison. The now abundant evidence indicates that these women and children survived repeated and extreme gender violence, and find themselves incarcerated in jails and prisons where their identities and bodies are further subject to control, searches, surveillance, and humiliation. Confinement operates to reduce prisoners to a powerless, dependent state of physical intimidation. Constant monitoring, the lack of privacy, the inability to remain in touch with children and families, strip searches and frustration, unhealthy food, boredom, and inactivity—the threats and sexual violence—all replicate women's past experiences with pervasive violence and control, and are re-traumatizing. The uniforms, the rules about what color clothing we could send in, the ever-changing regulations about books, food, phone calls, and mail work to enforce a dependency and frustration that is relentless. Yet the resilience of women in prison persists in ways that make it impossible to think of them only as victims; they are also survivors, inspiring and brilliant, creative and anguished, engaged and passive, mature and paternalized. We were witness to their graduations from high school, college, and graduate school while incarcerated; were audience to their performances and poetry; observers to their grit and creativity in the most innovative popular educational prison programs on HIV/AIDS prevention, hospice care, and treatment; and onlookers to their struggle to parent in countless ways from a distance.

Since relatively few white women are in prison, even fewer of the incarcerated women are Jewish. One spring, when our boys were nine, six, and five, the rabbi who worked part time at the prison encouraged his synagogue to help prepare a feast to celebrate Passover in prison and the prisoners were able to invite family guests. The children were excited to be sharing a prison event that was outside the ordinary visits, beyond junk food from the machines. There was the challenge of carving the roasted chickens with the plastic knives and forks available. Of course we had grape juice, not wine.

The rabbi led the service and the children, being New Yorkers, were familiar enough with the ritual and prompts. It was special for the prisoners to be able to talk to other visitors and their families, because the rule in the visiting room during normal times was No Cross-Visiting; prisoners were not allowed to sit or talk with families of other prisoners. When it came to the hunt for the *afikomen* (a piece of matzah wrapped in a napkin and hidden by the rabbi at the start of the service), Chesa, Malik and Zayd were determined to find the treasure and win a prize. Malik found the *afikomen* in a corner of the room under a chair. As the reward, the rabbi told the children that they could make a wish to come true during the year. Without missing a beat, Malik said: "We wish that Kathy would be free." Taken aback but flexible, the rabbi noted that, yes, Passover was a celebration about freedom and that we could wish for the freedom of all the women present. In part this visit remains memorable because it was extraordinary in its gesture toward normalcy; the boys babbled excitedly on the drive home, retelling the story about their search and their wish because they felt that they were playing a role in the effort to free Kathy.

As with every visit, leaving was the hardest part. As an infant and baby, Chesa would go to sleep immediately upon leaving a prison visit. There would be a guard's shout that there was five minutes left to visiting hours. Voices became simultaneously louder and softer. There was the scraping of chairs, a permissible goodbye hug, walking to the front of the visiting room where there was a thick line painted across the linoleum floor. A lingering goodbye. Leaving by separate doors. We went one direction, back out the multitude of locked doors, trying both to imagine and yet not think about Kathy being body-searched on the way back to her cell.

Family prison visits with David Gilbert were and are of a different order altogether, no matter which of the numerous New York State correctional facilities for men we visit. Men are rarely defined by their fatherhood, surely not male prisoners. There is no child care center, only long, wide, and scarred tables, hard to reach across, stretching the length of the visiting room, with prisoners all on one side in regulation jumpsuits, and a gaggle of relatives or girlfriends on the other side. Often families are assigned seats right next to each other despite scores of empty seats at other tables, making private conversation impossible. Guards at one end watch over the room and reprimand children who won't sit still. Elder parents are visiting their sons. Stylishly dressed and coiffed women are visiting their men on weekends, momentarily showing no signs of the all-night, ten hour bus ride to get to the far side of the state. Children are watching, sometimes playing cards or chess with an older brother or their father, running back and forth to the machines to buy Spaghetti-Os or popcorn. And the men in New York State correctional facilities are 75 percent African American and Latino.

Our favorite family times visiting David were the annual outdoor cultural picnics in the spring. David, rather uniquely, was invited to numerous ethnic picnics: Italian Day, Puerto Rican Day, African American Day. The Italians secured the best food; it appeared to have been catered by some local but well-connected restaurant, and it was abundant. Malik spent two hours making a baseball out of wet napkins and paper towels, and then thirty people—men, women, and children—engaged in a lively baseball game with paper plates for the bases, a game shaped and defined by players aged five to fifty-five. David, not known for his athletic prowess, was affectionately called "the professor" by the Italian prisoners, who admired his principled resistance to the government, if not his politics about white supremacy. All three children clung to David when we said goodbye.

Twenty-five years later, Zayd and I drove up with his baby daughter to visit David at Clinton Correctional Facility in Dannemora, near the Canadian border. We traveled by ferry across Lake Champlain, trying to time the drive so that she wouldn't be napping when we went in and had to be searched. David was surprised and happy, and the baby met another beloved family member. But another generation has begun prison visits.

It's hard to know what children make of prison visits, but they were a fixture in our lives. Our children saw hundreds of other children visiting parents in prison, but rarely other white children. They observed people laughing and playing; they witnessed arguments and tears. They were eyewitnesses to a tiny part of the prison drama of family life, severed and segregated by race and poverty. We have an elaborate collection of Polaroid photos of Chesa and his brothers taken during prison visits, some with palm tree backdrops. The boys were not afraid of going to prison or of the prisoners. They were curious, interested, and hostile to the rules.

As a high school student, Chesa became an activist for children of incarcerated parents, writing and speaking across the country for the ten million children who are separated from fathers or mothers but who categorically did no wrong themselves. He and other youngsters who grew up in similar circumstances, like Emani Davis, have opened a window to a formerly invisible group of victims, suffering because of America's addiction to caging African American and Latino/a men, women, and children.

***

I did time in the federal correctional center while the children were young, and they visited me separately each week. With Zayd, who was five, I did elaborate homemade crossword puzzles, we read books, and then talked about why the other women in the visiting room were incarcerated and who was visiting them. He jumped into my arms to tell me about the long wait downstairs, the searches, and the ways in which guards shouted to waiting families about dress codes and contraband. He sat on my lap for the whole visit, and when he left with the comforting friend who always brought him, he would wave to me from across the street until I flashed the lights in my cell as a final goodbye.

Visits from two-year-old Malik were excruciating but deeply satisfying. He almost always went directly to sleep in my arms, so I could breathe in his toddler smell and nuzzle his cheeks and neck, examine his hands with impunity. Although he was verbal and articulate, able to say that his suddenly new brother Chesa "can't have my mommy," he chose silence during the visits. Chesa, already visiting his biological parents in prison as a one-year-old, visited me less often.

The Metropolitan Correctional Center is at the edge of Chinatown and across from the New York City police headquarters in Lower Manhattan. From certain cells, we could see the Brooklyn Bridge. Only one floor of the tall, narrow pre-trial building housed women; we were some eighty women in a prison of more than a thousand men. That made every venture away from our unit an unpredictable voyage: entry into a packed elevator of male prisoners and guards; processing in the lawyers' visiting area with shouting male voices vying to hear each other; unexpected conversations in line waiting to see a medic. Because none of us were yet convicted, we did not endure the routine strip searches and internal examination of bodily cavities that characterize women's prisons, nor were we routinely subjected to sexualized violence.

The women on our unit were African American if they lived in New York City, or Latinas direct from Colombia or Mexico who spoke only Spanish. The women from Latin America had seen only Kennedy Airport and MCC in North America; they cried and said rosaries and were humorously willing to try to teach this ignorant *gringa* Spanish. All were charged with carrying drugs into the U.S. as "mules"; none were major or even regular drug dealers but each had taken one crazy, terrible risk in the hopes of getting money to help their children have better lives. The women were being prosecuted primarily to "flip" them, to give evidence against male higher-ups. There was no word yet for *globalization* but these women were an advance wave of the so-called war on drugs and the escalating incarceration and criminalization of women. At the current rates of incarcerating women, there will be more women in prison in 2010 than there were all prisoners in the U.S. in 1970. Such is the taken-for-granted of what passes for "crime control."

My closest prison friend was Cheryl, ten years older and able to beat me regularly at Scrabble. Cheryl spent a good part of the day on the pay phone doing numbers; she was openly proud that her craft (hotel boosting, or robbing hotel rooms) required wit and never violence. Cheryl taught me to count to ten slowly whenever it appeared that a fight was jumping off between women prisoners, and she schooled me in the fact that women were likely to shout, to get in each other's faces, but that if a punch had not been thrown by the number ten, it would stay verbal. In fact, the women on the unit were generous and kind to one another, organizing efficiently to nurse a new prisoner who was detoxifying and miserably sick by sitting with her in shifts, sponging her face, offering clean sheets. They knew how to get through holidays together. We shared books and cosmetics. We plotted how to get out along with the guards if there were a fire in the building. Some were geniuses at sewing and making the miserable navy blue uniforms look tight.

My term in prison was indeterminate and bizarre. I was jailed for refusing to obey the order of a judge to cooperate with a federal grand jury by giving samples of my handwriting. I was held in civil contempt of court, although my lawyer and I argued that the government was in possession of rooms filled with my handwriting, since they had seized files and letters from my apartments during COINTELPRO (a secret and illegal FBI program), and I had subsequently been a federal fugitive for eleven years. It was anguishing to be separated from our young children, but I saw resistance as a question of principle. During our years outside the law, scores of people refused to cooperate with grand jury witch hunts, organized by the Nixon administration to try to find members of the Weather Underground. The government grand jury strategy failed because ordinary people, innocent people, refused to cooperate. I could not do differently, even in different circumstances.

The dilemma was that there is no sentence when you are held in contempt. The idea of the prosecutor is to coerce your testimony, a relic from the British Star Chamber proceedings. So we (there were fifteen women who defied the grand jury, all of us at MCC) were ordered to be held until we cooperated, or until the U.S. attorney decided to indict us, or until their interest moved on to other matters. I had been back in ordinary life, above ground, for just a year, working first as a waiter, then at a law firm, being a mom of three boys, and thinking about how to reinvent myself as an activist at the age of forty. Bill visited me every single day, parented three small children, and tried to cope.

As it turned out, I served just seven months. I was released on a motion that argued that since I would never cooperate, because I was willful and stubborn, the contempt sentence had become "punishment" instead of "coercion." The other grand jury women were similarly released, or were charged in huge RICO conspiracy indictments. I thought I would never forget my prison number, never want to read another murder mystery, or do yoga again. But back with my family, we began the prison visits to Kathy and David that would characterize the next twenty years.

***

Today in the U.S., more than two million two hundred thousand of our fellow citizens are in prisons and jails on a given day, the majority incarcerated for nonviolent offenses. When I first visited Cook County Jail as a fresh out-of-college caseworker in 1963, there were less than two hundred thousand people in U.S. prisons. Now there are over two million—20 percent of the world's prison population at a cost upward of $50 billion a year to incarcerate them. While African American men make up about 6 percent of the overall population, they constitute half of the nation's prison inmates. One-eighth of African American men are disenfranchised for life because of their encounters with the criminal justice system. A deadly parallel is documented by Franklin Zimring and analyzed by numerous scholars: If you mapped the lynchings of African Americans in the first quarter of the twentieth century, county by county, and overlaid that with a map of legal executions carried out by death penalty states in the last quarter of the twentieth century, you'd see an astonishing overlap. Or is it astonishing?

In 1998, I attended and spoke at a turning-point conference in Berkeley, California, called "Critical Resistance: Beyond the Prison Industrial Complex." This gathering of three thousand people reflected the enormous amount and variety of prison organizing work that came before, and served as a catalyst for building a robust and more connected network of the Critical Resistance Movement across the country. The intellectual work and organizing skills of Angela Davis, Ellen Barry, and a cohort of young activists deepened and politicized the analysis of incarceration, made room for the leadership of former prisoners, and contributed scholarly and activist strategies linked to global movements.

The prison industry is stamped with race: a modern manifestation of white supremacy, where whites, for the same behaviors and with other variables held steady, have the privilege of largely avoiding incarceration. Due to the Critical Resistance Movement, no one can credibly claim they don't know; only the willfully ignorant in the U.S. can be unaware that quite near our homes and jobs, financed with our tax dollars, the unspeakable takes place every day, with no particular nexus to its alleged justification, public safety. As James Baldwin said: "The American situation is very peculiar, and it may be without precedent in the world. No curtain under heaven is heavier than that curtain of guilt and lies behind which white Americans hide."

The readily available dollars for prison construction, the employment of prison guards, the competition among small towns across the land for new prisons, the counting of prison populations in local census data, the isolated distances at which people are incarcerated from their families, the coerced, indentured inmate labor, the growing privatization of for-profit prisons, the evisceration of parole, the escalation of sentences through policies such as abolishing good time, three strikes, and drug, weapon or gang enhancements—these are the building blocks for what is now known as the "prison industrial complex." It stretches across every state and has not only reshaped criminal justice policy, it has transformed the labor force by expanding indentured servitude, created a growth industry for guards and their unions, nurtured flourishing new concentration camp construction businesses and private prison industries, while it destroys potential, families, and hope.

Death-row inmate and journalist Mumia Abu-Jamal notes: "The U.S. ... today supports a prison industrial complex that cages more black men, women and juveniles per capita than South Africa during the Botha regime." He and other political prisoners, including Leonard Peltier, Herman Bell, and the Cuban Five, continue to resist domination and defeat, while analyzing the system that incarcerates them and demanding freedom.

There are some sixty federal and state supermax prisons and scores more ultra-security units, places characterized by permanent solitary confinement, constant surveillance, isolation and sensory deprivation. African Americans and Latinos are generously overrepresented in supermax prisons and control units. These facilities appear to have blazed the path to Guantanamo and Abu Ghraib. And the globalization of the U.S. prison gulag has produced a rapidly growing export: Guantanamo, Abu Ghraib, the black sites, military prisons, and U.S. technical assistance about incarceration to subjugated or allied countries.

Today's prisons have their source and inspiration in chattel slavery—that distinctively U.S. form of forced labor that relegated those of African descent to the status of property. It is not a leap to trace the slave codes of the South to the Black Codes that followed Reconstruction and criminalized "vagrancy," idleness, and disorderly conduct, to the systems of convict leasing and chain gangs, to the web of incarceration that characterizes today's landscape. Frederick Douglass noted the tendency "to impute crime to color." Should a stranger from Mars land in Chicago today and peer into Cook County Jail, s/he would be astounded to see it filled, almost exclusively, with more than nine thousand eight hundred young African Americans and Latinos who constitute the average daily population: over ninety-nine thousand "admissions" per year. Imagine the international uproar if it were ten thousand Irish men, or ten thousand Jewish women!

Once the prisons and jails are built, it becomes necessary goal of the industry to fill and replenish them with prisoners, despite plummeting crime rates. To this purpose, police practices, harsh legislation, and the stoking of public fear are essential. The 1988 presidential election featured an attack ad using a mug shot of Willie Horton, a Massachusetts prisoner who committed armed robbery and rape while released from prison on a weekend furlough. It was an ad calculated to promote racial fear among white voters, and it worked to elect President George H.W. Bush and to defeat Michael Dukakis. Ronald Reagan launched his presidential campaign outside Philadelphia, Mississippi, where three civil rights workers were murdered in 1964. These examples of peddling fear involve coded but well-understood "race talk" and the demonization of African Americans, which tragically continues to resonate among the white population in the U.S. Fear of crime and fear of the other impacts virtually every election and each allocation of massive public resources; fear plus white supremacy determines who is subjected to official violence and who has impunity.

***

In 1969, a young man named Jon Burge returned to Chicago from military service in Viet Nam. Part of his assignment in Viet Nam was to guard and accompany detainees who were interrogated as suspected Viet Cong guerrillas at Dong Tam base, south of Saigon. Army records show that 1,507 detainees were interrogated in the three-month period starting November 1, 1968, when Sergeant Burge was assigned to the Ninth Military Police Company of the Ninth Infantry Division. Back in Chicago, he joined the Chicago Police Department in 1970, and was assigned to Area Two, a police station on Chicago's south side. Over a period of twenty years, as is now widely acknowledged, a group of white police officers engaged in the routine torture of more than one hundred African American suspects at Area Two stationhouse. The torture methods included electrically shocking suspects' testicles, tongues, and ears (using a "black box" from Vietnam and cattle prods), burning suspects by shackling them to boiling radiators, and putting lit cigarettes on their arms, legs, and chests, suffocating them with typewriter covers, forcing gun barrels into their mouths to simulate mock executions, and deprivating them of water, food, and sleep. All of the victims were African American men. More than thirty-five years later, not a single person has been indicted for these crimes—a pattern of total impunity.

For the past three years, I've had the distressing but dynamic experience of teaching a law school seminar on torture. Simultaneously, I've had the good fortune of participating in the Chicago Coalition Against Police Torture with a large circle of activists who will not remain silent. In fact, the most recent report from the intrepid coalition of community activists, lawyers, and human rights organizers documents that the taxpayers in the City of Chicago and Cook County have spent some $6 million to defend Jon Burge and his cohort, and up to $45 million to settle wrongful conviction civil rights claims dating from the current Mayor Richard J. Daley's time as state's attorney, plus an estimated $20 million in legal fees for those cases. Taxpayers footed the $7 million bill for an investigation by special prosecutors that took over three years to complete. Their 292-page report found "beyond a reasonable doubt" that numerous defendants had been tortured, but concluded that "the statute of limitations bars any prosecution of any officers."

Another $20 million is part of a settlement by the city of Chicago on torture claims by Madison Hobley, Stanley Howard, Leroy Orange, and Aaron Patterson, four men who served a total of seventy years on death row in Illinois for crimes they did not commit. They were convicted and sentenced to death by prosecutors under then State's Attorney Daley, based on false confessions extracted through torture. These four men were pardoned (based on innocence) and fully exonerated in 2003. They are among nine innocent Illinois men sentenced to death and two dozen others sentenced to prison for crimes they did not commit during this period. Some twenty men remain in prison based in part on evidence obtained under torture from the white officers of the Area Two police station.

The People's Law Office's Flint Taylor, civil rights attorney Standish Willis, and clinical law professor Locke Bowman, who together fought for justice for the Burge torture victims, their families, and their community, show no signs of slowing down. In the summer of 2007, the Cook County Board of Supervisors voted unanimously to support making torture a new crime as defined by international law, without a statute of limitations; to initiate new hearings for the twenty-six Chicago police torture victims who remain incarcerated; and to support any action taken by the U.S. attorney to investigate and prosecute crimes of torture by the Chicago police. As a result of a resolution signed by twenty-six of the fifty Chicago aldermen, the Police and Fire Committee of the Council held a well-publicized open hearing on July 2, 2007, to examine the failures of the special prosecutors' investigation and to explore remedies that the council can take with regard to Jon Burge and the police torture scandal.

For the mayor and the current state's attorney, this is the case that just will not go away. Not until 1993 was Jon Burge fired from the Chicago police force. He lives today in Florida, with a full police pension, on his boat called *Vigilante*. The torture of one hundred twenty-five Black men from 1973–1993 has, to date, only required him to return to Chicago, to take the Fifth Amendment in depositions, and to face demonstrators.

In 2005, after receiving no satisfaction from local or federal authorities, the Chicago Coalition Against Police Torture decided to go international. We brought torture victims and community members to the Inter-American Commission on Human Rights of the Organization of American States in Washington, D.C., to ask the Commission to hold hearings in Chicago on the blatant violations of The Organization of American States charter, and to bring the Special Rapporteur on Racial Discrimination in the Americas to Chicago to investigate. In the spring of 2006, the coalition participated in a shadow report to the UN Committee on Torture in Geneva, which was holding hearings based on a report by the U.S. State Department on their compliance with the Convention Against Torture (CAT). The committee was stunned to learn about the well-documented cases of police torture of African American men in Chicago. The CAT committee's final report includes a highly critical section on the Chicago Area Two torture cases, smack between their responses to the U.S. government about torture at Guantanamo and Abu Ghraib. A month later, Joey Mogul presented the Burge torture cases to the UN Human Rights Committee, again before a substantial delegation of U.S. State Department officials, again with an official demand that the U.S. government explain the absence of prosecutions for documented torture against Black men in Chicago.

These allegations of police torture were no secret. They circulated in the African American community for years, and by the late 1980s everyone who practiced in criminal court was aware of the tortured confessions and open secret of racist punishment and pain being used and defended by officials up the chain of command. A book was written (*Unspeakable Acts, Ordinary People* by John Conroy, 2000), a documentary film was made (*The End of the Nightstick*, directed by Peter Kuttner, 1993), Amnesty International issued a report on the cases (1991), and there have been thousands of newspaper reports about the cases, the victims, and the perpetrators.

On October 21, 2008, former Chicago Police Commander Jon Burge, 60 was arrested by FBI agents at his home on Florida on two counts of obstruction of justice and one count of perjury for allegedly lying about whether he and other officers under his command participated in torture and physical abuse of one or more suspects in police custody, dating back to the 1980s. He faces prosecution in federal court in Chicago, with a maximum penalty of twenty years for each count of obstruction of justice and five years for perjury. Prosecutors noted that the investigation is continuing.

So the war in Viet Nam did come home—in a damaged and deranged manner—as will the Iraq and Afghanistan wars and the so-called War on Terror. African American men experienced the full force of "collateral" damage through the practices of police interrogation techniques, trials using tortured confessions as evidence, and disappearances into the prison industrial complex. One of the consequences of the returning troops and military personnel and private security forces to the U.S. will be the domestication of new violent technologies and new brutalizing techniques that will again be used by law enforcement at home. Enhanced interrogation, coercive interrogation, "fear up harsh," cover-up and secrecy, and legal impunity will migrate back, whether or not we call these practices torture or "just" cruel, inhuman, and degrading treatment or punishment. In the Chicago Area Two police torture cases, no one can avoid the documented evidence of systemic, racist torture directed solely against the Black community over two decades. We can contemplate the level of harm to individuals. We can imagine the impact on family members and on an entire community. We can stand in awe at their humanity and survival. We can see the resonance with historic examples of white domination and terror. We can decide not to be innocent, to insist on seeing and on official accountability. We can surely address the question of justice and reparations.

***

Now our sons are grown. We receive fewer telephone calls from prison. For one, Chesa does not live at home to receive the regular calls. For another, David Gilbert is our sole family prisoner. In September 2003, Kathy was released on parole after serving twenty-two years in prison. Her release was due to a combination of her remarkable work with women inside, a robust campaign for her freedom, her a first-rate lawyer and—in no small part—to the tireless and intelligent work of Chesa. He traveled the state, wrote articles for New York papers making the case for parole, and made inroads into the community where the crime had occurred. Kathy left behind hundreds of women who also deserve immediate release. Her discharge, much like our own freedom, was also due to the workings of white supremacy, the privileges and power attached to being white and with access to resources. She is devoting her energies to working for the parole and release of long-term women prisoners as well as men longtermers, and making available to them the tools of balanced and restorative justice. It remains her work, Chesa's and ours, to obtain the releases of David, the scores of political prisoners who remain incarcerated, and the rest of the prison populations whose involuntary servitude does nothing to enhance public safety or create a better world. With one-third of all young African American men in prison or on parole or probation, the legacy of slavery is alive and well. Abolition is again on the agenda.

EMANCIPATE YOURSELVES FROM MENTAL SLAVERY

Bill Ayers

The paradox of education is precisely this—that as one begins to become conscious one begins to examine the society in which he is being educated. The purpose of education, finally, is to create in a person the ability to look at the world for himself, to make his own decisions, to say to himself this is black or this is white, to decide for himself whether there is a God in heaven or not. To ask questions of the universe, and then learn to live with those questions, is the way he achieves his own identity. But no society is really anxious to have that kind of person around. What societies really, ideally, want is a citizenry which will simply obey the rules of society. If a society succeeds in this, that society is about to perish. The obligation of anyone who thinks of himself as responsible is to examine society and try to change it and to fight it—at no matter what risk. This is the only hope society has. This is the only way societies change.

—James Baldwin

In 1965, I was arrested with dozens of others for sitting-in and disrupting the operations of the Selective Service—the draft board—in Ann Arbor, Michigan. Convicted of disorderly conduct, I spent ten days in the county jail where I got to know some wonderful people, including folks who'd just founded a small free school affiliated with the Civil Rights Movement. I decided to have a look, and I walked out of jail and into my first teaching job. My peculiar and twisty pathway into the classroom has forever linked in my mind teaching to social justice.

The Children's Community was founded by three energetic young mothers who wanted to create a space of peace and racial harmony for their own kids, and at the same time to launch a model that could impact schools more generally. I'd never seen any place like it—every child seemed to be engaged in a project or a work activity or a book, the place was fairly buzzing with lively energy, but no adult was giving orders or driving things forward, and no one seemed concerned—or even to notice—that there was no schedule, no timetable, no uniform set of tasks to be accomplished. The atmosphere was calm purposefulness, unlike any school I'd attended.

The school director tutored me in an alternative idea about teaching driven by a belief that, in a democracy, the aim of every school ought to be the creation of free human beings associated with one another on terms of equality. "In this school," she said, "we teach democratic living by living democratically; we don't want to learn *about* democracy from a distance so much as we want to learn *from* democracy up-close and personal." This theme carried through in every other aspect of school life: We tried to learn *from* nature rather than *about* nature, from participation in community life rather than looking at community from a distance. The school credo was this: an experience in freedom, integration, and democracy.

The school stood against racism and segregation, authoritarianism and cynicism, violence and war, irrelevance and fatalism and avoidance. We thought of ourselves as pioneers in a movement to remake the world, and we knew we had to become new men and new women if we were to succeed. We had to shed as best we could all the baggage from the larger culture—racist baggage, the baggage of capitalist culture—in order to free ourselves to free the nation. It was a lofty goal to be sure, but we had large ethical ambitions to achieve.

The materials and activities and opportunities in the classroom were supplemented by a stream of trips into the community—to the bakery and the orchard, the fire station and the county jail, the lake and the machine shop, a union hall, a picket line, a music studio—and a parade of community visitors into the school. Learning was taken to be a constantly buzzing collective dialogue with one another and with the world.

***

I became a full-time teacher, and I was a full-time activist in my spare time. Activism, organizing, and teaching overlapped significantly for me until they blended into one large project powered by hope and possibility. I searched for mentors and models, for examples and inspiration. There was a growing chorus of radical educators, and I was influenced early by the work of Jonathan Kozol and Herb Kohl, Septima Clark and Ella Baker, and Annie Stein and Myles Horton, and, importantly, Charlie Cobb and the Mississippi Freedom Schools.

In 1963, Cobb, then a student at Howard University, wrote a brief proposal for a Summer Freedom School designed to re-energize and focus the Civil Rights Movement in Mississippi. Cobb claimed that while the Black children in the South were denied many things—decent school facilities, honest and forward-looking curriculum, fully qualified teachers—the fundamental injury was "a complete absence of academic freedom, and students are forced to live in an environment that is geared to squashing intellectual curiosity, and different thinking." He named the classrooms of Mississippi as "intellectual wastelands," and he challenged himself and others "to fill an intellectual and creative vacuum in the lives of young Negro Mississippi, and to get them to articulate their own desires, demands and questions." Their own desires, their own demands, their own questions. For African Americans living in semi-feudal bondage, managed and contained through a system of law and custom as well as outright terror, this was thought to be beyond imagination—until a group of teachers and organizers and ordinary people imagined it anyway.

Cobb was urging students to question the circumstances of their lives, to wonder about how they got to where they were, and to think about how they might change things if they would—his proposal was insurrection itself, and he knew it. He was crossing hard lines of propriety and tradition, convention and common sense, poised to break the law and overthrow a system. His proposal was designed to shake the settled while it plowed a deep and promising furrow toward the unknown. He was teaching the taboo.

Charlie Cobb thought that one way to challenge the brute force of segregation and injustice was to create and develop the power of counter-institutions—alternative schools, work cooperatives, health clinics—as sites of liberation and struggle, places where the goals of the Black Freedom Movement could be enacted and where people could affirm their own humanity and experiences, building their projects on the rock of their own strengths, their own wisdom: "If we are concerned with breaking the power structure," Cobb wrote, "then we have to be concerned with building up our own institutions to replace the old, unjust, decadent ones..." His proposal—a single typed page—was typical of the strategy and tactics of the Black Freedom Movement at its best: It articulated a radical critique of the status quo and demanded fundamental social change while simultaneously enacting on the ground a vision of participatory democracy and simple justice in an unjust world. People imagined and named a world that could be, but was not yet; they organized themselves to live against the grain of oppression and injustice; they built a community in this spot, for this moment, where they could breathe that freer, more vibrant, and robust air, and from which they could storm the heavens.

Cobb and the other organizers understood that all education is political, that there is no such thing as a neutral education. Education stands *for* something and *against* something else. The Freedom Schools were organized to uproot an oppressive system, and they said so.

The curriculum included an academic component as well as arts, recreation, and cultural activities, but the core was what they called the "Citizenship Curriculum," a sustained inquiry into politics and society. In the published version, the academic part takes up two pages, the citizenship section twenty-five pages. The "Citizenship Curriculum" was a question-asking, problem-posing affair:

> *Why are we (teachers, students) in Freedom Schools?*
> *What is the Freedom Movement?*
> *What alternatives does the Freedom Movement offer us?*

The 1964 Freedom School Curriculum was based on dialogue—teachers listened, asked questions, assumed that their students were the real experts on their own lives: Why? What's the problem? What's the evidence? How do you know? Is that fair or right? What are you going to do about it? It was a pedagogy of lived experience with the goal of allowing people to collectively question and then challenge their circumstances and their situations. The deeper lessons were these: As human beings we are living in the flow of history and neither the current state of affairs nor the future is inevitable; we are each a work-in-progress who can link with others and make ourselves subjects in—rather than objects of—history; what we do or don't do makes a difference. I was captivated—learning with a purpose, education as revolution. We tried to learn from and adapt the whole approach to our little Children's Community.

Cobb's indictment of Mississippi's schools forty years ago can be applied verbatim and with chilling accuracy to contemporary schools in New York or Chicago or Los

Angeles, and most places in between: "a complete absence of academic freedom," "an environment that is geared to squashing intellectual curiosity." While generally accurate, this miserable description divides along the color line, an expression of white supremacy that finds its truest application in schools for poor, Latino, Native, and African American youngsters. Here students encounter something that looks and smells and walks and talks exactly like an antiquated and brutish colonial system: a school experience designed to pacify and domesticate, to promote and police the existing hierarchies of privilege and oppression in which poor youngsters know their place (the street corner, the charity line, the prison) and accept it with a minimum of bitterness and with zero resistance. After all, the authoritative voices repeat in icy chorus, whatever structural obstacles that might have once existed—segregation, say, institutionalized hierarchies built on color and caste and class—were happily swept away long ago and we are, all of us, free at last. Which do you believe?—your own unreliable eyes, or the categorical and commanding account of the experts, always majestic, triumphant, and settled.

Further, "Your reading levels and test scores don't lie"—you earned your failure, now own it. For students to question the circumstances of their lives—as they spontaneously and consistently do outside of school—is unacceptable; to persist is to become resistant, and then recalcitrant. It's a short step from recalcitrant to disruptive, and it's just a hair's breadth from disruptive to suspended. Expulsion lurks around the next corner, and from there arrest beckons. The school to prison pipeline. Either way—compliance or rebellion—the humanity of students and young people lies precariously in the balance.

Imagine a "Citizenship Curriculum" inviting debate, research, writing, reading, and more, around a revised set of questions for this moment:

What are schools for? Who decides? What do people learn in school besides reading, writing, and arithmetic? What do they learn about other societies? About jobs? About race and racism? About democracy? About government? About economics?

Are all public schools the same? What are the differences? Where do the differences come from? Who decides? What is the cost of education? How are schools funded? Are schools funded fairly? How do you know?

What is academic success? Who decides? What is standardized testing? Is it fair? How do you know? How big is the testing business? Has it always been this way? Who profits? What is history? Who makes history? Is history being made today? By whom? Who else?

How many prisons are there in Mississippi? In Illinois? Who does time, and for what crimes? How much money goes into incarceration, and how much into education? Who decides? Where is the nearest prison or jail? Are prisoners allowed to vote? Why not?

Where is the Mississippi Delta in relation to Chicago? Is there a link? Where are Chicago and the Delta in relation to Mexico City, Caracas, Ha Noi, Panama, Montreal, New York City, Baghdad, Jerusalem, Ramallah, Cape Town? Is there a link?

Who said, "No Black man should go 10,000 miles away to fight for a so-called freedom he doesn't enjoy in Mississippi"? Do you agree or disagree? Why?

Is our country at war? When did it begin? Who is the enemy? What are the objectives of the war? When will it end?

What youth gangs exist in our community? What appeals to kids about gangs? What are some thing gangs offer that are OK? What things are destructive and harmful to participants, to the larger community?

What makes you an American? Who decides? If someone questioned your right to call yourself an American, what story would you offer as proof? What image, object, or document could you produce that would be persuasive?

It's hard to stop writing questions—one thing leads to another. And once we take a step into this kind of curriculum and teaching we recognize that power is hidden in every question, and that everything is connected if we pursue it deeply enough. La Escuela Fratney, a public elementary school in Milwaukee, is a fountain of such ideas. When the second- graders were talking recently about Lake Michigan, one of them asked innocently, "Who owns the water?" Speculation included George Bush, Bill Gates, and the police. The wise teacher who pursued this question led an exploration of discovery and surprise that swept into areas of pollution and environmental science, the meaning of water in Milwaukee versus Oaxaca, the role of water in civilization, the art and poetry of water.

El Puente Academy for Peace and Justice, a public high school in New York City, develops curriculum around a fundamental question: Who am I? Kids read Piri Thomas and Junot Diaz, but they also integrate all the disciplines as they build skills of social analysis and public action around, for example, lead paint, asbestos, and blood pressure studies in the community. The "Sugar Project," begun in 1996, continues to this day as students investigate the Domino Sugar refinery in their neighborhood, trace economic and political history to Puerto Rico, and dive into chemistry, labor, health, oral history, and more.

Emancipate Yourselves From Mental Slavery

There is no real contradiction between asking critical and probing questions of the world in front of our eyes and teaching academic skills. Posing powerful questions and pursuing them to their furthest limits does not have to be mere musing—a dreamy kind of waste of time—nor does it have to compete with or become a substitute for skill-building. Indeed, the best teachers tend to tackle the latter with energy and commitment in the context of the former. A group of fifth-graders in Chicago, for example, decided with their teacher to investigate the dilapidated condition of their school building; they approached the inquiry with investment and passion, and nine months later, when they were given a civic leadership award, they could also note with pride that each had learned to write better, to do sustained library research, to get a range of information from the Internet, to analyze statistics and present findings with charts and graphs, and to speak with clarity to a variety of audiences including the press, the school board, and the mayor's staff. Another group of students in California—high school kids—who combed the press every day with their teacher in search of stories they wanted to pursue further, came across a seemingly insignificant obituary of a teenager in *The Oakland Tribune* that led to a sustained study that unearthed the largest illegal smuggling ring of indentured servants in California's history. Those kids also learned a wealth of academic skills along the way. We have to teach skills in light of something, why not in light of opening our eyes and looking critically at our shared world and then asking deep and authentic questions?

People concerned with justice continue to raise the demand for access and equity in our schools, and it's a worthy demand: The government should live up to its responsibility to all its citizens, the nation should realize its promise to all its people. But access and equity, while a beginning, are not the end: Social justice also requires full recognition of the humanity of each person, and this demands an entirely new kind of education, one geared toward transformation rather than transmission. Education as transmission always demands obedience and conformity; it assumes that students will act in scripts already written for them, mostly focused on "workforce preparation." Transformative education asks students to become artists, actors, activists, and authors of their own lives. To change themselves, to make the world their own.

The children of poor and disadvantaged or oppressed communities—whether in Louisiana, the Mississippi Delta, the west side of Chicago, the South Bronx, or the Navajo Nation—are deprived of many things (from decent facilities and adequate educational resources to full access to the larger community as a site of learning and growth) but the most profound loss, as Cobb noted decades ago, is the deprivation of the right to think. To alienate youngsters from their own judgments is to turn them into objects; to prevent them from naming their predicaments is a form of violence. The assault on thinking—on being able to look at the world through one's own eyes, to name it, to decide for oneself what is fair and just and true, to question one's circumstances, to wonder about alternatives—is the deepest and most lasting injury. And taking that injury as a challenge is the first step in teaching as emancipation.

***

There's a biting bit of satire from season twelve, episode fifteen of *MADtv*, available on YouTube. The scene: A group of tough-looking and unruly Black and Latino teenagers gathered together in a disheveled classroom where they lounge on the desks and admire their lethal-looking weaponry.

The ominous, stentorian voiceover: "Inner-city high school is a dangerous place. A place where hope has lost out to hate, where your homework isn't about math, it's about staying alive."

Cut to a Latina student with maximum attitude, close-up, full face: "If you Black, Latino, or Asian, you *will* get shot—that's a *fact.*"

Voiceover: "There's only one thing that can make these kids learn—"

Before we finish that sentence, let's locate ourselves in the narrative thus far: We know that teenagers are trouble, that African American and Latino kids are particularly problematic—more than indifferent and self-absorbed, they are prone to mindless violence. And while city schools are chaotic and dilapidated, there is a single, straightforward solution somewhere close at hand: "only one thing that can make these kids learn…" And what is that miracle, that one thing? The narrator finishes with a flourish: "—a nice white lady."

Most of us could have written that script ourselves—our culture, after all, is steeped in the cliché. Practically every teacher film from "Blackboard Jungle" through "Stand and Deliver," from "Dangerous Minds" to "Freedom Writers" follows the formula faithfully: tough kids, a savior teacher willing to sacrifice everything to rescue children and youth from the sewers of their circumstances (including their dreadful families), triumph, transformation, redemption. The plot points are all so predictable, the outcome so insistent that it ends up overwhelming our own lived experiences, making us wonder why our efforts don't ever quite measure up, why the heroic outcome eludes us—never, what's wrong with this picture, but, rather, what can I be doing wrong?

"Nice White Lady" lasts just over three minutes, but somehow packs it all in: As a young, innocent Amy Little introduces herself to the jeering students, the narrator intones, "With the odds against her, she'll do the unthinkable."

An older colleague, eager to temper her idealism and wake her up, barks, "Forget it!

These are minorities—they can't learn and they can't be educated." She won't be deterred: "With all due respect, sir, I'm a white lady—I can do anything."

She implores her students to let her teach them, but they resist, one girl giving her a standard street lecture: "What you think is going to happen here? You think you going to inspire me? Break through my tough-girl act and see the beauty that's within? Is that what you think?" She shoots the girl an intense and meaningful look, pulls out a pen and a notebook and pushes it toward her saying, "Write that down!"

Soon everyone is writing up a storm, weapons are holstered, and their troubles are gone. Before long Amy and her students are dancing in the aisles as the narrator intones, "When it comes to teaching inner-city minorities, you don't need books and you don't need rules—all you need is a nice white lady."

Every part of "Nice White Lady" is well-known, and all of it stands on a rampart of received wisdom and racist orthodoxy. All of it stands, as well, as an obstacle to effective teaching and meaningful effort. It's a bit of domineering common sense—and there is nothing more resilient than common sense, nothing more dogmatic and resistant to change.

The desire to help, always hierarchical and tied to privilege, typically feeds on sensationalism and images of the exotic, and often results, regardless of intent, in some form of colonial relationship. This is why "service" is such a miserable motivation for teachers, and ought to be challenged and opposed in favor of solidarity—working *with* not *for*, learning *from* not *about*, moving *horizontally* not *vertically*. The stance of solidarity asks us to learn from one another—there is no outside expert to consult, no Lady Bountiful in the wings, no foundation or government grant that can replace the wisdom on the ground—and to note that while the world is not yet decolonized, we can each struggle to decolonize our own minds. As teachers we can resist the missionaries within ourselves while we find ways to work with the people.

***

Some of this sentiment is embodied in a poster directed at visitors that hangs today near the headquarters of the revolutionary Zapatista movement in Chiapas, Mexico: If you have come to help us, it says, please go home; If you have come to join us, welcome. Pick up a shovel or a machete and get busy.

Ella Baker, one of the leaders of the modern Black Freedom Movement and the elder most revered by the young militants of the Student Nonviolent Coordinating Committee, promoted the idea of student volunteers working in the Freedom Schools and on voter registration projects in rural Mississippi and Georgia and Alabama in the early 1960s. The work needed doing, and the volunteers were willing, but she was deeply skeptical about the help these students would actually bring to the share croppers and peasants of the South. She pointed out—in a radical reversal that was typical of her—that the students from colleges and universities all over the country had everything to learn from the oppressed people themselves, and that the volunteers—with all their formal book-learning and their degrees and their professional futures—were in deepest need of help. "The people you've come to help know better," she said. So she urged them on, not in the posture of do-gooders, but in the stance of seekers and learners. *Ella Baker and the Black Freedom Movement* by Barbara Ransby is a masterful study of a life devoted to participatory democracy and internationalism, community education, and grassroots organizing with the dispossessed. She recognized and advocated that the best teachers are first and foremost students of their students.

This reversal of power and privilege became a defining feature of the culture and the politics being built in the struggle against the racist Jim Crow system. The Movement incubated and then sent forward its transcendent leaders—the visionary Reverend Martin Luther King, Jr., the determined and courageous Rosa Parks, the intrepid organizer Bayard Rustin, the revolutionary Stokeley Carmichael—but its character was shaped as well by the uncommon common people—Fannie Lou Hamer, Esau Jenkins, Bernice Robinson—pushing from the ground up, fueling a sense of urgency, and making connections between crummy schools, segregated facilities, and meager wages, for example, with a fatally flawed and fraudulent democracy: The rotting shack as an objective correlative for a rotting system. They had the problems, and they also had the solutions—they were the ones who kept the Movement moving.

THE ANCHOR OF RACE

What to the American slave is your Fourth of July? I answer, a day that reveals to him more than all other days of the year, the gross injustice and cruelty to which he is the constant victim. To him your celebration is a sham; your boasted liberty an unholy license; your national greatness, swelling vanity; your sounds of rejoicing are empty and heartless; your denunciation of tyrants, brass-fronted impudence; your shouts of liberty and equality a fraud... There is not a nation of the earth guilty of practices more shocking and bloody than are the people of these United States at this very hour.
— Frederick Douglass

The recurrent U.S. story—dominant, habitual, profoundly functional—is a tale of democracy and freedom, uplift and forward motion, perpetual improvement and never-ending progress. While there are important grains of truth in that story, told and retold in official and scholarly and popular venues over and over and over again, it echoes in our consciousness until it achieves the exalted status of a truth beyond doubt, a plain American fact: "America is the greatest country on earth"; "Land of the free, home of the brave"; "God bless America." To wonder about or interrogate any of this is like questioning whether down might be up, or white black. No sensible person dare ask.

Like everyone we learned the incessant, authoritative story of American freedom and democracy in school and at home, on TV and in books. It was drummed into our brains, and as we grew, every crack we encountered in the story became a little earthquake in our heads: Scottsboro, crack, Don Pedro Albizu Campos, crack, Greensboro, crack, Birmingham, crack, Selma, crack. And then the war, the marches, the hope and the assassinations. We had to know more, to find out the truth in order to choose whom to be.

Start at the beginning, when the Puritans provided one of the most durable symbols of the "American experiment," a symbol that is as resilient and resonant today as it ever was: America was to be a city on the hill—our exalted place, chosen by God—whose inhabitants, the chosen people, would engage in an errand into the wilderness, their task to shine their countenance upon the darkened world and thereby to enlighten it. There were some twenty million indigenous peoples already here, according to the most recent scholarship; 90 percent would be exterminated.

The project of a blessed people bearing civilization and progress and truth offers a ready justification for anything—conquest, theft, and mayhem, ultimately mass murder: We come in peace, we are messengers of God, we embody the greater good. Opposition is nothing but the Devil's handiwork.

(A brief parenthetical aside here: Beyond political calculation and opportunism, military advantage and strategic aims, imperial dreams and desires, this foundational symbol goes some way toward explaining many U.S. misadventures, including the shock-and-awe bombing and occupation of Iraq and the unconditional military support the U.S. offers Israel today. That nation, too, was built by a determined band of people who suffered and survived, arose phoenix-like to discover "a land without people," they claimed, "for a people without land." They, too, were a chosen people, a lighter-skinned

European people claiming the leadership, who "made the desert bloom," and they planted their plucky little democracy in the midst of hostile and threatening and notably darker-skinned neighbors. Perpetual but righteous war would become the necessary order of the day for the forces of goodness. And so it is, in settler Israel as in the settler U.S. End parenthesis.)

Before the improbable and treacherous migration to North America, people in Europe thought of themselves as English or Irish, Dutch or German, Italian or Greek. As soon as these exiles and pilgrims landed in a "new world"—a land populated by a complex network of indigenous tribes and civilizations soon to be massacred and driven into reservations, a land soon enough abounding with captured Africans, and, as it conquered a continent, Mexicans and then Chinese indentured servants—every European *became* white. Made-in-America. Race achieved and exploited this singular success: the creation of whiteness as a union of disparate peoples, classes, backgrounds, and histories. Oddly, whiteness is the most dehumanizing of all categories, for it can only be expressed as a negative—not Black, not colored. It has no content of its own; it surely has no science; it's always experienced as a negation.

Many readers know this early history better than we do, so skip ahead if you like. We include a dramatically abbreviated version here as a marker of our own lurching toward learning, something that came as a shock to us and then left its imprint as we made our ragged ways into the world.

When the First Continental Congress met in Philadelphia in 1774, over a century and a half after the first Africans arrived in chains in Jamestown, the abolition of the slave trade was named as one of the goals for the new nation. But when the Founding Fathers ratified the Constitution after the Revolutionary War, instead of abolition, they wrote slavery into law.

The Declaration of Independence, which dissolved the legal and political ties to Great Britain, is stamped with white supremacist thinking, but it's the Constitution of the United States, in Article I, Section 2—the infamous "3/5 Clause"—that embeds white supremacy in its heart, accommodates the new nation to slavery, and sets in motion all the political layered and social and economic privileges and disadvantages still flourishing:

> *Representatives and direct taxes shall be apportioned among the several states which may be included within this union, according to their respective numbers, which shall be determined by adding to the whole number of free persons, including those bound to service for a term of years, and excluding Indians not taxed, three fifths of all other Persons.*

Gouverneur Morris of Pennsylvania provided a voice of dissent:

> *Upon what principle are slaves computed? Are they men? Then make them citizens and let them vote. Are they property? Why then is no other property included?*

> *The admission of slaves into the House when fairly explained comes to this: the inhabitant of Georgia or South Carolina who goes to the coast of Africa, and in defiance of the most sacred laws of humanity leads away his fellow creatures from their dearest connections and damns them to the most cruel bondages, shall have more votes in a government instituted for the protection of the rights of mankind, than the citizen of Pennsylvania or New Jersey who views with horror so nefarious a practice.*

In Article I Section 9, Congress is prohibited from abolishing the international slave trade until 1808; in Article IV, Section 2, the various states are prohibited from emancipating fugitive slaves; in Article I, Section 8, Congress can call up militias to suppress insurrections, including slave uprisings.

On and on: commerce, taxation, representation, unamendable clauses. Slavery and its antecedents—a large and easily identifiable underclass—had several alluring advantages from the ruling class point of view: the suppression of wages and the ruin of a possible laboring-class unity.

Of the first five U.S. presidents, four owned slaves and, overall, twelve presidents owned slaves, eight while in office. Hundreds of senators, congressmen, and judges—highly esteemed men, some of them revolutionaries—owned slaves. George Washington, father of the nation, owned slaves, freed his personal servant upon his death, and said of slavery in 1786: "I can only say that no man living wishes more sincerely than I do to see the abolition of [slavery]. But when slaves who are happy and content to remain with their present masters, are tampered with and seduced to leave them ... it introduces more evils than it can cure."

James Madison, the fourth president, owned slaves his entire life, but freed them in his will. In 1819 he said: "A general emancipation of slaves ought to be" gradual, equitable and satisfactory to the individuals immediately concerned, and "consistent with the existing and durable prejudices of the nation... To be consistent with existing and probably unalterable prejudices in the U.S. freed blacks ought to be permanently removed beyond the region occupied by or allotted to a White population."

John Tyler, tenth president, owned slaves and said, "[God] works most inscrutably to the understandings of men; the negro is torn from Africa, a barbarian, ignorant and idolatrous; he is restored civilized, enlightened, and a Christian."

Zachary Taylor owned more than a hundred slaves, and declared in 1847: "So far as slavery is concerned, we of the South must throw ourselves on the Constitution and defend our rights under it to the last, and when arguments will no longer suffice, we will appeal to the sword, if necessary." Taylor later served as a lawmaker in the Confederate government.

Historian John Hope Franklin observed that "racial segregation, discrimination, and degradation are no unanticipated accidents in the nation's history. They stem logically and directly from the legacy that the founding fathers bestowed upon contemporary America."

Whenever we hear about the Founding Fathers and their "original intent," let's remember just what kind of fathers we're talking about, and wonder a bit about the purity of their intent. They were human, of course, filled with contradictions—isn't everyone?—and apologists point out that they lived in their own time, not in ours. True. But even and especially in their own time, values and standards were contested, as they always are—there was Cinque as well as Jefferson, Wilborn as well as Washington, Frederick Douglass and John Brown and Toussaint L'Overture as well as Zach Taylor. And in that contested space the Founding Fathers were fundamentally, to a man, undeniable white supremacists.

At the end of the Civil War, this young country again had an opportunity to confront the legacy of white supremacy and set things right. Congressman Thaddeus Stevens and Senator Charles Sumner proposed to seize slaveholders' lands and divide them among the former slaves, offering what was to become the iconic and legendary "forty acres and a mule" as reparations for generations of slavery and exploitation and oppression, and to give the newly freed people an economic foothold in the future. The failure to follow through on this potentially powerful gesture allowed the resurgence of the brutal system of white supremacy in new but also lethal forms.

The slave economy, a consistent and efficient exploitation of labor, was always more than a simple labor arrangement—it was the first thoroughly race-based system ever invented, and now, at the 400th anniversary of Jamestown, it is possible to see that despite significant modifications and hard-fought transformations, it has defined every aspect of U.S. history, from the development of capitalism, to the odd federalist political system with its disproportionate Southern power, to our daily interactions. Race anchored slavery. It intended to dehumanize Africans and it failed; it never meant to dehumanize white people, but indeed it has. We live in the world slavery created.

So in fact the U.S. was *conceived* as a white supremacist nation, and the American idea and experience was, from the very start, shot through with the assumption of white superiority. The consequences of this for African Americans are too familiar. Both the corrosive and advantageous implications for whites remain only lightly examined and largely misunderstood. While white supremacy has always been resisted and contested—primarily by its victims—it has never been upended, never massively rejected, never defeated. It changes form and shape from time to time, it is shot through with contradictions and even exceptions, but back it comes, again and again, living within and among us right up to today. In other words, white supremacy has proven itself an astonishingly enduring social and cultural system, and the U.S., in spite of its happy rhetoric, remains fundamentally dedicated to structures, institutions, and ideologies that construct and enforce white domination.

JOHN BROWN'S SEMINAR

Now, if it is deemed necessary that I should forfeit my life for the furtherance of the ends of justice, and mingle my blood further with the blood of my children, and with the blood of millions in this slave country whose rights are disregarded by wicked, cruel and unjust enactments, I submit: so let it be done!

—John Brown

"I love Walt Whitman!" the young waitress said enthusiastically as she noticed a button on Bernardine's shirt depicting a nineteenth-century man with a luxuriant white beard. We nod our agreement. "Me, too. Walt Whitman is great. But this is John Brown." Eyebrows jumping, uncertainty. "You know, Harper's Ferry, war to free the slaves?" A puzzled nod. We needed a pamphlet, a CD, a website.

When we were young, John Brown was unknown to us, too. Perhaps we might have remembered a grainy black-and-white photo in our American history textbook, burning eyes, hollow cheeks, the look of a wanted poster—surely a fanatic. Or was that William Lloyd Garrison, wild-eyed editor of *The Liberator* newspaper? Both were described as lunatic zealots. In today's post 9/11 political world, they—along with Nat Turner, Harriet Tubman, and Sojourner Truth—would surely be labeled and then dismissed by the authorities as terrorists.

The image on the button is a photograph of a bigger-than-life statue of Brown from North Elba, New York, where the farmhouse of John Brown and his large family is tucked into the valley below snow-covered Mount Marcy (Tahawus, or "Cloudsplitter," to the Algonquin) among the ridges of the Adirondack Mountains of upstate New York. Brown, his wife, and his sons made this isolated farm a third major artery of the Underground Railroad. Here they picked up fugitive slaves who made it to the nearby free Black farming community of Timbuctoo or the Irish iron-mining compound Tahawus and drove them a harrowing, long night's drive North in their wagons, up through the dense, mountainous wilderness passes. They would deliver their "goods" to the Quaker stationmasters up at Port Kent or Plattsburgh on Lake Champlain, where they would travel by boat into Canada or continue directly by wagon across the Canadian border to emancipation. This secret pathway between the two established lines—one through Niagara, and the other up the Hudson Valley—had circuitous and treacherous roots from the Adirondacks down to the Appalachian Range and directly into the arteries of Virginia slavery.

Unlike many notable white abolitionists, Brown allied himself concretely with African Americans—in this case the small and heavily armed Timbuctoo, established on rocky, unforgiving soil by runaway former slaves and freedmen. He did not trust well-meaning whites, but relied instead upon his own family members or the African Americans whose lives were at stake. Contrary to mythology, John Brown consulted, planned, and strategized with the great Black leaders of his day: Frederick Douglass, Harriet Tubman, Martin Delaney, J.W. Loguen, and Henry Highland Garnet. Toward the

84

end, Brown recruited political, economic, and military solidarity and support from the mobilized and growing community of some fifty thousand Canadian Blacks. There he convened a quiet conference of African American leaders and a handful of white men at Chatham, where an anti-slavery constitution was adopted and Brown's general military strategy was approved. Significant sectors of these forces would stick with him through the wars of Kansas and up to the historic raid at Harpers Ferry.

We gathered there at North Elba in 2000, some three hundred of us, one brilliant May day, on the occasion of the 200th anniversary of Brown's birth (May 9, 1800). With two dear friends we drove up from Albany toward Lake Placid, drinking in the rich variety of greens that cover the mountains: bright spring greens, yellowish greens, deep velvety fir greens, tiny mountain lakes, Heart Lake.

Before arriving at the Brown farmhouse, we attended a convening at a perfectly restored church in Elba, where the novelist Russell Banks spoke about the funeral procession that had brought Old Osawatomie, as Brown was known, from the Virginia scaffold where he was hanged, back up to their valley home where he—and the sons who died with him—were buried under an enormous stone boulder. The journey of John Brown's body, said Banks, became a rallying point for the free Northern Blacks and the Abolitionist forces. Ordinary people turned out to watch it pass, to see the casket move from train to barge to wagon, and to pay their respects. It may have taken some courage to come out to watch John Brown's body pass; surely a part of the swelling crowds included slavers who feared and despised Brown, and now felt triumphant. Within a half-year of the hanging, though, the Civil War began and Union troops went into bloody battle singing, "John Brown's body lies a mouldering in the grave, but his soul goes marching on."

The nerve, the chutzpah, the arrogance of a white man who set himself on a course to take up arms against the system of slavery! For years he studied, planned, and trained for a guerrilla war that would be waged by freed African Americans from the North joined by liberated men and women from the heart of the slave South and their white allies. The raid, the military strategy, the conception failed. And yet—a white man willing, even determined, to die for Black freedom! How was that possible?

We filed out of the church, an unlikely crowd of Black youth up from Albany, and New York City, aging radicals, Black and white, local residents—also Black and white—caretakers of the Brown homestead, and independent activists. Spilling out into the bright chill, we walked through the cemetery up the dusty road to the Brown farmhouse.

The gigantic grey boulder that looms in the front yard is unruly and looks slightly ominous. No tended rows of gravestones here. Nowadays, the rock is surrounded by the recognizable fencing of official state monument sites across the country, and marked with a formal plaque telling the story to visitors. The farmhouse is restored, open for scrutiny. It feels better to be outside, up a little rise on the land, looking from the bottom of a bowl into the dizzying and ancient mountains. One can imagine the harsh winters, the welcome moment of the June sun, the hardscrabble struggle to grow food, to make an isolated living.

Another year Bill Fletcher spoke at the same spot about John Brown. We made the pilgrimage again to that craggy, obscure location near the Vermont and Canadian borders. Fletcher, longtime labor activist and leader of TransAfrica, the Black Radical Congress, and the Aurora Project, brought the clear, analytical perspective of a radical African American trade unionist. His talk was sober, analytical, rousing altogether. He pondered the incongruous forces of class and race that maintained the slave system and keep us divided today; he ruminated about the determined efforts of free Blacks, religious allies, slave uprisings, and comfortable Abolitionists who came together to pressure industry, labor, and complicit politicians into standing up against slavery. He wondered about Brown's break with nonviolence, his zealotry, his legacy. We strolled up to the farmhouse, thinking about all the unfinished business that is the real America.

It's an alarming if totally predictable fact that while John Brown's body was turned over to his widow after his hanging, and two weeks later the bodies of two other white comrades were turned over to their families, the bodies of two Black raiders, John Copeland and Shields Green, were tossed in makeshift graves and then dug up by a group of medical students who used them as subjects for dissection—the relentless assault on the Black body. Although three thousand mourners gathered in a church in Oberlin, Ohio, to commemorate the life and heroism of John Copeland, his body was not present.

To us in the late sixties, "white mother-country radicals" as the Panthers called us, John Brown became a symbol of that rare white person ready to put his body on the line, to cross the invisible but tangible boundaries of white privilege and safety, to see and feel and think that the bondage, lashing, and ownership of a people based on the color of their skin was a continuing assault against *him*. We ignored the parts of Brown that made no sense to us: the deep religious passion and Calvinist Christian conviction, the authoritarian and absent father, the failed businessman. Brown organized his life around ending slavery, and that was good enough for us—his actions in Kansas and Harpers Ferry were the legacy we excavated and embraced.

Beginning in 1854, settlers and armed militias were pouring into the Kansas territory from both North and South, some hired, some ideological, some drunken louts up for a fight, some motivated by the word of God—all enlisted in the contest over whether Kansas would be free or slave. The method was slaughter and intimidation prior to the pending vote on statehood. Kansas would tip the fragile balance between slave states and free, and in Kansas, it was no holds barred.

Brown had to leave behind his second wife, Mary Day, and daughters Ruth, Annie, and Sarah at the North Elba farmstead. Mary married John Brown at the age of sixteen, inheriting five of Brown's children; she bore thirteen more, and saw four children die of dysentery in the winter of 1843. Brown said goodbye to Mary and his daughters to travel with six sons and a son-in-law, Henry Thompson, to Kansas. By 1856, he was an old man, determined to learn the art of war by going to war, to practice for the grand strategy he was hatching, to rehearse the inevitable coming conflict, to test his men and himself. They lived marginally in Kansas, struggling against the rain and cold, disease and mud. Some of their band left, and others arrived. There were skirmishes and armed defense of civilians in Lawrence and across the state.

And, finally, there were Osawatomie and Pottawatomie. Both were settlements of pro-slavers too poor to own slaves themselves, other poor folk, and failed farmers much like Brown himself. The Southern whites who came to Kansas were not the powerful, the plantation owners who were migrating West with their slave property, demanding a reopening of the African slave trade. Kansas whites were not even those smaller white farmers who owned a few slaves themselves. These were the poor white workers of the South, those five million white Southerners who held no slaves and were described as ruffians and rabble, crackers and adventurers; "not the leaders ... but the dogs which were to worry the free state men to death," Du Bois called them. Some few included the slightly more prosperous slave overseers. They were set on seizing opportunity from Kansas and becoming pioneers, and they saw their economic future threatened by the prospect of free Black labor. Further incited and armed by powerful pro-slavery forces, they were driven to wrest Kansas for themselves and to exclude the free Blacks. They wanted free soil and demanded Black exclusion from labor and the vote. Kansas was the first battle, the dress rehearsal for the gathering Civil War, and blood soaked the land.

In May 1856, in retaliation for the sacking and burning of Lawrence, where there had been no resistance, Brown and his forces murdered five pro-slavery men, seized in their sleep and hacked to death on the banks of the Pottawatomie River. It was a cold-blooded reprisal, grisly and harsh, difficult—maybe impossible—to justify. Yet the guerrilla warfare, these battles and skirmishes, including Pottawatomie, turned the tide in Kansas, from slave state to free. On August 30, the battle of Osawatomie was fought when pro-slavery forces from Missouri attacked the town, which was defended by Abolitionists including Brown. His son Frederick was killed in the defense. Brown left Kansas, and was known for the rest of his life as Old Osawatomie.

John Brown's searing focus on the system of white supremacy and his renunciation of its privileges, its silences and its complicity, fired our imaginations, and we —in the student movement and then in the Weather Underground seized upon him for three linked reasons—for better or for worse. First, we celebrated his dedicated insistence to the cause of Black freedom as the key to everyone's freedom—to his, to ours. Second, his years of activism developing and preparing the Underground Railroad served as one of our few domestic models for clandestine networks. Third, we were taken with his conclusion *as a white person* that taking up arms and being willing to fight was essential to implementing the Abolitionist goal. Few others in U.S. history met that triple test.

Brown appeared to us to identify fully and viscerally with the suffering and experiences of Black America, to have a laser perception of the violent subjugation that was the basis of slavery, and to simultaneously resist romanticizing or objectifying African Americans—enslaved or free. He took African Americans to be fully human, chock-full of foibles, ignorance, and tragedy. He despised the institution of slavery, recognized how totally it corrupted white who benefited from it—rich and poor alike—and expected both whites and Black people to resist the slave system.

So it was John Brown's humanizing enterprise that captured us, seeing it as our obligation as humans/citizens to act to transform the situation of the most dispossessed. It was his insistence over decades that the issue of race—Black subjugation and white supremacy—fundamentally defined the American reality.

The Underground Railroad was a sparkling fact of the American experience that excited our radical imaginations. Reaching up to Canada and down to Mexico, the methods of escape from slavery, flights to freedom, consecutive shelter with a train of anonymous supporters, border crossings, invented new lives and identities—these were the ingredients of strategy, organization, and purpose. The goal was to remain invisible to the slavers, the state, and the organized terrorists, and hyper-alert to the possibilities of bountyhunters, kidnappers hired by slaveholders or agents hired to return lost or stolen "property," or even betrayal by tentative supporters.

Of course, the slavers had the law on their side: As long as escaped men and women were characterized as property, the law set out to enforce their return. Runaways were described as violent criminals—neither as freedom fighters nor as human beings dashing for liberty.

Today, most of us are certain that were we alive during the 1850s, we would surely have sheltered runaways and been part of the Underground Railroad in some capacity. But the vast majority of whites in the North, as in the South, failed to support an end to slavery in any concrete manner until the Civil War wrapped it in a nationalist frenzy. Henry David Thoreau excoriated his fellow citizens for their failure to demand the freedom of a Black man arrested and imprisoned at the Boston Court House under the Fugitive Slave Law of 1850: "I had thought the house was on fire, and not the prairie... What should concern Massachusetts is not ... the Fugitive Slave Bill but her own slaveholding and servility. Let the State dissolve her union with the slaveholder." White clergy and formal religions largely failed to demand an end to slavery. Individual citizens mostly closed their eyes, turned their heads, or rationalized the fear and risk: What about our children and their safety? What about not knowing who might betray us? What about our job, home, spouse?

Brown lived and breathed the violence of the slave system. After Harpers Ferry, Thoreau spoke out immediately in support of John Brown by conjuring up the daily reality that was so easy for whites—including Abolitionists—to ignore: "The slave-ship is on her way, crowded with its dying victims; new cargoes are being added; in mid-ocean a small crew of slaveholders, countenanced by a large body of passengers, is smothering four millions under the hatches, and yet the politician asserts that the only proper way by which deliverance is to be obtained, is by 'the quiet diffusion of the sentiments of humanity,' without any 'outbreak.' As if the sentiments of humanity were ever found unaccompanied by its deeds."

Those who spoke out after his capture but *before* the hanging included the Black churchwomen of a Brooklyn and Williamsburgh congregation who offered to raise funds to help support Brown's family. They wrote to Mary Brown a week before Brown's scheduled hanging, a letter published in *The Weekly Anglo-African* newspaper in New York.

> "He is our honored and dearly-loved brother..." the women said, signing the letter, "pray your loving sisters." "We wanted to tell you how we have met again and again in prayer for you, and those who are still in bonds, and how, in offering this word of sympathy to you now we desire to express our deep, undying gratitude to him who has given his life so freely to obtain for us our defrauded rights..."

We were fixed by John Brown's revolutionary blood feud with slavery. Armed self-defense was well recognized in the Black Freedom Movement of our day, from the efforts of the Deacons for Defense and Justice during the Southern Civil Rights Movement, Robert and Mabel Williams (authors of *Negroes With Guns*), to armed Black students seizing the administration building at Cornell University, and the Black Panther Party for Self-Defense. Self-defense was one thing, but carrying the war to the oppressor and those who sided with them (pro-slavers are fair game) seemed both unthinkable and inevitable. Brown refused to permit the physical risks of resistance, the suffering and dying, to rest solely on the Black community. We aspired to be like him.

On the day of Brown's hanging, his farewell note, handed to one of his guards, wrote of his identification with the sorrows of the slave population and the guilt and penance of whites: "I John Brown am now quite certain that the crimes of this guilty, land: Will never be purged away; but with Blood. I had as I now think: Vainly flattered myself that without very much bloodshed; it might be done."

When Brown launched the raid on Harpers Ferry in 1859, he had a grand vision of what might be possible. He and his comrades would seize the weapons in the arsenal and cross the Shenandoah River to the Virginia mountains. There, within Faquar County, lived some ten thousand enslaved African Americans, 650 free Blacks and 9,875 whites. Adjoining Black counties with a majority of people in bondage constituted what the historian W.E.B. Du Bois called the Great Black Way. Brown anticipated leadership from Canadian Blacks, and he contemplated raids down from the mountains to release the enslaved Blacks, to disperse arms to them, and to encourage uprisings across the South. He was relying on small guerrilla raids, but in some writings and conversations he anticipated an insurgency, a full-throttled rebellion like those of Nat Turner and Denmark Vesey on a massive scale.

He was wrong. The attack was a blunder, a bungled raid filled with miscalibrations and folly. Brown was wounded and captured alive by a regiment commanded by Robert E. Lee, indicted for the crime of treason—"an enemy of Virginia, an enemy of the Union, a foe of the human race"—convicted as well of conspiring with slaves to rebel and murder in the first degree. "In the first place," Brown said at sentencing, "I deny everything but what I have all along admitted: of a design on my part to free slaves ..." And yet the attack and the trial, the national commentary and the hanging, accelerated events, led to his martyrdom, and became a major catalyst for the Civil War.

Visiting Harpers Ferry brings all the magnificence of the setting, the geography, and the strategic location into view. It includes, of course, the inevitable wax museum and gift shops, family-style diners and miniature villages. Like most historical sites, one must challenge the official narrative, taking it with a skeptical ton of salt.

Brown couldn't know that the next year would bring the firing on Fort Sumter followed by a five-year Civil War with the issue of slavery invariably at its crux, fatefully intertwined with the struggle between Northern capital and Southern plantation agriculture. The meaning of Harpers Ferry was not, in the end, what his band of anti-slavery activists anticipated. But they made their meaning grand meaning, and this inflamed and inspired us.

The transcendentalist Thoreau wrote: "John Brown's career for the last six weeks of his life was meteor-like, flashing through the darkness in which we live. I know of nothing so miraculous in our history." Du Bois, in addition to his magnificent 1909 book on John Brown, tangentially and tellingly mentions John Brown three times in the thousand pages of his collected writings. While discussing Harriet Tubman, he notes that she was one of John Brown's "closest advisors" and was prevented from being present at Harpers Ferry only by severe illness. Du Bois also places Brown in an honorific list of ethical lives: Jeremiah, Shakespeare, and Jesus, Confucius, Buddha, and John Brown. And in a brief essay on books, written in 1931, Du Bois suggests the essential African American library include some sixty indispensable volumes—one is *The Life of John Brown.*

When Brown raised the alarm, he shattered a certain silence, placing his and his children's bodies concretely in the service of the goal: death to slavery. With his actions and his resistance in captivity he declared an emergency. It is so easy for whites not to see, to keep the bondage of "others" invisible, to deny the cruelties, indignities, inequities, and powerlessness, to misread the rage and the obsessions. There are always other interpretations, individual flaws and explanations—things are more complicated. And, of course, they are. But John Brown's ferocious focus on the system of slavery itself allowed him to empathize with African Americans, to see them as full human beings no less than himself. It's a rare thing: a trustworthy American white person.

THE LENGTHENING LEGACY

When someone else strives and strains to prove to me that black men are as intelligent as white men, I say that intelligence has never saved anyone; and that is true, for, if philosophy and intelligence are invoked to proclaim the equality of men, they have also been employed to justify the extermination of men.

—Frantz Fanon

All the attempts through the centuries to divide human beings into the fiction of races—173 in one "scientific" rendering two hundred years ago, 57 in another—would seem folly if they didn't represent such murderous and bloody projects. But they always do. The invention of whiteness as a permanent symbol of the fully human, the just-us, as a chit to be traded on in tough times, is the condition that creates the other, the stranger, the less-than-fully human. That's why the historian Noel Ignatiev calls for the abolition of whiteness—abolition would open a space against negativity and for humanity. Wherever we find the marshalling of science to define visible human difference as races, we find conquest on the agenda and ruin at the horizon. The invention and glorification of race is ultimately a recipe for murder.

Race bristles with significance, and yet when we speak of race we pull from a curious sack of meanings and a specious base of knowledge. Race might refer, and often does, to a people or nation or tribe of the same stock and background—the German race, the Jewish race, the Japanese race. That this has a preposterous edge comes as no surprise, for practically no one really believes any longer that those broad strokes of background are somehow immutable, that tribal stock is really static, or that national identity is stone-like. And yet, not so long ago crime statistics in Chicago, for example, were broken down into categories that might strike some today as odd: Irish, Italian, Jewish, Negro, white. How would one know? Today crime is reported as Black, White, Hispanic, Asian. Again, how does anyone know? It all depends on the angle of regard. Today Eastern Europeans are surprised to acquire a new identity as they arrive—they become "white," just as Koreans, Filipinos, and Vietnamese are newly-minted as "Asians." Surely some ethnic immigrants have become—are still becoming—"white." It is hard, however, to claim much in the way of progress here.

The "science of race" is by now a thoroughly discredited myth: "The genes that regulate the amount of melanin beneath the skin are simply not expressed in the brain," according to an interview with Dr. Robert Pollack by Patricia Williams. Pollack was a colleague of James Watson, the Nobel laureate and co-discoverer of DNA, who had made a string of racist comments in late 2007 that Pollack wanted to challenge. "The social responses to race are real; race is not," he said. "Race is a choice."

***

Every story of oppression begins with the cries and groans of unjustified suffering, undeserved harm, unnecessary pain—stories of human beings in chains or under the boot. It begins, say, with slavery, not an American invention, but, rather, a frightening commonplace in human experience. Americans, even today, like to point glibly to slavery's historic banality, its ubiquitous quality through the ages, particularly in Africa, as if that trumps the "peculiar institution" slavery became in the land of Native Americans, in this land, in the hands of "our" forefathers.

A word like "slavery," a word that points to something so large and so ghastly, can conceal as much as it reveals, can provide a protective gloss so that the unspeakable—in being spoken—is reduced and falsified. Torture, genocide, slavery—we search out the words to name the world, to understand, to see, to grasp, and perhaps to change all that we find before us. But sometimes, through misuse or overuse, words become clichés, and then morph again into slogans. The rough edges, the specificity is sanded off and smoothed out. The imagination collapses and the mind closes down. Whatever horror the word pointed to in the first place becomes opaque; the word blinds us and erases the world. When we utter the word without weeping, we can be pretty sure our souls are in peril.

Slavery is dreadful—we can mostly agree there—but the word has come to a condition of little depth and meager detail. This is apparently why John Brown was reported to have regularly read aloud with his family detailed accounts of the physical conditions of specific runaway Africans from advertisements posted by their owners in Northern newspapers: Jacob, forty-two years old, missing one eye with a deep scar on his left cheek made by an ax; Celia, thirty, both arms and back showing the braided marks of a whip. Brown opposed every fact of slavery—not only institutional and structural, but also personal and human.

Orlando Patterson notes that the African American people was an enslaved group for 248 of its 387 years in this country, two-thirds of its existence. Captured Africans were subjected routinely and legally to exploitation and rape and torture and violence at the whim of their white owners, and they were also at the mercy of whites generally; a consistent assault attempted to reduce the Black family was reduced to an exclusively reproductive unit through the white supremacist system; African Americans as a group have struggled for survival under the most obscene conditions—stolen from their homes and forced across an ocean onto a new land; worked as animals in the fields; freed from slavery only to be forced into a serf-like existence on low-density farms; pushed from South to North, from peasant shacks to overcrowded urban slums; now *caged* in record numbers, disenfranchised, discarded. And, yet, "still here, still rising.

But we might also think for a moment, not of the general condition, but of a particular young man with this specific human face, a mother and a father, a past and a future. He has a name that points to his ancestors, his father's father's name, and beckons toward a future of promise and redemption. He is in love, for the first time perhaps, and his partner is pregnant with their first child, a sign of productivity and abundance, their hope for tomorrow. He works every day in the fields and the forests, minding crops and animals, gathering food, attending to the requirements of his home and his village. Almost every evening he smokes his pipe with the men before he rests.

And then in one blinding and violent moment his life is crushed. The sudden, searing struggle overwhelms him, cripples him, leaves him bloody and gasping. Whipped and chained and transported in the hold of a ship for thirty-four torturous days of puking and dying and starving and living in human wastes, he arrives in a strange and brutal place only half alive.

He endures, he survives. The pain is never entirely gone, but the mind shuts down and the raw and open wounds become scars. He lives for forty-two more years, fathers two more children but knows neither one, dies without family or mourners, his remains placed in an unmarked slave yard near the fields.

How can we understand such a thing? Everything the young man had was taken, but more than this. Everything he was, everything he might have become was also stolen from him, and the slave system attempted to transform him from a person of depth and dimension into a thing for the use of others. His humanity was reduced by the slave traders to a crude property transaction, his hopes and dreams, his aspirations and capacities smashed to dust on the ground.

This single act is a monstrous, primal crime, to be sure. But, rather than multiply this single act by, say, ten million lives, if we take it life by human life, each story specific in its brute humanness, its horror and its hope, each particular, then the long, torturous arc of Black dispossession and dislocation comes into clearer focus. The telling of it makes the pain distinct, understandable in human terms. It commands us to face facts and to take account of the various roles played by white people over centuries, complicities that encompass the whole range of human behaviors: active participation, acquiescence, silence, retreat. Such an accounting is a necessary condition of repair.

And then there is necessarily the slave trader's side of the story, the birth of the institution of white supremacy, a story with its own warp and weave. We remember the film *Roots* tracing Alex Haley's family history back to Africa. Early in the story, the captain of a slave ship, a man who considers himself a Christian and a liberal and finds, he claims, the transporting of slaves odious work, confronts his first mate, a crude, unpolished fellow who regularly rapes and abuses the human cargo, often throwing people who resist overboard, and taunting the captain for his squeamishness. The captain, all worry and hand-wringing, implores the brute to treat the slaves a bit better, insisting that they are also human beings and God's children. The first mate looks him squarely in the eye and responds with astounding lucidity: Of course they're human beings, he says, and if we're to profit from this enterprise we'd best convince them and everyone else that they're dogs or mules—anything but human. You see, he points out, if they're fully human, there's absolutely no justification for our business. Only if they're inferior—in their own minds *and* in the minds of the exploited but relatively advantaged whites—will we stand to gain. We must, if we are to benefit, insist that they are beasts, nothing more. Pretending that Blacks are inhuman, the slave trader dehumanizes himself, and the captain, retreating into his ineffectual fretting and whispered prayers and entreaties, undermines his own humanity in the process as well.

Prejudice and the idea of inferiority based on race grows from and is fed by the need to justify and perpetuate this dreadful inequality, this domination and control. And while discrimination and slavery go back to antiquity, the system of chattel slavery based on race—that is, the enslavement of an entire people and their transformation into commodities without any family, property, or human rights whatsoever, bound for life and for generations into the imaginable future, and simultaneously the invention of whiteness as an immutable marker of privilege even among the poorest of whites—is the "peculiar institution" born in North America of the African slave trade. Racism as a primary social and cultural dividing line in the United States, and in varying forms down the rest of the hemisphere—developed from a greed for profit and achieved by deception and a monopoly of firearms, not by some imagined biological superiority— is the legacy of that institution.

At the core of the rotten reality, as W.E.B. Du Bois explains so clearly, is exploitation and profit. The bad idea is neither its own source nor foundation, but is brought forth and rests on that heavy base of caste and class injustice. The imposition of white supremacy is then rationalized by religion, culture, and myth, encoded into law, defended by force and violence. Fighting racism in the realm of prejudice alone, or only in the world of language and ideas, without resisting and undermining the core inequality and unjust structures that give birth to those ideas, is in the end a hopeless mission.

Slavery was a form of super-exploitation and it was based on violence and on terror— and all whites benefited in large ways and small—regardless of whatever social intercourse might be observed between particular people on any given day, just as colonial conquest, occupation, imperial expansion is always violent at its core, and all U.S. people benefit (as well as suffer) in some measure.

***

The edifice of racism as bigotry is built, then, upon the hard ground of race as a convenient invention for violent exploitation. That is what Du Bois had in mind when he declared the problem of the twentieth century "the problem of the color line." Now that we're finished with that century—a hundred years marked by unparalleled degradation and violence against people because of color, ethnic background, and national origin, and by extraordinary efforts on the part of the downtrodden and disadvantaged of the earth to achieve and extend human dignity and freedom—Du Bois's words remain lucid and significant. The problem of the color line persists.

What is to be done?

We're drawn to "Letter to My Nephew on the One Hundredth Anniversary of the Emancipation" by James Baldwin, and we, with a sense of eavesdropping, read and re-read it, captivated, in our youth. The searing letter, "My Dungeon Shook," is the opening pages of *The Fire Next Time*. Baldwin wastes no time indicting the United States: "This is the crime of which I accuse my country and my countrymen, and for which neither I nor time nor history will ever forgive them," he begins, "that they have destroyed and are destroying hundreds of thousands of lives and do not know it and do not want to know it." Baldwin amasses a bill of particulars: "You were born where you were born and faced the future that you faced because you were black and for no other reason... You were born into a society which spelled out with brutal clarity, and in as many ways as possible, that you were a worthless human being." He tells his nephew that "it was intended that you should perish in the ghetto, perish by never being allowed to go beyond the white man's definitions, by never being allowed to spell your proper name." Baldwin argues that even though "the details and symbols of your life have been deliberately constructed to make you believe what white people say about you," his nephew—along with other Black people—must "remember that what they believe, as well as what they do and cause you to endure, does not testify to your inferiority but to their inhumanity and fear." Too many white people, Baldwin believes, "are, in effect, still trapped in a history which they do not understand, and until they understand it, they cannot be released from it."

For Baldwin, the remedy is painful and complex but available—white Americans must look unblinkingly at history, face our constructed and cushioned reality, confront the tears of the wounded, the consequences of that wickedness; we must harness ourselves, then, to a great collective effort toward justice. Baldwin finds hope in an image of "the relatively conscious whites and the relatively conscious blacks, who must, like lovers, insist on, or create, the consciousness of the others in order to end the racial nightmare, and achieve our country." Action and commitment fueled by both rage and, yes, love— like lovers, he said. But nothing until we summon the courage to look honestly at the world as it is: "It is not permissible that the authors of devastation should also be innocent. It is the innocence which constitutes the crime."
We fight to see through and beyond the construction of race, even as we must note

without equivocation the powerful consequences of our humanly constituted, profoundly racialized world—*both*. If we are to be responsible, we cannot pretend to be colorblind or deny privilege, but neither can we stay mired in useless guilt or stumble in our attempts to destroy white supremacy and eliminate domination.

Facing reality involves confronting our history, acknowledging our past, including its deceptions and its discontents, its dishonesties and its disasters. Racism, we re-discover, is not a little secondary subplot in the U.S. story, but a central and permanent theme coloring every other. It's built up over centuries of misbehavior and oppression, infecting our attitudes, our assumptions, our behavior. We wake up, we open our eyes. We are not innocent then, but neither are we paralyzed. As the legal scholar Derrick Bell writes, "Perhaps those of us who can admit we are imprisoned by the history of racial subordination in America can accept—as slaves had no choice but to accept— our fate. Not that we legitimate the racism of the oppressor. On the contrary, we can only delegitimate it if we can accurately pinpoint it. And racism lies at the center, not the periphery; in the permanent, not in the fleeting; in the real lives of black and white people, not in the sentimental caverns of the mind." Racism is the main channel in the North American river, not a small trickle at the edge.

For Bell, this recognition is not cause for despair, but rather for "engagement and commitment," and it calls forth the same demand that Black people have faced since slavery: "making something out of nothing. Carving out a humanity for oneself with absolutely nothing to help—save imagination, will, and unbelievable strength and courage. Beating the odds while firmly believing in, knowing as only they could know, the fact that all those odds are stacked against them." Bell urges action to create meaning, to name oneself in resistance, to oppose the void. He counsels "the pragmatic recognition that racism is permanent" side by side with "the unalterable conviction that something must be done, that action must be taken."

In "The Space Traders," Bell creates an allegory about race in America that is both illuminating and chilling. It happens that a fleet of spaceships bearing aliens arrives with what appears to be incredibly advanced technologies and loads of good will. They can provide many of our immediate needs: Cheap and clean energy, gold, an abundance of food, environmental restoration, and much more. They ask only one thing in return for their materials and know-how: The U.S. must bring all African Americans to the East Coast where they will be loaded into the spaceships and taken away forever. There is no coercion or hint of threat involved—no indication that the Black people will be hurt or harmed in any way—simply an invitation to a trade.

After some debate and confusion—and resistance from a few white people—whites essentially say, Why not? We get all this wealth and technology, and at the same time we get rid of a seemingly intractable problem, the problem of Black people, something that's bedeviled us for years. What's the downside?

When Bell presents his allegory to Black people, he reports that they are unanimous in their belief that it reveals a harrowing truth of their condition. White folks aren't so sure, and they're divided in their reaction—denial, guilt, confusion—united only in their discomfort.

The allegory hinges on questions many would like to leave unasked: Do whites think Black people are human in *exactly* the same ways they are themselves? Do we assume a unity of human experience and being? Is the presence of Black people, we hesitate to say it out loud, more a burden than a gift?

White people, in all our dimensions and identities, who aspire to stand up to oppose racism, a plague out there in the world as surely as it is in here, inside our own minds and hearts, are foolish to parse matters—I'm better than Mark Fuhrman, we're tempted to boast, I'm neither a Nazi nor a Klansman. The important thing is not to slide off into self-congratulation, but rather to find the courage to be counted, to stir from indifference and inaction, to love the world enough to oppose the domination. Baldwin, again: "It is not necessary that people be wicked, but only that they be spineless" to bring us all to wrack and ruin. Amilcar Cabral, the African liberationist from Guinea-Bissau, noted that in today's world, it is not necessary to be courageous; it is enough to be honest.

Those who embrace this colossal effort must fix one eye firmly on the world as it is, while the other is looking toward a world that could be but is not yet—a future fit for all our children, a place of peace and justice. We can, with bell hooks, learn to create little sites of freedom, small locations of possibility: "To labor for freedom, to demand of ourselves and our comrades, an openness of mind and heart that allows us to face reality even as we collectively imagine ways to move beyond boundaries, to transgress." We can identify obstacles to our collective well-being and link up with others in acts of hope and love.

***

The illusion of white superiority can be found at the heart of our language: "White" means "free from spot or blemish," "free from moral impurity," "not intended to cause harm," "innocent," "marked by upright fairness," and then there are all the familiar phrases like "white knight," "white horse," and "white hope." "Black" doesn't fare so well—"dirty," "soiled," "thoroughly sinister or evil," "wicked," "sad, gloomy, or calamitous," "grim, distorted, or grotesque." Associated terms include black art (sorcery), black and blue (discolored from bruising), blacken the character (become evil), blackball (to exclude from membership), blackmail (to extort by threats), black market (illicit trade), blackout (to envelop in darkness), black heart (evil), black mark (doomed), black day (characterized by disaster), and so on. It's absolutely exhausting.

And then there are all the color-free euphemisms that are recognizably color-coded: at-risk youth, high-needs neighborhood, achievement gap, hard-to-staff schools (in the world of education); super-predator, gang-involved, violent-prone (in the world of juvenile justice). The words "urban" and "city" evoke a color when used as adjectives, as in "urban riots," "urban decay," "city schools," "city transit system." And, of course, a neutral-sounding word like "public" gets colored when we speak of "public welfare" or "public housing" or a "public hospital."

Color and ethnicity are embedded in our language, at the core of our ability to think and act. A coward is "yellow," an angry mood is "black," a victim of fraud is "gypped" or "Jewed." Women and girls are ..., well, the list is endless. Sports mascots are "Indians," and "Braves," and "Chiefs," immigrants are "aliens" or, if Arab, "terrorists." In a country brutally divided along racial lines, founded and sustained on a constructed and interwoven hierarchy of color and class divisions, language itself is encoded with privilege, oppression, bias, bigotry, and power. Our thinking debases our language, and our language simultaneously shapes our thinking. Modern American English tells us who we are, where we've been, and where we're going.

***

We read the boys to sleep every night of their childhood. They tore through the boy books Bernardine never knew: *Black Beauty, Robinson Crusoe, Huck Finn,* and *Crazy Horse,* but the reading list also included *Little Women, Little Men,* and *Jo's Boys* as well as all of *Dickens*. Many, perhaps the majority, of the American classics involved virulent racism (Little House on the Prairie) and rampant sexism (Shel Silverstein's The Giving Tree). So the challenge was whether to change the gendered or ethnic language or to interrupt, interpret, and repudiate. Of course it was never so simple, and for more familiar books, read over and over (Winnie the Pooh, Charlotte's Web, Stuart Little), Zayd, Malik and Chesa knew the text by heart and objected to any deviation, even as they were drifting off to sleep. How do children imbibe the essence, the discipline of white and male supremacy? We assumed that words matter.

***

Toni Morrison talks of the "evacuated language" of the powerful, of the "systematic looting of language" geared toward "menace and subjugation." "Oppressive language does more than represent violence," she writes, "it is violence; does more than represent the limits of knowledge; it limits knowledge." She argues for the rejection and exposure of "obscuring state language or the faux language of mindless media," "language designed for the estrangement of minorities, hiding its racist plunder in its literary cheek." She describes "sexist language, racist language, theistic language" as "typical of the policing languages of mastery" that "cannot, do not, permit new knowledge or encourage the mutual exchange of ideas."

We can resist the language, of course, and we should—it's good exercise and it can be cleansing and clarifying to refuse to simply be at the mercy of repetitive and oppressive language. Our kids attended a day care where the adults worked diligently to create a liberating and empowering environment for young children, struggling constantly with language. The school was founded and directed by an extraordinary young woman renowned for her advocacy of liberating and anti-racist perspectives; the multiracial community of parents and staff tended toward public activism for equity and social justice. We all wanted to free ourselves from the constraints of a racist and sexist society, and so it became natural and not jarring in that school to hear conversation laced with terms like "mail carrier," "police officer," "cowhand," and, one of our personal favorites, "waitron." Not only did "firefighter" replace "fireman" but the dramatic play area had a poster of a Black firefighter in action and the block area had a unique collection of little figures including a white male nurse and a Black woman firefighter. "Firefighter, firefighter, firefighter."

Our little school was lodged just across the street from a New York City firehouse and the firehouse was staffed exclusively with white males. The children visited the firefighters, tried on their hats, rang the bell, and got to know a few of them. One day Megan, five years old, asked a fireman, "Why are all the firefighters men?" When, she continued, did he expect there would be Black women in the station house? The firefighter exploded in derisive laughter: "Never, I hope. The neighborhood would burn down."

"That's not fair," Megan said softly then, and, when back at school, more forcefully. The class wrote letters of protest to the fire chief, the mayor, and the city council pleading for justice.

The non-sexist language and the anti-racist materials were in hard and steady combat with facts on the ground, and changing language did not in itself change worlds. Our adult responsibility, as far as their education was concerned, included the obligation to present the concrete situations they encountered as problems that challenged them and called for some response.

James Baldwin noted that language is always a political instrument—a "proof of power," he said. "It is the most vivid and crucial key to identity," connecting one with—or separating one from—whole communities.

Baldwin is entering here the debate about the use, status, and reality of Black English, and he locates it in a long history of subjugation and struggle, a language born of necessity whose rules and traditions are "dictated by what the language must convey": "The brutal truth is that the bulk of white people in America never had any interest in educating Black people... It is not the Black child's language that is in question, it is not his language that is despised: It is his experience."

It's impossible to be a good teacher to a child who is despised, and on the other side, difficult to learn from someone demanding the repudiation of one's experience, of "all that gives sustenance," as the price of the ticket for an education. Baldwin concludes that in a country characterized by so much hypocrisy and bigotry and denial, "in a country with standards so untrustworthy... a country unable to face why so many of the nonwhite are in prison, or on the needle, or standing, futureless in the streets," many youth "have concluded that they have nothing whatever to learn from the people of a country that has managed to learn so little."

***

Because race is a social construction, an agreed-upon covenant, a dynamic relationship rather than a fixed category, a hundred years ago the Irish had to *become* white, as Noel Ignatiev convincingly demonstrated, and Jews only entered what Bertolt Brecht called "the Caucasian chalk circle" after World War II. The bizarre history of the U.S. Census Bureau's attempts to categorize people has recently come to this: "Choose Your Race."

Whiteness has proved itself to be both remarkably durable and notably flexible, but race as social relationship means that its construction is active, not naturally occurring, that it requires actors with some degree of agency in order to shape and reproduce it. That means, again, that as a dominant and domineering idea, race is insecure and unsettled, and that it can only be analyzed and understood in motion, embodied, and mutable, itself on the run.

It's been said that the Civil War of 1860-1865 was the last battle of the American Revolution. It's also been said that the Southern Civil Rights Movement of 1954-1965 was the last battle of the Civil War. What will be the last—or even the next—battle of the Black Freedom Movement? When will we achieve racial justice?

A standard response to the mythology that today surrounds the struggles for civil rights of half a century ago—and a most convenient alibi for inaction now—is that the struggle was somehow easy then: "The outrages were so blatant"; "The enemy was so apparent"; "Everyone agreed on what had to be done;" "The Movement won." These are the clichés repeated at every turn. But is any of it true? Let's look a little more closely: Was there unanimity then? Did the Movement win? What really happened? Is racism really so difficult to see or understand now? Are we now post-racial, trans-racial, beyond race? What might we *learn* if we give up the fiction of being "good whites"? How might we listen if we reject both the self-promoting stances as well as the self-flagellating postures? Who might we become if we insist on reaching forward as whole people with bodies as well as minds, with hearts as well as heads, with emotions and spirits and feelings beyond reason? Where would we find ourselves? And when? There will necessarily be a next battle—will you, will we be a part of it?—because the racial hierarchy is intact and ongoing.

There's no point in making a claim of racial innocence—those days never existed, and there's way too much water under that bridge anyway. Racial innocence simply leaves a hierarchy of privilege and oppression based on color unchallenged and intact. Insisting on not seeing the domination that's in front of our eyes is, as Mab Segrest says, "the metaphysics of genocide." Our only options, then, are racial responsibility or racial irresponsibility. Here we are again in the territory of choice—mystified, to be sure, murky and obscured—and paths that will be taken whether we intend to take them or not.

The myth of white superiority is dynamic: its survival over centuries has depended on its ability to adapt to massive changes—from revolution, war, and Abolition to Suffrage and the end of Jim Crow, from decades of agitation and activism to widespread civil rights legislation from the class integration of some to the emiseration of many— without losing its grip on society. It is adapting now, before our eyes, in the face of immigration from Asia and Africa and Latin America, new class configuration and globalization. One marvels at its endurance, its flexibility, its tenacity.

Let's interrogate first the hidden curriculum of white supremacy and the logic of privilege, and then look toward the stance that racial responsibility might ask of us. When we refuse to acknowledge or understand our own history by inventing a fairy tale of goodness and beneficence, we disarm ourselves and we make it impossible to know who we are in the world or how we might move forward. The initial refusal becomes the anticipatory mindset for ongoing delusion and denial, for the perpetuation of injustice in the garb of innocence.

White evasion is central to the logic of privilege, and it comes in a thousand guises:

colorblindness ("I don't even notice a person's color"); containment ("In Minneapolis we don't have a race problem because there are so few Black people"); diversity and assimilation ("We work together so well, and some of my best friends..."); beyond race ("Class is the only real issue"); whitewashing (silent bonding and the assumption of monolithic racial solidarity across differences); white flight ("I know it's heavy, because I've been oppressed too,—hey, how about those Yankees."); disappearing (living, working, and schooling in all-white enclaves while Black men and women are driven into the gulag). In each case, inequitable power remains intact, justice is circumvented and denied, confronting the consequences of racism is avoided, and the speaker remains inside the comfort zone of privilege.

Race is a fiction, then, but racism is simultaneously the hardest of bedrock realities. To understand the fiction—the active process of social construction—and to miss the reality is to barricade behind denial. To see the reality and to act as if it's just there, like a tree or a hole, is to evade responsibility.

Denial is ready and waiting, and evasion is easy to embrace. But there are other choices. More difficult and yet responsible is to look both backward and forward, to examine the political impact of racism, to see its very stark social consequences—and then to notice the ways in which race matters, the ways it distorts and disfigures, the ways whites benefit and the ways whites are gnarled and misshapen, the ways in which we are each and all implicated and must find ways to become accountable.

Here are a few random racial realities we might fail to notice if denial and evasion are our creed:

- The average income of an African American today is 74 percent of the average white income.

- There's a 50 percent chance that a member of an all-white jury has decided a Black defendant's guilt before de-liberating. (The figure drops to 33 percent if the jury is mixed).

- Almost a third of Black families have a zero or negative net worth.

- In 1865, African Americans owned 0.5 percent of the total worth of the U.S. In 1990, 135 years later, African Americans owned 1 percent of the wealth.

- Two hundred years of unpaid slave labor amounts to something—most economists start their estimates upward of $1 trillion.

• Only once in our history was compensation paid by the government—in Washington, D.C., $300 per slave upon emancipation was given to the former slave owners for their loss. Nothing to the former slaves.

• Half of African American families are too poor to qualify for the full U.S. child tax credit.

• A Black youth with no prior jail time has a forty-eight in 100,000 chance of going to jail on a drug offense; a white youth has a one in 100,000 chance.

• The income gap between white and Black families is greater now than it was forty years ago.

• A third of the Black men living in Alabama are disenfranchised because of a drug conviction.

• There are about 10,000 inmates in Chicago's Cook County Jail on any given day. About 75 percent of them are African American, another 20 percent Latino.

• The Chicago Public Schools—a half a million kids, overwhelmingly Black and Latino—educate 80 percent of the bilingual kids and 50 percent of the poorest kids in Illinois and yet spend only half the money per child to educate them compared to surrounding districts that are predominantly white.

Supreme Court Justice Harry Blackmun noted that "in order to get beyond racism, we must first take account of race," to confront what Toni Morrison calls "the thematics of innocence." Not race as scientific fact, but race as social/historical practice with terrible consequences and measurable impacts.

FROM ACTIVISM TO RESISTANCE

...some Some Negroes my own age and younger say that we must now lie down in the streets, tie up traffic, do whatever we can—take to the hills with guns if necessary—and fight back. Fatuous people remark these days on our "bitterness." Why, of course we are bitter.
                                        —Lorraine Hansberry

Our paths crossed as we emerged from Cleveland and Chicago, each drawn to a meeting of Radicals in the Professions: Bernardine one month out of law school and living in New York City, working as an organizer for the National Lawyers Guild; Bill teaching at a radical alternative school in Ann Arbor. The gathering was early in the Summer of Love, June 1967, and was composed of former students who wanted to figure out how to live our whole lives as political radicals, casting our lot with the people of the world. The Newark rebellion had ignited the day the conference began, and our comrades from the community organizing project there never arrived.

The conference divided between those who thought that race prejudice and military excess were problems to be reformed, and those of us who saw empire itself and the system of white supremacy as an entrenched and intractable enemy. Finding ourselves in the same incendiary corner of the room, and, later, dancing in the dark, we were instant allies. It took a few more years of shared struggle to discover that we were also soul mates who would become life/love partners.

We had each been involved in the Movement for years by then—marching, protesting, sitting-in, standing-up, organizing door-to-door. We'd each tried in various ways to disrupt the military draft, that bureaucratic machinery for sorting soldiers from civilians, the living from the dead—issuing, we concluded, toxic warrants to kill and to die. We organized draft resistance workshops, stood freezing on icy early mornings at the Chicago Armory as buses mustered up. We barricaded the doors of draft boards, spoke at coffeehouses outside military bases—we'd become electrified by the injunction, "Don't let your life make a mockery of your values." Activism and organizing, we'd each concluded, would become our way of life.

The bloody U.S. assault on and occupation of the small Asian nation of Viet Nam from 1965-1975 was an example of white supremacy gone international, and sanctioned modern-day terror on a gigantic scale. The Vietnamese patriots were called "slopes" or "slants" or "gooks" by the U.S. military—the racialized dehumanization part and parcel of the project of murder and domination. The official dispatches from Viet Nam were designed only to deceive: The Vietnamese fighters committed "random acts of violence," brought "terror to the villages," had "no regard for human life," and on and on and on. Slowly young journalists covering the war called the official news conferences "the Five o'clock Follies" and began to photograph and write their own truth. Their anti-war writings became classics, beams of light against the monotone party line of the networks and big media.

The invasions had all the markings: the air war, the artillery, the naval barrages, the bombing campaigns targeting whole populations, entire regions. Crops were destroyed, bridges downed, roads ruined. There was often a ritual feeling to the destruction, as witnesses from Congress and the media were flown in for optimal viewing. The slaughter was designed by a small hard core, but all U.S. citizens were called upon to identify, to celebrate, to link up. The suffering was often entirely random—whole regions of Viet Nam were designated "free-fire zones," cities were bombed indiscriminately, puppet governments were replaced, civilians were murdered by the hundreds of thousands, and this was not mere "collateral damage," the perverse Pentagon term-of-art for mayhem and murder, but deliberate, cold-blooded policy. The intent was extermination of the leaders and control of the many through intimidation.

From 1965 onward, a growing number of people organized, spoke up, wrote, and demonstrated against this murderous U.S. policy, and we were arrested in escalating acts of opposition. By 1968, the overwhelming majority of Americans had been won to oppose the war, in no small part because of the position of returning veterans, but the war continued and escalated. We didn't know it then, of course, but after President Johnson was driven from office, the war would go on for another seven years and over 1.5 million more human beings would be sacrificed to the American-built death chamber in Southeast Asia.

Several developments in the early years of the war dramatically shifted the balance and altered the scene. For one thing, U.S. political leaders—blind and arrogant as they took over the failed French colonial mission—were certain they would triumph easily over a poor peasant nation and be welcomed as liberators by the natives—a tired, delusional conceit of every would-be conqueror, as displayed today in Iraq and Afghanistan. But the Vietnamese refused their assigned role in Washington's script, and the National Liberation Front resistance wouldn't quit; they retreated when necessary, holed up underground as required, and reemerged suddenly to beat back the invaders. At enormous cost, the Vietnamese refused to lose.

Those who opposed the war invented a thousand different ways to organize and to educate our fellow citizens. We marched and picketed and resisted—it's true—but we also drew up fact sheets, created teach-ins, embraced music, murals and agitprop, circulated petitions. The resistance organized as mothers, as students, as teachers, as lawyers, as returning veterans, as union workers, as churches, as whole communities. Sites of protest included draft boards and induction centers, coffeehouses set up outside military bases across the country and in the Philippines, ROTC offices and campus institutes of war research, Dow Chemical (maker of napalm, an incendiary liquid used to deforest the jungles of Viet Nam but also regularly used against civilians), and every politician associated with the administration. The earlier peace movements to ban the bomb and prohibit nuclear testing contributed direct action and theater.

One of the most difficult and exhilarating projects was Vietnam Summer, a concerted effort to knock on every door in working-class neighborhoods across America and meet people face to face, listen to their concerns, and engage them in a dialogue about war and peace. The more we tried to teach others, the more we ourselves learned—about Viet Nam, about white supremacy, about violence against women, about the cost of the war at home for housing, health care and schools, about culture, politics, and possibility, about ourselves. These front door encounters became an entire education in the concrete consequences of war and empire on ordinary people: loss, dislocation, confusion, sadness, anger. We became more and more radicalized as we made the connections between foreign war and domestic racism, between economic hierarchies and the hollowing out of democracy for the majority, between the sexual exploitation of Vietnamese and Thai and Filipina women to service the military and the subjugation of women at home. Eventually we thought of ourselves as revolutionaries, committed to overturning the whole system.

Critical leadership in the Black Freedom Movement came out early and unequivocally against the war in Viet Nam. The Student Nonviolent Coordinating Committee issued a statement saying, "No Black man should go 10,000 miles away to fight for a so-called freedom he doesn't enjoy in Mississippi." SNCC leader James Forman wrote *The Life and Death of Sammy Younge* about the murder of a returning African American GI. SNCC, Malcolm X, Muhammad Ali, Dr. King, and the Black Panther Party thus became—but are rarely recognized as—leaders of the anti-war movement. As poet Elizabeth Alexander notes, "The sixties has become an iconic time in memory, and we think we know what we mean when we say 'Black Power.' But a careful look at the text and testimony of the time (as any) reveals various black powers more richly nuanced and textured than glib summaries represent. Who we leave in and out of our political canons has a great deal to do with how we call the young forces of the present to the task of productive political and culture-work." As the war dragged on, large numbers of African American and Latino GIs fought against racism in the ranks of the military, and, disillusioned with the war, became a massive force of opposition in Viet Nam and back in the U.S. Without question, the rising radical Black political consciousness within the military heightened contradictions of racism and empire and led to a deeper disillusionment and awareness among Latinos, Asian Americans, and poor whites. At home, African American support for the war plummeted—Black youngsters were dying in disproportionate numbers for the imperial dreams of a handful of powerful men, and the community said "No."

All of this shook the country to its core, and perhaps the last straw was the large numbers of vets returning from Viet Nam who came out publicly to tell the plain, recognizable truth. With the antiwar movement at its height and hundreds of thousands of people demonstrating in the streets, Black, Latino, Native American, and white GIs joined the freedom and peace movements in droves, bringing along with them an infusion of urgency and purpose. They created their own anti-war organization, Vietnam Veterans Against the War, which in turn inspired new levels of militancy in our ranks. The Movement, which had been organizing with GIs from the start, embraced the vets as a strategic priority, and since the average age of the soldiers in Viet Nam was just nineteen, many vets found a natural ally in the Movement, discovering they had more in common with their young activist peers than with the old fat cats in power. In ground-breaking events like Operation Dewey Canyon III, the iconic demonstration where one by one, military veterans, many wounded, stood before a microphone giving their name, rank, and serial number, the names of the medals they'd been awarded, and then tore their war decorations from their chests and threw them down on the Capitol steps, they initiated a new dimension to the crisis.

So when the president stepped away from office in the face of advice from his core advisors that the war could not be "won," those of us who had worked for peace felt vindicated and triumphant. We thought we'd achieved a key victory, and that now the war might end.

But five days after Lyndon Johnson bowed to reality in Viet Nam, Martin Luther King, Jr., was assassinated in Memphis and cities around the country erupted. Nina Simone sang the heartbreaking "The King of Love is Dead" and announced from the stage, "I ain't about to be nonviolent, honey." The audience erupted. Fire in the streets—within six blocks of the White House, in fact—martial law, machine guns mounted on the Capitol balcony and the White House lawn, tanks and troops patrolling downtown. One hundred twenty-five cities erupted, and when the smoke cleared, 46 citizens had been killed, 2,500 injured, and some of the 70,000 mobilized national guard troops had refused orders and revolted.

Three months later Robert Kennedy was assassinated. Henry Kissinger emerged with a "secret plan to end the war," Richard Nixon was elected President over a liberal Democrat who would not come out unequivocally against the war, and by the winter it was clear that the war would *not* end—it would instead escalate and expand in spite of the wishes of almost everyone.

The war became deadlier and deadlier—each week it dragged on, thousands of innocent people were murdered by the United States government. *Slaughtered.* And there was no end in sight.

***

When Fred Hampton and Mark Clark were murdered in 1969 in a west side apartment in Chicago, we thought we were witnessing the Gestapo-like tactics of a burgeoning police state up close and in vivid color—the certain and clear face of assassination and terror, an impending American fascism we thought. Fred was the charismatic young leader of the Black Panther Party, and our SDS offices were just blocks away on Madison Avenue. The Party used our huge and modern off-set printing press—a key technology at the time and a gift from Anna Louise Strong, an American revolutionary living in China—and we saw each other every day. Fred was our friend, our critic, our comrade.

We'd been subject to escalating police harassment ourselves—our apartments regularly ransacked, our cars vandalized, and we were increasingly arrested and beaten in a growing number of raids. The toppling of the Haymarket monument in Chicago, a huge statue of a police officer as an official representation of the defeat of the great anarchist-led labor struggle in 1886, triggered a police "declaration of war" against us. We felt increasingly besieged, but we knew that the worst was reserved for our Black brothers and sisters—twenty-seven Panthers had been shot down by police forces from L.A. to New York in 1969 alone, and we saw nothing ahead to slow the pace. And now Fred and Mark were dead.

We'd encountered the political and criminal terror of the cross-burners and marauding mobs of hateful white supremacists, but when Fred Hampton was murdered we experienced the machinery of state-sanctioned violence and state-generated justification ultimately. Fearful assessments by the Chicago police and the state's attorney blanketed the news: The Panthers are a violent gang, they said, authors of random acts of lawlessness that terrorize ordinary citizens; the Panthers brought this tragedy upon themselves by initiating a shootout; the police were merely defending themselves. The truth was brought out immediately by the surviving Panthers and the intrepid People's Law Office attorneys, and proven over the next decade: The police assault on the Panther apartment was deliberate and unprovoked and sustained and overwhelming and unanswered; Fred had been drugged by a police infiltrator and was unconscious in his bed when he was riddled with police bullets; the Chicago police were operating in secret concert with the FBI in planning the bloody assault. Fred was called a violent terrorist by law enforcement, but he was in fact targeted and assassinated—the forces that killed him were both federal and local, a small part of a vast and wealthy system of official terror, armed to the teeth. In a series of brilliant strokes, the Panthers and the People's Law Office photographed and seized the bullet-ridden apartment door and hid it in a church basement, organized public tours through the bloody apartment, and opened Fred's casket for viewing by tens of thousands of Chicagoans who paid homage to the young leader and defied the police lies—echoes of Emmett Till.

The murder of Fred Hampton altered the reality we saw—it was a crash course in revolution. How could we act in solidarity with the Panthers? How could the

Movement correspondingly escalate and move forward?

Living through that time of aggression, assassinations, imperialist war raging in our names, and uprisings, rebellions, resistance, and disaffection at home, it seemed as if we were experiencing terminally cataclysmic events and permanent war: a revolutionary moment. Looking back we can see that even if it felt that way, it wasn't so—that while it was monstrous and bloody, the war in Viet Nam lasted for a decade, killing 3 million people, and then it was done. The U.S. was defeated militarily, in a rout, as well as politically—hearts and minds were never won by the invading occupation. Millions of Vietnamese, Laotian and Cambodian civilians were needlessly killed, and close to sixty thousand U.S. military were dead, at least twice as many injured, poisoned, and left to live with the anguish of battle. The Black Freedom Movement was targeted, jailed, splintered, and sustained in new forms. But in those days, with the outcome far from certain, we had to choose our actions within a shifting, complex, and speculative world. Should we oppose the war? How? Could whites play a productive role in dismantling white supremacy? On what basis? How far should we go in order to prevent more senseless slaughter and dismemberment? Could we be part of mobilizing a more widespread resistance? Could we perhaps go beyond ending this war, and end the system that led so inevitably to war after war?

Some of us burned out. Others left for Europe or Canada or Africa. Some ran for office, while others rushed to create the communes of California or Philadelphia or Vermont where we might strive to live in harmony with our values and with nature, becoming new men and women. Some dug in. Others dropped out. Some created what they thought would become vanguard political parties and went into factories to organize the industrial working class, while others joined the Democratic Party with the hope of building a powerful peace and justice wing within it, and still others moved on in their professional lives. Some made a religion out of making love, others made a mess of making revolution. No choice was the obvious best choice, none in retrospect was up to the challenge.

A small group of us—young, determined, somewhat despairing at that time—chose to build an organization designed to survive the escalating repression at home, and simultaneously to create the capacity for illegal and armed resistance to both the war and the structures of racism. The Weather Underground stormed fleetingly across the landscape at the tail end of that mythical and iconic age now simply called the Sixties. Originally a militant formation inside Students for a Democratic Society, a catalytic radical student group, the Weather Underground rose, hot and angry, to—in our own terms—smite the warmongers and strike against the race-haters. We went over the top. We hoped the Weather actions would speak for themselves. Our efforts would be stained by mistakes because we could never see fully or far enough; we were ourselves limited, our theories flawed. Still, we concluded that the greater crime would be to do nothing, or not enough. The U.S., we now know, unleashed a secret, violent, dirty war against Black leaders, and a companion campaign of arrests, threats, and dirty tricks against white radicals. Stepping into history, we would be inadequate to the task. Staying aloof from history would be its own choice and error. Inaction was the option of cowards. We would fight using direct action, but in new ways: We would bring the war home as we had boasted, but with measured force, with precision; we would draw an angry sword against white supremacy, retaliate for racist attacks, and fight a parallel battle with our Black revolutionary comrades, but from a new and liberated space. And with care. And so, believing in the immense power of people to challenge fate and accomplish the unthinkable, holding on to a profound sense of personal responsibility, we plunged ahead.

The Weather Underground issued a first communiqué—a word we borrowed from Latin American guerrillas—in a tape called "A Declaration of a State of War," read by Bernardine Dohrn, in May 1970. It was packed tight with defiance and hyperbole, and in it the organization threatened to bomb "a major symbol of American injustice." When, a little more than two weeks later, the promised explosion rocked the New York City Police Headquarters on Centre Street after a warning call—and there were no injuries—the Weather Underground was fully launched. The mayor of New York offered $25,000 dollars for any information that would lead to an arrest. A new communiqué arrived at *The New York Times* and was rebroadcast widely, and through it the organization instructed the FBI—and through them police forces everywhere—on its odd reliability and quirky authenticating signs. We were in communication:

> Tonight, at 7 P.M., we blew up the N.Y.C. Police Headquarters. We called in a warning before the explosion. The pigs in this country are our enemies. They have murdered Fred Hampton and tortured Joan Bird. They are responsible for six Black deaths in Augusta, four murders in Kent State, the imprisonment of Los Siete de la Raza in San Francisco and the continual brutality against Latin and white youth on the Lower East Side....

Within months a pattern of action was established—retaliation for attacks on the Black and Latino struggles, and offensive actions against the imperialist war machine. Weather's signature MO was to phone a middle-of-the-night warning call to some sleepy guard inside a building or to the nearby police or to a journalist, a call that provided calm and detailed instructions to clear a specified area. Weather then sent letters of explanation—sometimes exhorting, sometimes threatening, sometimes still barely decipherable beyond the knowing—that claimed credit and publicly defended the actions as politics by other means, as political theater, as propaganda-of-the-deed. The communiqués were signed and delivered simultaneously to several major news outlets in different cities across the country seconds after the blast. The FBI and the big city police separated what they came to know as an authentic Weather action from the other tens of thousands of political bombings, direct actions, and threats carried out by different, distinct insurgent groups during those magnificent and terrible years.

Each letter had a logo hand-drawn across the page—our trademark thick and colorful rainbow with a slash of angry lightning cutting though it. New morning, it signified, changing weather. Oddly, as intense as it all looks and sounds, in our minds it seemed cautious and responsible, a huge de-escalation from the apocalyptic, military rhetoric of just months earlier. In any case, we embraced the symbol of peace and reconciliation balanced by that fiery bolt of justice.

We and our comrades wanted our life underground—eluding capture and striking back—to have a meaning beyond the narrow and the particular. Within the year the FBI's Ten Most Wanted List would include Angela Davis, H. Rap Brown, and student militants from Madison and Boston as well as Bernardine. FBI wanted posters were torn down from post office walls, reappearing in windows with a new slogan: "Those Wanted Welcome Here." Widespread popular support—even from those who disagreed with our tactics and choices—sustained and fortified fugitive resistance. And multiple undergrounds we discovered, as we obliquely passed by undocumented workers, lesbians and gays with new identities, AWOL military personnel, draft resisters, and distributors of psychedelic potions in the crowded underground passageways. We searched for meaning by participating as fully as we could in all aspects of life, and we tried to understand everything in order to make ourselves subjects in history and not simply passive objects to be used and discarded. We embraced our utopian dreams, we struggled to make history. We hoped to participate in a public insurgency that would collapse the empire's death machine and liberate us—flawed as we were—and all human beings, to reach the fullest measure of our humanity. *Revolution.*

SCENES FROM AN IMAGINED INTERROGATION

Do you believe in violence?

"Believe" is an odd word here. We see violence everywhere and we detest it, but we don't think we should discuss this as a religion. Violence isn't a faith but a fact.

What do you mean, a fact?

Violence is a terrible reality, the remnants of displaced violence, silent violence, are everywhere apparent and unavoidable if we would just open our eyes.

You saw the video of the recent protests?

The burning cars, the young people throwing rocks and bottles, the shock troops of empire...

"Shock troops of empire"?

So they looked to us—the high-tech helmets, the shields, the uniform anonymity...

And what about the rioters, weren't they dressed alike, and also as shock troops?

There's a difference.

The difference, of course, is that they can't achieve their goals legally and so they turn to violence, destroying anything in their path, provoke the police and the army to respond, isn't that the difference?

Well, it depends on where you start the tape.

Start the tape?

Exactly. It depends entirely on where you choose to begin. The countries you're inclined to defend turn to violence systematically, routinely. They are typically born in violence, and surely sustained by violence. Some would say the "cycle of violence" begins there.

So you side with the rioters?

At least we should understand them.

And here, as elsewhere, you justify violence?

No, not at all. But we can understand it without justifying it. Violence terrifies us. But we distinguish violence against people from violence against property. We admire the teachings of Martin Luther King, Jr., his actions sharp, gentle, fearless, tough.

King thought the proper way to resist violence was nonviolence.

King exposed the hidden violence that had always been there—the violence of racism, of rights denied. He led a movement that disregarded the official disregard of people's rights—he negated the negation—and what surfaced all around him was violence: the barbarity of the police, the threats of the mobs, the ongoing brutality of the racist terrorists, the complicity of the law, the indifference of those who profit. He exposed a system of violence, and he was left exposed himself, and he was murdered. The White House, fearing that other Black leaders would "exploit the anger in the ghetto," said, "nothing is achieved by violence," and the National Guard was summoned.

And isn't that true? What is achieved by violence?

Institutionalized violence—the violence of slavery and rape, the anguished shattering of the Black family, lynching, racial apartheid or segregation, prisons, economic exclusion, danger, threat and terror, for example, in any country—is the normalized violence that the powerful employ to achieve their privileges. Whole generations might grow up, get old, and die and never lift a hand against one another, and yet a master/slave relationship, adequately examined and understood—yes, observed from the start—is violent at its very core. When slaves did rise up against their masters—Harriet Tubman, say, or Nat Turner—they were met with incomprehension and rage, they were called violent terrorists and they were hunted, they were slaughtered. Today their photos hang in urban school hallways (rarely in suburban ones). Colonialism is the institutionalization and globalization of such a relationship.

During U.S.-led wars like Viet Nam and Iraq, every American is implicated in acts of violence. We know what is being done in our names, we see and read about instances of the terror in gory detail: shock and awe, the bombing of cities and the mass murder of civilians, the flattening of Fallujah, the torture of Abu Ghraib, the lawless CIA black sites. State violence is pervasive and real. We have the opportunity to remain silent or to resist; many remain silent, and others resist. We admire and practice non-violent resistance. Ourselves, and have nothing but admiration for all those who put their bodies on the line against injustice. Some condemn the dissenters and tolerate state violence, and that's the highest hypocrisy. Some fight with their lives in the hope of saving others.

Ghandi and King were able to make moral claims through nonviolent resistance. British colonialists and Southern white racists were exposed as the perpetrators of historic violence. Wasn't the great success of unarmed civil disobedience that it made visible the brutality of injustice and oppression?

King, exposing a system of violence, was left exposed himself, and he was murdered.

So was Fred Hampton. So was Malcolm X. Advocating resistance "by any means necessary" didn't save anyone.

No, but there was legitimate moral justification for armed self-defense, for taking up arms against an oppressive apartheid state. Sometimes it's necessary and appropriate to use violence in the pursuit of freedom or justice. Look at Nelson Mandela and the ANC in South Africa. Look at John Brown. Look at George Washington.

Who decides? If you make the claim that violence is sometimes justified, aren't you opening the floodgates to fanatics of all stripes who argue that they are allowed to kill and maim in the pursuit of their dogma? Isn't this the justification of reactionary zealots like Timothy McVeigh and Osama bin Laden?

But that's an important point. Violence isn't an ideology. Tactics can be grossly misused. But terrorism surely includes state terrorism arial bombings in Lebanon, Fallujah, Afghanistan, for example—as well as group and individual terror. All levels of violence are, in fact, always employed by the established power, and most often used indiscriminately by the forces of reaction and fundamentalism. The 20th Century is a horror of human suffering and escalating civilian deaths through war.

Give an example of violence properly used.

Again, Mandela and the ANC were called terrorists during their resistance to apartheid. They participated in bombings, kidnappings, even assassinations, and not all defensible. But the armed uprising weakened the regime and emboldened the struggle.

Nonsense. It was the turning tide of world opinion that ended apartheid in South Africa.

But Mandela's fighters helped turn the tide. Or look at the Cubans ousting Batiste and the U.S. Mafia. Or John Brown and the raid on Harpers Ferry.

A botched military action that resulted in the deaths of several innocent people, including African Americans. If John Brown played any role in ending slavery, it was as a martyr to the violence of the State of Virginia, not as an armed revolutionary.

That's impossible to say. It was important that somebody—a white person, at that—was willing to put his life on the line to end slavery. He became a symbol precisely because he matched his words with his actions. All opposition to slavery was important: Thoreau and Emerson, Frederick Douglass and Sojourner Truth, but Toussaint L'Ouverture, John Brown, Nat Turner, and Cinque had key roles to play, too.

So do you think it's acceptable that innocent people should be killed sometimes in pursuit of a greater good?

No, it's always unacceptable. But the violence of the status quo, the mass murder quietly executed, is unacceptable as well.

So you do believe in violence?

FIGHT BACK

If a population is under violent, relentless threat from a dominant, predatory group with whom it shares its environment, if the dominant group after centuries of enslavement, lynchings and brutal oppression and public dishonoring continues to so manipulate the environment so that the threatened group has been cornered like rats in blocked sewers which we call ghettoes, if the only options offered by the most powerful leaders of the dominant population is the socially moronic policy, the scorched earth "contract," of more incarceration in already over-filled jails and more state-sanctioned executions in already overcrowded death-rows, then it is both brutally logical, in socioevolutionary terms, and highly intelligent for the threatened group to arm itself to the teeth and behave as murderously threatening and aggressive as it can.

—Orlando Patterson

What white Americans have never fully understood—but what the Negro can never forget—is that white society is deeply implicated in the ghetto. White institutions created it, white institutions maintain it, and white society condones it.

—The Kerner Commission

Weather practiced public storytelling, and the subtext was our own hopeful little message: *The revolution has begun, and you can't catch us.*

We took them by surprise—neither law enforcement nor the media imagined that white youth would escalate in this way. Surely our anguished parents and families were unprepared. Court appearances and dates came and went—a fair number of us were gone, and more mobilized to support the new outlaws. We struck a chord in part because we crystallized and distilled in pure form the spark of outrage that anyone feels coming face-to-face with injustice: Even critics had a tiny little Weather person lurking in their hearts. And yet this was also a time when we were referred to as "home-grown American terrorists." That's what *Time* magazine called us, and *The New York Times*, too, and that was the word hurled in our direction from the halls of Congress, the FBI, and the CIA, which wanted to invent nonexistent foreign ties: *Terrorist.*

We imagined a pale anarchist figure dressed in an oily overcoat, feverish, eyes blazing, beard and hair wild and unkempt, sitting in the back of a theater with a round black bomb and a sparkling fuse in his pocket. Nothing at all like us. Terrorists terrorize but, we wanted to educate; terrorists employ the rhetoric of fear and threat against people; we directed our fire at the symbols of terrorist state itself. *No*, we said to ourselves, *we're revolutionaries, not terrorists.*

We'd been organizers and activists, national officers of SDS, and then among the founders of the Weather Underground, and in 1970 we were indicted with other comrades on two single-count conspiracies, one for crossing state lines in order to create a civil disturbance—the "Rap Brown Law"—the other for crossing state lines to destroy government property by transporting explosives. We had no intention of answering in federal court—by then we'd seen too many activists entangled in lengthy trials and, no matter what the verdict, neutralized and effectively kept off the streets—and so we took off and lived on the run for what stretched into the next decade. We thought of ourselves immodestly as freedom fighters, but we knew that the words "armed and dangerous" were tattooed over every inch of us by law enforcement, justifying their well-publicized shoot-to-kill orders.

The Weather Underground's symbolic actions directed against property were meant as an emphatic and dramatic protest against the empire's lethal acts of sustained and premeditated mass slaughter, both at home and around the world. Consider the U.S. war crimes committed at My Lai. In a matter of hours, U.S. soldiers raped, looted, maimed, and tortured the residents of a Vietnamese village; they burned homes, slaughtered animals, and killed 347 villagers. The My Lai massacre embodied the unvarnished horror of the Pentagon's murderous frenzy in Southeast Asia.

In contrast, Weather's actions embodied the prolonged intensity of the resistance and, except for the terrible 1970 accidental deaths of our three beloved friends, Diana Oughton, Terry Robbins, and Ted Gold, no one was killed or wounded. During the early 1970s over twenty thousand government targets inside the U.S. were bombed—with one tragic death of researcher Robert Fassnacht at the Army Math Research Center in Madison—all directed against political property targets. The Weather Underground took responsibility for a couple of dozen.

We opened to a world of words and they tumbled from us in a crazy flash flood of awakening zeal. We wrote open letters to the militant Catholic Left—and they wrote back urging us to temper our actions with compassion—and to the Panther 21, who warned us about the dangers of American exceptionalism, cautioned about being seduced by youth drug culture, and urged us to blast away at colonializing racist power everywhere, no equivocation, no holds barred. We argued with both, we agreed with both, and we argued among ourselves.

We scribbled to old friends—roommates from an earlier world, favorite teachers, brothers and sisters. We invented words; we constructed culture. We fought back, we dreamed out loud. And we were, like others, forever explaining, defining, correcting, implying, editing, translating in sometimes delighted, often dogmatic and rhetorical and desperate efforts to be understood. We were ill-equipped gunslingers, and we became word-slingers instead.

When our pick-up truck broke down on a highway, the state trooper who pulled us over found us not only respectful and engaging but open and grateful for his presence. We were practicing verbal jujitsu. Soon he offered to give a push to the nearest service station, and we asked for his name so that we might send a letter of gratitude to his commanding officer (he refused—the helpful push was outside regulations.) We were conscious of the protection of white privilege and we were determined to use it to penetrate the monster—the Pentagon, the Hall of Justice, the police station.

The preface "Weather" had become as prominent among us as "Mc" is in the wider world, and just as colonizing. We talked of Weathermen and Weatherwomen, Weatherkids and Weatherstories, Weather documents and Weathersymps. The leadership was, of course, the Weather Bureau, a leaflet was a Weather Balloon, and the anti-imperialist struggle was the Weather Going Tide. Recruits went through what amounted to an informal Weather Berlitz in order to become functionally bilingual.

When we began doing clandestine work, we needed a word that cloaked our intentions and so we spoke of the North Star, and then of the Dash—I'm spending this morning on the Dash, someone might say, implying both a censor's beep, a word unspoken, as well as the mad dash we anticipated to the underground railroad, following the North Star toward freedom. When we were actually on the run, we inoculated ourselves from fear and called our fugitiveness "the Joke"—Have you told your new boyfriend the Joke? Or: I don't think anyone here knows the Joke. Our organization, publicly the Weather Underground, became "The Eggplant," from an obscure rock lyric about "the eggplant that ate Chicago."

Our political manifesto issued from underground was called *Prairie Fire*, as in the Chinese proverb "A single spark can start a prairie fire." We named our clandestine newspaper *Osawatomic*, after that spot in Kansas where old John Brown, his sons and sons-in law, and a handful of allies entered the fight over whether Kansas would enter the nation as slave state or free.

Homegrown, as American as cherry pie, the underground was in other ways an internal "foreign" country—we spoke patois and did things differently there.

On August 7, George Jackson's seventeen-year-old brother Jonathan stormed a courtroom inside the Marin County Civic Center carrying a submachine gun and freed three San Quentin prisoners and took five hostages, including Judge Harold Haley. Outside, police and guards opened fire. Jonathan Jackson, the judge, and two others were killed. Angela Davis was accused of having purchased some of the guns used in the kidnapping. She was underground for two months before being captured. The next year she was tried and acquitted on all charges.

Two months after the bloody shootout, the Weather Underground placed a bomb in the same Civic Center:

> We dedicate this act to the prisoners of San Quentin, Soledad and New York, and to all Black prisoners of war. Fighting where there is no place to hide, they have turned every prison in Amerika into an advance guerrilla post of the war against pig Amerika.

***

On October 1, 1970, inmates, fed up with the appalling condition of the New York City jails, took seven hostages in the Long Island City branch of the Queens House of Detention. In the next few days, prisoners in three other jails took their own hostages, and the standoffs continued until the end of the week when the New York police stormed the jails and wrested control from the insurgents.

A few days later an anonymous caller phoned police in the middle of the night and said: "This is the Weatherman calling. There is a bomb planted in the court building that will go off shortly. Clear the building." Ten minutes later a bomb went off in the Long Island City courthouse. The device had been jammed behind a telephone booth on the third floor. No one was hurt. The only person in the building at the time was a janitor, who told reporters, "I heard a big blast. I thought the boiler blew up." The communiqué:

> *Ho Chi Minh once said, "When the prison door is open the real dragon will fly out." This week, in the concentration camps of New York City, the courage and humanity of the people broke through the fortress of the pigs. In the slave ships of the 20th century Nat Turner rises again. The Viet Cong say that prison is a school of revolutionaries—but the jails, like the streets of every city have become free fire zones—Watts and Detroit taking place behind armed guard and iron bars.*

***

"They've pushed me over the line from which there can be no retreat," George Jackson wrote. "I know that they will not be satisfied until they've pushed me out of existence altogether." On August 21, 1971, guards at San Quentin shot Jackson to death, claiming he was armed and attempting to escape. The gun, variously described as a revolver and a pistol, was never found. In the context of his long war with the California prison authorities, Jackson's death was suspicious, to say the least. "We may never know exactly how he died," wrote a local alternative newspaper. "But we damn well know why he died."

At 2 A.M. on August 28, a week after Jackson's death, a woman called a telephone operator in Sacramento. "This is the Weather Underground," she said. "There's a large explosive device at 714 P Street. Don't move it." Police cars rushed to the offices but before they arrived, the device—three to five sticks of dynamite—had already detonated. "The explosion," *The Los Angeles Times* reported, "turned the rest room into a mass of twisted pipe and splintered wood, blew gaping holes in the roof, knocked out an elevator door, cracked walls, ripped up the floor and several electrical lines and water mains." No one was hurt.

A minute or so later, a second bomb exploded in the Department of Corrections offices on the San Francisco waterfront. The wordy and analytic communiqué that arrived at *The San Francisco Examiner* later in the day began:

> *On Saturday, August 21, 1971, George Jackson, Black warrior,*

revolutionary leader, political prisoner, was shot dead by racist forces at San Quentin. Murdered for what he had become: Soledad Brother, soldier of his people, rising up through torment and torture, tyranny and injustice, unwilling to bow or bend to his oppressors. George Jackson died with his eyes fixed clearly on freedom.

***

Less than a month after Jackson's death, on the morning of September 9, 1971, an argument between inmates and guards turned bloody inside western New York's Attica prison. Within minutes, the inmates had control of D-Yard and by nightfall they were surrounded by heavily armed state troopers. "WE ARE MEN!" the prisoners wrote to the outside world. Negotiations involving lawyers and designated journatlists lasted for four days. Then Governor Nelson Rockefeller ordered electricity to the prison cut off, and on the morning of September 13, helicopters dropped tear gas into the yard and New York State Troopers opened fire. Twelve minutes later, eleven guards and thirty-two inmates were dead. Official reports that guards had been killed or castrated by inmates turned out to be false. Among the inmates shot and killed by the troopers that day was Sam Melville, a self-described independent sort of Weatherman doing time for a 1969 property bombing of a Manhattan military induction center.

Four days after the massacre, newspapers were informed that a bomb would explode in the office of the New York State commissioner of corrections. Police cleared the building just as the detonation smashed the cinder block walls on the ninth floor:

> *By now everyone is aware that the Monday slaughter did not have to take place. If this was a civilized society, the Attica men in power would not need to kill those who demand their freedom and to be treated with the respect due to every human being.*
>
> *Attica Prison is a place where eighty-five percent of those held there are Black or Puerto Rican. All the guards and administrators of the prison are white. This is not an oversight by some dumb bureaucrat. This is how a society run by white racists maintains control.*
>
> *Everyone knows about high bails, the box, beatings by white racist guards carrying "nigger sticks." Everyone saw Governor Rockefeller, Commissioner Oswald and the rest of those racists lie, and then attempt to justify their lies as to the alleged "killings" of the hostages.*
>
> *It is not a question of being ignorant of the facts. In their manifesto the*

prisoners said: "The entire incident that has erupted here at Attica is a result of the unmitigated oppression wrought by the racist administration network of this prison. We are men, we are not beasts. And we do not intend to be beaten or driven as such. What has happened here is but the sound before the fury of those who are oppressed..."

Mass murder is not unusual in this country: it is the foundation of American imperialism. In our lifetime we have seen four Black girls killed by a bomb explosion in Birmingham, Alabama. We have seen Black students gunned down at Orangeburg, South Carolina, and Jackson, Mississippi. We have seen Watts, Newark, and Detroit. Amerika has murdered Malcolm X, Martin Luther King, Fred Hampton, and two weeks ago, the authorities in California assassinated George L. Jackson. We have seen white students shot and killed at Berkeley and Kent State.

And in Southeast Asia this country now bears the responsibility for the deaths of over a million Vietnamese people. Amerika's genocidal war will be more devastating than that waged by the Nazis—poisoning a people and a land for many generations to come.

Children grow up in this country knowing that Lt. William Calley can be convicted of the murder of twenty-two unarmed Vietnamese civilians and be congratulated for it by a President more interested in his re-election than the lives of any human beings on Earth. The main question white people have to face today is not the state of the economy (for many, the question of selling their second car) but whether they are going to continue to allow genocidal murder, in their name, of oppressed people in this country and around the World.

Tonight we attacked the head offices of the New York State Department of Corrections. Tomorrow thousands of people will demonstrate in New York and around the country against this racist slaughter. We must continue to make the Rockefellers, Oswalds, Reagans, and Nixons pay for their crimes. We only wish we could do more to show the courageous prisoners at Attica, San Quentin, and the other twentieth century slave ships that they are not alone in their fight for the right to live.

Weather Underground

***

Around five o'clock on the morning of April 28, 1972, a New York City police officer investigating a taxicab holdup shot and fatally wounded Clifford Glover—four feet eleven inches tall, all of ninety pounds, and Black—in South Jamaica, Queens. At ten years old, he was thought to be the youngest person ever killed by a member of the NYPD. The officer, Thomas Shea, was later tried for murder and acquitted by an all-white jury.

On May 18, around 3:30 A.M., a bomb detonated from beneath a patrol car parked outside Shea's 103rd Precinct. A transit patrolman, walking to his own car at the time, was hospitalized with chest pains. Half an hour after the blast, the switchboard operator at *The New York Times* was told:

> *This is the Weathermen, and we are moving in on the 103rd Precinct in Queens for the death of the little boy killed last week by the police.*
>
> *At the recent demonstration at the 103rd Precinct someone held up a sign which read "We call you pigs when you murder our children." Our action against the Precinct is in sympathy with the families and communities of the dead and in solidarity with the living—those in prison, those who continue the struggle.*

***

Sooner or later everything in America becomes commodified or disappears. Just so "the sixties," something we didn't even know existed as we lived through it. No one experiences the flow of life in neatly defined chunks, certainly not in decades—"Oh, my, it's January 1, 1970, I'd better change my clothes"—everyone is an intergenerational person, but the imagined Sixties are a bounded myth, constantly being retold, constantly being repackaged and resold as a containable cultural unit. The pitchmen are a shock: Janis Joplin's image employed to sell Mercedes-Benz, Dennis Hopper and Peter Fonda on choppers hyping Diners Club for when you're on the road, Jimi Hendrix, John Lennon, Martin Luther King, Jr., himself.

We were a small part of the mighty Civil Rights Movement as well as the largest international antiwar movement in history, a movement that limited the options of the war-makers, allowing a range of progressive options and a surge of new liberation movements to emerge and flourish inside one heartland. The Vietnamese people themselves, mobilized and united, were the decisive element and force in their own national liberation. We were part of a culture of opposition and we struck a resistant stance in the world. Inevitably, that posture was seized, sanitized, and commodified. Even in the 1960s, "the sixties" was being sold back to us as a product, bell-bottom pants or Afros or revolutionary deodorant. Now, in the fog of polarization, demonization, and nostalgia, it's worse—"The 60s, Inc." with an established group of scholars and reactionary commentators who attack all radical or even renegade accounts of the significance of that time, and who defend their authorized views, their patents, through an echo chamber that begins in tiny, right-wing blogs, works its way to Fox News and the pundits, and stutters into the big media. A new wave of scholars, historians and artists have taken over, uncovering classified documents, interviewing survivors, analyzing and making meanings. But the culture itself was and is—as always—deeply contested territory.

So the war, to explain the war (and the U.S. defeat in Viet Nam), continues to be waged still, a linchpin in the conflict over today's wars in Iraq and Afghanistan. The war against Viet Nam was a national and international disaster, it's true, and the current received wisdom is like a stuttering script of repeating slogans—often contradictory but always untroubled. These are some of the fabricated but sacred articles we are all supposed to know by now: Viet Nam was a quagmire sucking the U.S. down, the well-intentioned and innocent first steps transformed in the Asian jungles into something unspeakable, but it was not our fault, never our fault; the war was bad or wrong or a mistake, the media was heroically and consistently truth-telling throughout, and right-thinking people opposed the war, they were responsible protesters now part of our proud democratic tradition; the vets suffered most, both in the field and a second time when, on returning home, they were shunned or even spit upon by anti-war folks. Like most clichés and myths, these are false, and they fail to heal, fail even to inform. Each has a thread of truth to hang itself on, while each dissolves complexity and destroys the contextual content. But their tenacity is more a function of their seemingly endless repetitions—the Big Lie-style refrain chanted at every turn—on how they allow us to cling to our childlike view of the world. They mostly wilt and die under scrutiny.

Take this last cliché—the vets were reviled at home. It's true that their government, which had used them so cynically, so murderously, failed them again at home in a thousand ways—broken promises, lack of jobs and education, inadequate health care—and then threw them away. When Richard Nixon began his run for the presidency, he based his campaign on a falsehood: the vaunted "secret plan" to end the war. A corollary to this grand disingenuous gesture was another—to stick up for the GIs, not against the war-makers, the brass, or the rotten politicians who perpetuated the deepening agony for their own puny careers, but, amazingly, against the peace movement itself. And so we are told that returning vets were spit upon by longhairs, and that fraudulent image was blown into an icon beyond truth—beyond truth because it is not true.

The Black freedom struggle, too, has been in part airbrushed in the retelling. What many of us experienced as part of a continuum—what Russell Banks in *Cloudsplitter* called "beads on string ... bubbles of blood on a barbed steel strand that stretches from the day the first enslaved African was brought ashore in Virginia to today, and we have not reached the end of it yet"—is recast to accommodate an uncomplicated conclusion. Martin Luther King, Jr., is recast as a saint with a dream rather than an angry pilgrim who became a radical activist, and Malcolm X as a memoirist with a bit of a chip on his shoulder rather than an evolving, growing revolutionary and internationalist. The received truth of history, then, becomes the common sense of the culture—and, frankly, there is simply nothing more insistent nor dogmatic than common sense.

The Sixties was prelude to the challenges we face today. Efforts to criminalize the Sixties as misbegotten, extremist, self-regarding lunatics-aging enemies within—is a despicably false narrative.—Which in part explains its endurance as contested territory. But nostalgia for that time, longing for a ship that's already left the shore, is also an empty exercise that can easily become a brake on activism today. A more hopeful approach is to trace the lines of resistance as a way to choose against war and racism—to act up for peace and balance, liberation and justice and freedom—right here, right now.

QUESTIONNAIRE

What is terrorism?

Is the concept—terrorism—consistent and universal? Does it apply to all parties engaged in certain actions or does it change over time?

Which terrorist had a £100,000 reward on his head in the 1930s? When did he become a "freedom fighter," his image rehabilitated?

How many Israeli prime ministers were designated "terrorist" by the British government at some point in their political careers?

Which group of foreign visitors to the White House in 1985 was hailed by Ronald Reagan as the moral equivalent of our Founding Fathers, "freedom fighters" against the "Evil Empire"?

What did George W. Bush call these same men?

Who offered the following definitions: "Terrorism is a modern barbarism that we call terrorism;" "Terrorism is a threat to Western civilization;" "Terrorism is a menace to Western moral values;" "[W]e have no trouble telling [terrorists from freedom fighters];" "Terrorism is a form of political violence"?

Which U.S. president said, "I am a contra," referring to the Nicaraguan group designated "terrorist" by international human rights observers?

Has there ever been a U.S. president who refused to employ "political violence"?

Are Muslims more likely to commit terrorist acts than Christians or Jews or Hindus?

Which form of terrorism—religious, criminal, political, or official and state sanctioned—has caused the most death and destruction in the past five hundred years? One hundred years? Ten years? Which has caused the least?

Do the numbers matter?

AFFIRMATIVE ACTION: FOR WHITES ONLY

Cast your eyes about, look as far as you can see; all, all is owned by the lordly white, except here and there a lowly dwelling which the man of color, midst deprivations, fraud and opposition, has been scarce able to procure... We have pursued the shadow, they have obtained the substance; we have performed the labor, they have received the profits; we have planted the vines, they have eaten the fruits of them.

—Maria Stewart

Pride and selfishness...never want for a theory to justify them—and when men oppress their fellow-men, the oppressor ever finds, in the character of the oppressed, a full justification for his oppression. Ignorance and depravity, and the inability to rise from degradation to civilization and respectability, are the most usual allegations against the oppressed. The evils most fostered by slavery and oppression are precisely those which slaveholders and oppressors would transfer from their system to the inherent character of their victims. Thus the very crimes of slavery become slavery's best defense. By making the enslaved a character fit only for slavery, they excuse themselves for refusing to make the slave a free man. A wholesale method of accomplishing this result is to overthrow the instinctive consciousness of the common brotherhood of man...

—Frederick Douglass

If a man or a woman, say, has been held in chains in a prison for his or her whole life, worked like a mule, been denied the right to coherent and stable human relations or to education or to any basic freedoms, it would perpetuate the cruelty to one day remove the chains without any reparations or resources for support, and put him or her on a street corner or a barren scratch of land.

Slavery ended just over one hundred forty years ago in the U.S., feudal quasi-slavery only a generation ago—all pretty recent history. And white supremacy still reigns. So those of us who hope to live beyond the racial nightmare must grope our way toward justice with some sense of how pervasive and entrenched this monster really is.

We begin when we understand the absurdity of the constantly stuttered assertion by white people that since they never personally owned slaves—and perhaps even their ancestors are unindicted—never discriminated in any way and that, from their perspective, don't have a prejudiced bone in their bodies, they are, then, free of any responsibility for the sorry state of things.

The confusion here is between social and individual ethics. The Constitution and the law allowed Blacks to be captives, first as chattels, and then, for another hundred years, as serfs and landless peasants and second-class citizens. The army and the police enforced the relationship. This situation means that everyone who enjoys the wealth of the nation benefits from the exploitation of slave labor so fundamental to the accumulation of American wealth and that every citizen, everyone who has a stake in the national polity, has an obligation to face our history and repair whatever wrongs we find. The previous and enduring harm and distortions caused by the "peculiar institution" and the century of apartheid that followed requires multiple kinds of action, affirmative and otherwise.

But white people, especially those of us near the top of the heap, like to fool ourselves about our situations, about the circumstances of our lives, about how we arrived where we are. "I work hard," we say in cheery chorus, and leave unstated a long list of virtues that implicitly belong to white people: intelligence, discipline, energy, honesty, good intentions, and a lot of pluck. OK, OK—maybe there was a little luck in there, too, but, in my specific case, and in mine and in mine, when it comes to choice versus chance, it's mostly about choice. "I work hard." Well, good for us.

It would be amusing if it weren't so tragic, if its consequences weren't so dire on all

134

sides. Any outside observer with an ounce of common sense and a tad of historical perspective and with eyes even blinkingly open would say that white people are suffering from some mass psychological illness when we talk that way: Privilege Avoidance Disorder (PAD), Delusional Innocence Dementia (DID). It can't be healthy to look out into the world and to pretend so consistently that we can't see what is right in front of us, jumping up and down and waving its arms frantically in our faces while screaming in our ears. "Privilege?" you ask dully, "What privilege?" It's got to be taking a toll.

So if white people worked hard and got ahead, the argument goes, Black people should do the same. "Set asides," "racial preferences," and "affirmative action" just make no sense. For one thing, white people never got those advantages—OK, maybe race-based slavery was a wee advantage for some of us—so affirmative action for Black folks would be unfair. But perhaps more important, those things would be bad for Black people themselves, creating a "culture" and a practice of sloth.

In reality, affirmative action has effectively served the ideology of white supremacy and the practice of privilege from the start—from at least the seventeenth-century when white indentured servants were replaced with captured Africans. They worked alongside one another briefly, but it soon became clear to the masters that the whole exploitative system could be fortified and survive through the generations if servitude became entirely race-based. And so the first affirmative action: You white people will have limited but new rights and entitlements and advantages based solely on your skin color, but in return you will have to police the boundaries of race and support the system. Deal? Deal!

Of course that's ancient history, so move on. Salim Muwakkil notes the intertwined connections of racism and immigration. In 1790 the Naturalization Act allowed European immigrants—"free white persons" only—a path to citizenship, and the right to vote, hold office, and even own property. In 1830 the Indian Removal Act forcibly relocated Native Americans to west of the Mississippi River and granted the stolen land to white people. Blacks had no access, of course—not citizens. And, again, the Homestead Act of 1862 authorized the granting of free land to homesteaders—whites only—carved out of what had been the Indian Territory of the West. More than 270 million acres, 10 percent of the total land area of the U.S., was passed exclusively to white people in a massive *affirmative action* gesture.

Alien Land Laws in several states prevented Asian immigrants from owning land— *affirmative action for whites*—and racial barriers to citizenship were in place until 1952, racial preferences in immigration until 1965. Whites win again.

When the progressive Social Security Act was passed in 1935 guaranteeing an income after retirement, it specifically excluded domestic and agricultural workers—white advantage once more encoded into law without a word on race. And the Wagner Act in the same year—also part of the New Deal—protected and extended the rights and benefits of workers, but also acknowledged the right of unions to exclude Blacks. And the Federal Housing Administration, which allowed millions to own their own homes for the first time and in so doing to amass a mountain of wealth, also created a system explicitly tying loan eligibility to race, the infamous policy known as "redlining." Between 1934 and 1962 the government issued $120 billion in home loans, 98 percent to whites. Once more, *affirmative action for whites.*

Today, as a result of affirmative action for white people—usually called the creation of the "middle class"—the typical white family has a net worth that is on average eight times the net worth of a typical Black family. When Black and white wage earners with identical incomes are compared, whites still have twice the wealth of Blacks. *Affirmative action: for whites only.*

"Affirmative action" as a mechanism for promoting racial justice for the past few decades is on legal life-support, if not ready for the autopsy. The Supreme Court has not upheld a single affirmative action program since 1989, when it approved by a 5-4 decision a plan to encourage "minority ownership" of broadcast licenses. In 1996 a proposition prohibiting any form of affirmative action based on race or gender was approved by California voters, and in 2006 the Michigan electorate overwhelmingly voted to outlaw affirmative action based on race. In 2007 one Supreme Court rejected two longstanding, *voluntary* affirmative action programs. As a country we refuse to repair any of the damage done to an entire people based on color. We refuse to remember, or to acknowledge, or to invent new solutions, and that could drive a sane person crazy.

Let's return to the Homestead Act: After the Indian Wars of the nineteenth century, the U.S. government had a profound interest in promoting settlement in the Great Plains, but Southern legislators who worried about tipping the balance of political power against the slave states blocked all homestead legislation. When the South seceded, Congress quickly passed the Homestead Act of 1862 that granted anyone who was over twenty-one or a head of household, anyone who was a citizen or intended to become a citizen, the opportunity to claim ownership of up to a hundred acres of land in the West. The homesteader was required to live on the land for five years and to make improvements on the property. All that free land—for whites only, of course, because Black people were still property under the law.

Interestingly, the Homestead program continued in the Midwest and West until 1934, and the peak homesteading years were 1871, 1880, and 1902—years after the Emancipation Proclamation and the end of the Civil War. Experienced Southern agricultural workers—the formerly enslaved—were discouraged from moving West, and in 1866 Congress passed the Southern Homestead Act granting freed Black people and those loyal to the Union forty acres in Mississippi, Arkansas, Louisiana, and Florida. The land was poor compared to the hundred acres available in the West, and it required living in uncomfortably close quarters with former slavers. There was, predictably, fierce and violent white resistance. Plantation owners developed a feudal system of sharecropping, creating in effect a peasant class of Black laborers held in a permanent state of debt and dependency. The hope that freedmen could own and control the means of production was crushed with the betrayal of Reconstruction and the repeal of the Southern Homestead Act in 1876.

But the dream never died: In 1877, three thousand Black people petitioned the president seeking help finding land in the West or in Africa. Many emigrated to Liberia in this period to escape the terrorism of the Black Codes, Jim Crow, lynching, and structured and enforced poverty. Many more were gripped with "Kansas Fever," the idea that in the land of the great Abolitionist John Brown, a state now ruled by former Abolitionists, they would find land that would offer the next huge step toward liberation.

Enslaved human beings had been denied everything—to say that they'd been denied "equal opportunity" seems grotesquely tepid. Everyone recognized that without the support of land, or of transportation to new land, of a mule and a few tools—that is, without some public policy of positive action to redress wrongs, Emancipation would be gutted. In 1883, the Supreme Court struck down the Civil Rights Act of 1875 against discrimination in public accommodation, with the infamous conclusion: "When a man has emerged from slavery, and, by the aid of beneficent legislation, has shaken off the inseparable concomitants of that state, there must be some stage in the progress of his elevation when he takes the rank of a mere citizen and ceases to be *the special favorite of the laws*..." We still hear the echo: Black people get all the advantages, in 1883 on up through today. And so it was for Emancipation: Eviscerated. That's why, despite the odds, so many fled the South.

White supremacy, in spite of Emancipation, in spite of war, adapted itself for new times, asserted itself once more, triumphant.

During the Great Depression, Congress created the Home Owners Loan Corporation as an aid to refinance mortgages in the face of massive threatened foreclosures. The government would grant and guarantee loans, and the corporation developed criteria and surveyed neighborhoods to assess financial risk—a scale of A to D, color coded with an A designated as green, for most desirable, and a D as red. Thus, in 1933 the concept of "redlining" was born, and when the Federal Housing Authority was created in 1934 to guarantee mortgages and indemnify banks against the risk of default, it relied entirely on the corporation's standards. "Redlining" was official government policy, and it is alive and well today in spite of anti-discrimination laws and massive social upheaval.

A random but weighty example: In 1999 the U.S. Department of Agriculture paid a $300 million settlement to a group of Black farmers who had brought suit sixteen years earlier alleging racial discrimination in loans and subsidies. It was a pale and inadequaate victory—in 1920, 14 percent of the nation's farms were Black-owned; by 1992, that figure was less than 1 percent.

A story in the morning newspaper—deep inside, buried between the ads—opens with this head: "Accused of Discrimination, Clothing Chain Settles Case." The story describes a practice called "racial retailing"—store employees following Black shoppers, patterns of withholding shopping bags only from Black folks, and clerks refraining from inviting Black customers to apply for store credit cards. We knew about the racial divide in catching a cab in New York or Chicago, the well-known traffic offense of "Driving While Black," but "racial retailing" was a new formulation. While many of our white students—self-described good people and liberal, too—are amazed to hear of this injustice "so long after the victories of the Civil Rights Movement," African American students take the news with a kind of seething recognition, a familiarity that is at once knowing and outraged. Here we are again, they say. And, yes, here we are, face to face with American apartheid, a cruel and debasing separation and a hierarchy of racialized privilege and oppression with all its attendant self-justifications and mystifications. And white folks are surprised.

A few years later, the Adam's Mark hotel chain settled a class action law suit brought by Black guests required to wear orange wristbands during their stays. Adam's Mark executives stipulated in the settlement that they meant no harm. Of course not. And so, accompanying the oppression comes the consistent dissembling and the denying making it all so clamorously American. The structures of racial hierarchy are everywhere in evidence—changing forms from time to time, they are strictly enforced and remarkably consistent in substance—dragging the chains of an unresolved history along into each new year. And yet ... and yet white people, sleeping the deep, deep American sleep, stubbornly insist on beginning each day completely innocent.

White privilege, the pervasive and invisible fact of life in America, comes packaged as neutral, inevitable, and inoffensive policy, and has got deniability built right in. When states granted zoning authority to towns, they handed over the power to set lot and house size requirements and, therefore, the power to create exclusive enclaves. Add to that the federal tax code's mortgage interest tax deduction and the granted authority to set school attendance boundaries, and we have the entire recipe for publicly funded, exclusive privileged schools, or socialism for the rich. And yet no one—victim or beneficiary—is meant to notice.

138

Affirmative Action: For Whites Only

***

Today, in a public housing project near the University of Illinois at Chicago, where Bill is a professor, more a prison barracks where folks are warehoused and forgotten than a community, city services are spare to nonexistent, and the police, who patrol the border relentlessly, rarely venture into the area itself. Whenever a resident moves out, that apartment is boarded up, services are cut and a ghost town begins to emerge. In just a few more years public and private abandonment will destroy this community. But the cause is neither a culture-of-poverty nor a tangle-of-pathologies, neither a misguided permissive welfare state nor a geography of poverty. It is a clear instance of exclusion, suppression, abandonment, and desertion, a system of white supremacy plain and simple.

In the multiracial and largely middle-and upper-middle class Hyde Park neighborhood where we live, by contrast, the largest private police force in the world—the University of Chicago police—is always on the move, ever ready to help, "serving and protecting" with vigor. And because we have a huge and powerful institution and a politically demanding citizenry in the neighborhood, we are unlikely to suffer the withdrawal of streets and sanitation, water, parks and recreation, education, and public safety. When a streetlight goes out, it's quickly repaired; when a tree limb falls, it's removed. If this upkeep and care disappeared, all our smug sense of civility would no doubt disappear down the toilet in a heartbeat. This is the community that comedians Mike Nichols and Elaine May once famously described as "the only integrated neighborhood in Chicago—Black and white, shoulder-to-shoulder against the poor."

At the end of Chicago Freedom Summer described earlier, the summer of 1966, Dorothy Gautreaux, a Black community activist and tenant in public housing, sued the Chicago Housing Authority (CHA) and the U.S. Department of Housing and Urban Development (HUD) in a class action representing forty thousand other residents. The suit charged discrimination in the location of public housing projects— most built in the 1950s and 1960s—and in the assignment of tenants based on separate waiting lists of Black and white people, alleging that most CHA projects were all Black by design, deliberately and exclusively located within the "Negro ghetto," and that Blacks were steered, frustrated, and ultimately prohibited from moving into any of the few projects located in white neighborhoods.

In 1969 a federal judge found for Gautreaux and ordered the CHA to build the next seven hundred units in white areas of the city, and to locate 75 percent of all subsequent units outside the ghetto in what were called "scattered sites." Rather than comply, the CHA stopped construction altogether—no significant low-income housing was ever built again in Chicago.

That same 1969 decision absolved HUD of complicity in enforcing segregation—the excuse, as always, "we meant no harm"—and Gautreaux appealed. In 1971 the U.S. Court of Appeals reversed the lower court and found HUD guilty of aiding and abetting the CHA in a deliberate pattern of racial segregation. This ruling opened the gates to seek a metropolitan-wide solution, and the Gautreaux remedy came to be called "mobility-based" housing.

The Gautreaux decision and program morphed over time into a hugely complex social experiment, a twenty-two year odyssey filled with struggle, courage, risk, and, occasionally, meager satisfaction. Some say the price was too high—after all the obstructionism and foot-dragging, Dorothy Gautreaux herself was long dead before relief of any kind was conceived or realized. The Chicago City Council's refusal to approve construction sites cost the citizens of Chicago $50 million in lost public housing funds during that period. And the myopic focus on "mobility" took attention away from the problem of egregiously insufficient low-income housing, while the intense energy required for the effort took resources from community enrichment. In the end, while forty thousand people were members of the named injured class, and arguably hundred of thousands or even millions more suffered real harm, only seven thousand families moved out of the city. There simply is no fit between offense and reparation.

Families who moved from ghetto to suburb express an abiding ambivalence: happy to send their children to well-funded and relatively functional schools, but fearful that their kids are being unfairly labeled and channeled off into gleaming new sub-ghettos called special education classes; pleased to leave relentless street crime behind, but frightened by incidents of racial harassment, and suffering the dehumanizing grind of everyday social isolation. Again and again, Gautreaux class members provide searing insight into the dilemmas and contradictions of their own lived situations. For example, while prominent outsiders—including legal scholars and social scientists—describe urban crime in natural disaster or act-of-God terms, the participants themselves identify a system that had cast them aside, a system that concentrates and isolates poor people, and then deserts them in regard to public safety. "The police won't come fast enough," says Alesa Butter, and in that simple statement she captures a wide range of public policies that intentionally disregard the hopes and needs of Black people trapped in poverty.

And in a contrast that everyone can see by opening their eyes, the mothers describe the benefits of suburban schools: "There is a music program that is excellent;" "The beautiful school [offers] the first real football field [they had] ever seen. [It also offers] golfing, track, tennis, swimming…" They understand and describe the structured "savage inequalities" they face, and in speaking up for their own children their comments indict a whole system.

Residents know exactly what's happening. In the *Journal of Ordinary Thought*, an irregular neighborhood journal "founded on the proposition that every person is a philosopher" and that "expressing one's opinions fosters creativity and change," public housing residents describe the world through their own eyes:

> *My neighborhood has changed so much over the past four months. Any and everything is going on in my neighborhood, from police brutality, drugs, drug houses, to my son repeating everything he hears outside my door. I call the police to complain, but no change. I call the Alderman to complain. No change. I'm not expecting a change overnight. I'm trying really hard not to let these big problems run me away, but I have a child that I'm trying to raise, and no one is trying to hear me....*
>
> —Monika Ivy

> *Sometimes we get in a place and get real comfortable, and we don't want to leave. We can't really afford to. We're right at everything, and things are so easy to get to. Now the developers are talking about picking us up and moving us to some strange place, and we don't like it. What can we do about it? Let's put our heads and hearts and money together and come up with a solution.*
>
> —Denise Taylor

> *Buildings are being demolished, kids are being moved here and there, not settled in one place. Some are being given new housing, but some who have had problems or trouble can't get new housing and are having a hard time being placed. The plan: to move us out of the downtown area, the most popular area in the city now. So what is to happen with us? Who cares? Our trouble here has just begun. The old, smaller buildings are getting some people who don't want to be there, but have no choice, who have no one to come to their rescue. There are children who have to move into a different gang area and buy themselves more trouble. Moms are having a hard time. What to do? How to save my child or children? The cry is loud. Save our neighborhood.*
>
> —Sandra Shepard

Much of what is written and said about African Americans by whites—academics, journalists, social scientists—assumes white normativity. It floats along comfortably on a credulous folklore of our/their white invention. It assumes Black deviance and white normativeness. It allows a beneficent social engineering in which no one's motives are examined, no one's agendas questioned.

But what if poor African American communities, too, are fully human—complex, diverse, and mysterious? What if the benign idea of "dismantling the ghettos" turns out to simply move poor people around while serving a real-estate agenda with fangs? What if the remedy is teeny-tiny in relation to the harm?

Perhaps this is why, finally, the monumental and sustained Gautreaux program alone is entirely unsatisfying. There is not enough housing stock for poor people. Vouchers are insufficient in themselves and each is resisted mightily by receiving communities; a voucher ends up buying very little. Advocates find themselves defending all the things they set out to oppose: quotas, steering, and other restrictive practices; protecting the interests of white residents including passing stereotype-driven judgments about the re-locating families' "acceptability" to the resistant whites; and absolute paralysis in practice.

Gautreaux provides a cautionary tale whenever the fight for justice moves, as it must, to tactics. Even with the power of the federal courts and the mighty efforts of thousands of people, Gautreaux results were meager. Receiving communities resisted and much effort went into ameliorating or overcoming objections. Families that made the moves had neither adequate resources to account for nor sufficient help to repair the harm they had suffered. Racialized and oppressive housing patterns were neither disrupted nor breached. They are, if anything, more firmly in place. The more things change ... well, sometimes they just remain the same.

***

Legal scholars Derrick Bell, Charles Lawrence, and Sylvia Law point out that white privilege is so profound and pervasive—and still entirely unacknowledged—that it is embodied even in the heart of anti-discrimination laws. Here we are, living in our putatively post-Civil Rights world, more than forty years after the passage of the historic Civil Rights Act of 1964 and the Voting Rights Act of 1965, and white supremacy is not only alive, but thriving vibrantly, encoded in law and supported by legal precedent.

Before the historic Black Freedom Movement, racial discrimination was legal, blatant, explicit, and normal. When racial discrimination was finally proclaimed illegal in the U.S., it also became largely unacceptable in its blatant and explicit forms. But that was neither the end of things nor the bottom of it. In a famous anti-discrimination case, Duke Power Company, which had maintained two rosters of workers, one white, the other Black, and paid white laborers more money for exactly the same work, created two new categories: one list was for workers with a high school diploma, and the other for workers without. Sound sensible? While there was no evidence that a high school diploma had anything whatever to do with job performance, the high schoolers were paid more. The result: Black workers remained second class in terms of treatment, pay, and benefits; white workers got additional privileges.

In 1971, the Supreme Court ruled against Duke, agreeing that neutral-sounding rules like a high school graduation requirement—unrelated to a legitimate, demonstrable purpose of on-the-job performance—discriminate *in effect* and are, then, illegal.

The idea that discriminatory *effects* or consequences ought to count lasted only for a historic eye-blink with the U.S. Supreme Court. The court soon held that racial discrimination would be prohibited only when it was shown to be "deliberate and intentional." Now that's an extraordinarily high legal standard, almost impossible to prove. Black applicants to the Washington, D.C., police force, for example, unsuccessfully challenged a standardized test that excluded almost all Blacks, arguing that there was no evidence that the test correlated in any way with police performance. The court approved the test even though it was patently discriminatory *in effect.*

From then on, as Sylvia Law observed, "the only racial discrimination that counts in the law is explicitly articulated, intentional, conscious racism." This means that the anti-discrimination laws themselves embody white-skin-privilege: "The only perspective that counts is [that of] the white perpetrator. The effects on the Black victims are irrelevant." As the court said in 1979, "discriminatory purpose" means that a perpetrator must act "'because of,' not merely 'in spite of'" its negative impact upon an entire identifiable group. So if white people don't notice adverse impact on Blacks—a no-brainer—that impact doesn't count. The U.S. rejection of discriminatory *effects* stands in sharp contrast to the International Convention on the Elimination of All Forms of Racial Discrimination, a treaty ratified by the U.S., which prohibits both racially discriminatory *purpose* and *effect.*

When a lawsuit based on gender discrimination was brought by an associate against a white-shoes law firm, and it came before Judge Constance Baker Motley, the defense asked her to recuse herself since, being a woman, she could not be neutral in matters of gender, and, further, being Black, she might have overidentification with and unfair sympathy for a plaintiff claiming discrimination. She refused and, in a withering response, told the attorney that if he could find a judge who was neither *of* gender nor *of* race she would happily step down; until that day, she said, she was quite certain she could be fair.

COLORBLIND

[This is] a historic moment of unprecedented ungenerosity, when a mood for slashing social progress can be powerfully abetted by an argument that beneficiaries cannot be helped, owing to inborn cognitive limits expressed as low IQ scores.

—Stephen Jay Gould

Why is it so difficult for so many white folks to understand that racism is oppressive not because white folks have prejudicial feelings about blacks (they could have such feelings and leave us alone) but because it is a system that promotes donation and subjugation.

—Patricia Williams

White supremacy, Charles Mills argues, "is the unnamed political system that has made the modern world what it is today," and the accompanying "Racial Contract," while it is political and moral and epistemological, is also real and, in economic terms, "an exploitation contract." White skin privilege is rarely acknowledged in political or economic discourse, even when the "underprivileged" are briefly noted or paraded, and yet privilege is pervasive and structural and always hiding in plain sight.

In this system white people enjoy the comfortable conceit of conceiving whiteness as both normal and the norm—everyone else is simply trying to measure up, and usually not trying hard enough. When American white people are asked by researchers to describe themselves, they never mention race, while Black people in the U.S. almost always do. A large piece of white privilege, as the legal scholar Sylvia Law has argued, is the "privilege not to have to think about race." In *Honky*, a fascinating memoir of growing up white, Dalton Conley details the everyday privileges and codes of speech and action that are given if not asked for, and notes that whites always have "the right to make up the reasons things turn out the way they do, to construct our own narratives rather than having the media and society do it for us." Conley concludes that race colors our identity in fundamental ways and that, while he can't be sure exactly why one childhood friend got shot and another went to prison while he went on to a selective school and then university, the accumulated details form "the invisible contours of [racial] inequality... like the clogged traffic arteries of I-95."

One of the current popular whitewashes—a cultural bulwark around the blockhouse of white supremacy, promoted heavily by the powerful and endorsed as a kind of common-sense post-Civil Rights ideal by many—is the illusion (among whites) of colorblindness. Charles Krauthammer, a neoconservative writer, claims to "oppose affirmative action on grounds of colorblindness and in defense of the original vision of the Civil Rights Movement: judging people by the content of their character and not the color of their skin." And Vice President Dick Cheney, who as a congressman voted against both the resolution condemning apartheid in South Africa and the one to create a national holiday in honor of Martin Luther King, Jr., has said repeatedly that he honors the memory of the late Civil Rights leader by refusing to see race. "I think that what Reverend King was advocating," Cheney says, "was that we learn to judge people by the content of their character rather than the color of their skin. And that's what we should all try to do."

And so, in Cheney's logic, if large numbers of Black people live in substandard housing, or if disproportionate numbers of Black men are incarcerated, or if Black students are underrepresented in higher education—if any of a thousand obvious measures of social stratification demonstrate unequivocally the existence of a hierarchy of privilege and oppression based on color—it's the content of *their* characters that's at fault: "I judge them to be inferior because of character"—no longer skin color, even though the impact is identical. To notice the fact of the inequality, to mention the substance of it, to act on the reality of it, is to violate the spirit and besmirch the memory of Dr. King. The advocates and activists for racial justice become the bigots in Cheney's curious cosmology—he himself is merely living the dream.

It's a neat reversal: Justice John Harlan first used the word "colorblind" in a legal context in his 1896 dissent from *Plessy v. Ferguson*, in which the Supreme Court upheld a law requiring segregated railroad cars; William Rehnquist quoted Harlan's dissent in 1980 as he himself dissented from a court ruling requiring set-asides for African Americans. For Harlan, "colorblindness" meant that the state could not create hateful and oppressive racial categories; for Rehnquist, "color blindness" had morphed into racial neutrality—as if we live in a world where we can close our eyes and racism will simply vanish. Colorblind: A new code word in defense of the status quo, of power relations as they are, of white supremacy.

Stephen Colbert, the satirical faux right-wing know-it-all from Comedy Central, performs colorblindness as a central trope of his act. For the first year of the show he did a bit where he would ask the opinion of "my Black friend" whenever issues of race emerged—a variation of the old "some-of-my-best-friends" theme.

"I don't see race," he now says whenever he covers a story concerning Black people. When he interviews a Black leader or politician or scholar or artist, he inevitably busts out with "I'm told you're Black, but frankly I don't see race—are you Black?" If the guest responds affirmatively, he says, "Prove to me that you're Black, because I just can't see it—I don't see race."

Patricia Williams, the distinguished law professor from Columbia University, takes a different dig at the colorblind myth. She reports that in various social situations, when the conversation turns to race, she casually asserts that she is not Black. Whatever complexity race might signify disappears, and the reaction is universal: "Poof! Instantly I become Black again."

Stephen Colbert sometimes notes, "People say I'm white, but I don't see it. I guess I am because my neighbors say they're white and I live in a gated community for whites only, but I really don't see race." A more dangerous move in America would be this: "Prove to me you're white." Even those who agree that race has no scientific basis are uneasy with a challenge to the most solid anchor of their American identities. Prove whiteness? In a country where one drop of Black blood makes you Black, and a dozen white branches on the family tree won't guarantee membership in the Caucasian club? Better leave that whole business alone.

Colbert is sending up colorblindness, peeling back the comfortable justifications that have made it such a widely shared illusion, such a comfy commonplace. But, of course, the language itself is not colorblind, and as soon as someone evokes colorblindness as a quality there is an implicit and automatic acknowledgement of color, and of the abiding fact that color matters. On the historic occasion of Senator Barack Obama's presidential campaign, pundits bloviate on race, many insisting that it's "no longer about color"—and yet no one mentions either the "color" or the beyond-color theme when commenting on Hillary Clinton or John McCain: Whiteness is "neutral," "normative," the assumed default position. During the OJ trial an observer commented, "People don't notice that he's Black, so he'll get a fair trial." But to make that statement one has already, a) noticed that OJ is Black, and b) implicitly acknowledged that color counts profoundly in the criminal justice system.

Jose Saramago sketches a harrowing moral landscape in *Blindness*, his creepy allegory of a modern epidemic and the inevitable atrocities it unleashes. A man stopped at a red light in rush hour goes suddenly blind—a milky whiteness descends, and his sight is inexplicably gone. Around him horns honk, commuters become impatient and then enraged, a little chaos takes hold as people try to sort out what has happened. Someone helps the man home, and then steals his car.

By the next day it has become clear that an epidemic of "white blindness" is spreading, afflicting people at an accelerating pace. One after another, people open their eyes and feel as if they've plunged into a thick milky sea.

The authorities at first quarantine the ailing, locking them away in an empty mental hospital. When the guards go blind, their eyesight vanishing into the vast whiteness, the prisoners are abandoned, but not before a group of blind men organize themselves into a predatory gang, steal the food rations of the others, and humiliate and rape all the women, young and old.

When it seems the worst is upon them, when the brutality becomes overwhelming, one and then another and then all the people, just as suddenly, regain their eyesight. In jubilation, laughing and awkwardly hugging one another, they ask, Why? Whatever happened? Why did we go blind? Where did the milky whiteness come from, and where has it gone? Why do we now see?

The woman narrator responds: "I don't think we did go blind, I think we are blind, Blind but seeing, Blind people who can see, but do not see." She is reminding them— and all of us—that the opposite of moral isn't always immoral—it's more often indifference. Ethical action on one hand, and on the other cool detachment, negligence, apathy, cynicism, inattentiveness, incuriousness, aloofness. Blindness. Were they really blind? And now, sighted once more, can they really see? Can we?

"Blind people who can see, but do not see"—the nightmare Saramago evokes is the modern predicament in full, without window dressing. Blind people who can see. White people who can see race but do not see race—colorblind people.

Since each of us is a finite being in an infinite and expanding universe, we might begin by acknowledging our limits—we can see some things, but we cannot see everything. Normalcy is invisible—it's hard to see our own advantages, and it's exhausting to even look. One of the privileges of privilege is that it's anesthetizing. Each of us has large blind spots based on privilege, and the tautology ought to trouble us: We are blind to our blind spots.

Paradoxically, that recognition might allow us to go beyond, to step toward the not-yet- known, and to take our ignorance as a starting point rather than a dead-end. Whose perspective is left out? What's missing? Where am I not looking?

Our middle son Malik had long blond hair curling down to his waist well into middle school. He wanted long hair; he refused to have it cut except for his fourth birthda,y when his greatest wish was to go to the Village Barber and have his hair spiked, dyed purple, and gelled. Malik was regularly mistaken for a girl. "Man, that girl really can throw a baseball!" When people were quietly told that he was a boy, they launched into frantic apologies, stumbled over excessive remorse, noted that it was obvious that he was a boy now that they looked closely, and generally acted a fool. Malik calmly looked at them as is they were nuts. Perceptions and either/or classifications.

The biggest crisis came when he was to be batboy at Wrigley Field. After numerous discussions among ourselves, we sat down with Malik days before the epic afternoon game. We explained that some of the players in the dugout might be rude and ill- informed about people's right to wear their hair the way they choose. He could do one of three things: 1) Cut his hair; 2) tie it up under his baseball cap; or 3) ignore them. Malik wasn't conflicted. He would be himself. So we have great color photos of Malik lined up on the field alongside Ryan Sandberg and Andre Dawson, with Don Zimmer, the Cubs manager, arm around the kid with hair flowing down his back. Only one guy (white) in the dugout was a jerk that day. The other thirty players all told Malik stories about their days with long hair and afros and took him right in.

Because we are blind to our own blind-spots, where might we look for illumination? The answer became a defining feature of the Movements for civil and human rights, for racial and gender justice and for peace: *Look to those who suffer the consequences—* of racism, of war and colonialism, of sexism, of homophobia, of disability, of oppression of any kind. It was the Vietnamese at a certain point who could teach Americans about war and peace, but we had to open ourselves to them; primarily it is African Americans who can shine an irreplaceable light on race and white supremacy; women on patriarchy the poor on poverty. The lesson was this: If you want fundamental change, tie your fate to the most oppressed.

This is difficult to do for two main reasons. The first is that it requires giving up the comfortable position of privilege to which one is accustomed and from which one gains a false sense of stability in the here and now. The second is that we don't know the answers, the strategies to defeat racism. It is communities of color that define, decide, and lead in the broad sense. Yet, ultimately, whites, whether white women, workers, students or youth, are responsible for organizing, challenging, and defeating our identification with whiteness. This thrusts white radicals toward an uncertain and unknowable future. The South African writer Nadine Gordimer wrote, "the black knows he will be at home, at last, in the future. The white who has declared him or herself for that future, who belongs in the white segment that was never at home in white supremacy, does not know where he will find his home at last."

White people's general reluctance to see white supremacy, racial hierarchy, racism, or the oppression of Black people, has been true within social justice movements. All the clichés that clutter the mind—"Some of my best friends..."; "I don't see color..."; "I didn't have anything to do with slavery or Jim Crow, I wasn't even alive then..."; "I'm not prejudiced..."; "That's all ancient history..."; "Those people are making a mountain out of a mole hill"—shatter into tiny fragments and crash to the ground in the light of the experiences of the primary victims of racism. So that's where we must be looking for knowledge, for perspective, and for wisdom.

An incessant daily reminder of an assumed white supremacy is the ubiquitous and controlling term "minority" when referring to people of color (or women). The default is "white" men—somehow the majority. It of, course, all depends on where you stand—where are "whites" a "majority?" The messages about power, control, and inevitable are built into the language.

***

Peggy McIntosh invented the idea of an "Invisible Knapsack" of white privilege to explain how she and other whites are given "unearned assets which I can count on cashing in each day, but about which I was meant to remain oblivious." The pack is weightless and unseen, hidden behind her back and filled with "special provisions, maps, passports, codebooks, visas, clothes, tools and blank checks." Our youngest son Chesa, who has lived extensively in Latin America, names a similarly unacknowledged phenomenon for white Americans abroad—the "Gringo Wildcard."

The "Invisible Knapsack" is carefully hidden from those who carry it around. Nothing in white education or upbringing alerts us to the ways we are "unfairly advantaged," or active participants in a damaged and shattered culture. White lives are presented as "neutral, normative, and average, and also ideal."

Resisting all this, McIntosh begins to make a list of the contents of her "Invisible Knapsack." Pulling the contents out of the pack, lining them up on a table for all to see, counting them up, she figures, is a way to become more conscious and perhaps more effective in combating white supremacy. Here, then, are a few of the items from Peggy's knapsack:

> • *I can go shopping alone most of the time, pretty well assured that I will not be followed or harassed.*

> • *I can be sure my children will be given curricular materials in their schools that testify to the existence of their race and heritage.*

> • *Whether I use checks, credit cards or cash, I can count on my skin color not to work against the appearance of my financial reliability.*

> • *I can swear, or dress in second hand clothes, or not answer letters, without having people attribute these choices to the bad morals, the poverty or the illiteracy of my race.*

> • *I can do well in a challenging situation without being called a credit to my race.*

> • *I am never asked to speak for all the people of my racial group.*

> • *I can remain oblivious of the language and customs of persons of color who constitute the world's majority without feeling in my culture any penalty for such oblivion.*

> • *If a traffic cop pulls me over or if the IRS audits my tax return, I can be sure I haven't been singled out because of my race.*

It's a start—and it could be a useful exercise for whites of any class, gender, sexual orientation, or ability: Spend a week jotting down the daily experiences of white-skin privilege. It's oddly difficult to begin, but if you pay attention and stick to it, the pace accelerates and the items pile up quickly.

Let us add caution and complexity to this exercise—there's a danger that feelings of guilt will trivialize the problem of privilege, that politics and morality will be reduced to navel-gazing, meditation, or culpable hand-wringing, that action will give way to therapy. The country is proliferating with sensitivity trainers and diversity consultants and multicultural educators—all instructing white people in how to deal with Blacks. In this psychologizing of race, self-fulfillment and sentiment rule the day: If white people feel better and steadily improve ourselves, the world will follow along. Another warning is that the backpack is differently packed for queers of every race, ethnicity, or class, less full for every worker and underemployed person, for most all women, the majority of immigrants. The class complexity extends to middle-class and wealthy African Americans who may themselves have acquired some of these tools; the backpack is nowhere near full for homeless and destitute white people.

And so there's another essential step: All of the items from the "Invisible Knapsack" must be understood eventually as expressions built upon, propped up, and supported by larger and harder frameworks of historic flow, law and policy, social class and economic structure and condition. This is a call to stand up: recognition and love and acceptance, yes, but also solidarity, obligation and action. The goal is not peace of mind and a mellow acceptance of injustice, nor the Star Trek approach to multiculturalism— one of everything with a white man in charge. The goal is not diversity as entertainment and icon. Diversity in America—and globally—is actually a description of power and privilege and resource distribution more than anything else. The goal ought to be white folks working to regain our own humanity through solidarity; the vision is enlightenment and freedom; the benefits, justice then peace.

***

Some events become—for reasons sometimes obvious and as often mysterious—major shared cultural moments, inescapable in their reach and grasp. The assassinations of JFK and Martin Luther King, Jr., for example, were huge and defining if you are an American of a certain age—"Where were you when Kennedy was killed? How did you hear the news? What did you do next?"

September 11, 2001, cuts through our consciousness and it also splits time—there's a "before" and an "after" 9/11. Everything changed... or it didn't.

Even events that take on mythological proportions and achieve iconic status have layers of skepticism, doubt, and dissent inscribed on our hearts. And so the killing of Kennedy was a national tragedy, a dream destroyed, and the end of Camelot, but Malcolm X saw the wages of empire in the act and called it "chickens coming home to roost." And King's murder, massively mourned and igniting an unprecedented wave of urban rebellions, brought grim and secret satisfaction to legions of his opponents. The murder of Malcolm X electrified, energized, enraged, terrified, satisfied—depending on your angle of regard: Who you were and how you saw the world.

The OJ Simpson trial belongs somewhere on this list—the white Bronco, the ill-fitting glove, the notorious LAPD detective Mark Fuhrman and his "N-word"-laced tapes, and, of course, the verdict itself. "Where were you when—on national TV!—the verdict was read? How did you react?"

The answer to that last question is color-coded through and through. Chris Rock said, "Black people too happy, white people too mad—I ain't seen white people that mad since they cancelled '*M*A*S*H*.'" Rock debunks in two directions. To his Black audience: "Black people runnin' around saying', 'We won!' 'We won!' What the hell we won?" And for whites: "If Jerry Seinfeld caught in a double murder, and the person who found the bloody glove was from the Nation of Islam, he'd be a free man—Jerry be eatin' cereal today."

Ambiguity, complexity, reversal. An elderly barber in South Central L.A. ten years after the verdict, shook his head slowly and said in a quiet voice, "The shame of it is that they framed a guilty man." We were in a classroom in the Cook County Temporary Juvenile Detention Center when the OJ verdict was read. Oddly, TVs had been wheeled into every classroom—perhaps someone in authority felt that just because they were incarcerated (or perhaps precisely *because* they were locked up) the kids shouldn't have to miss this shared American moment. In any case, we crowded together—three adults and a dozen kids, each themselves charged with a crime—as Judge Lance Ito strode into the courtroom and all rose.

The kids were giddy with anticipation, and one of the more enterprising was giving odds and making book. "He was framed, man," said Antonio. "Everybody saw that the cops slipped the evidence in on him."

"OK," replied Big, "true. But there's two dead honkies out there, and you know for sure some brother's gonna pay."

On and on—laughter and teasing and, as the moment approached, tension.

When Judge Ito echoed "Not Guilty" over and over, the room erupted—cheers, high-fives, and manly half-hugs. And before the noise died down Freddy, sixteen years old and charged with two gangland-style murders, wheeled around on his heels, his huge smile morphing toward a pained grimace, and clasped the back of his left hand into the palm of his right: "Damn!" he cried out. "Damn! How can I get hold of Johnnie Cochran?" The joint erupted in laughter.

Meaning-making itself is racially segregated, and OJ a perfect blank slate on which to inscribe our assumptions, prejudices, stereotypes, and experiences. To white people, Black rage fits; to a group of young white women at Brown University, a narrative of male violence makes sense; and to large numbers of Black Americans, the possibility of white cops planting evidence and framing a Black man is way too close to their collective life experiences for comfort.

One indelible contribution of the OJ moment was the popularizing of a clever bit of shorthand meant to emphatically underline our post-Civil Rights, putatively new and improved colorblind society and dismiss out-of-hand race as a factor in any situation where people of color might level a charge of racism: "Playing the race card." Robert Shapiro, an OJ attorney who apparently had a change of heart as the trial proceeded and found his high-profile co-counsel's accusation that Detective Fuhrman's propensity for the "N-word" was irrelevant to the case before them, said that "Johnnie Cochran played the race card, and he dealt it from the bottom of the deck." Cochran was being duplicitous and devious, Shapiro implied, bringing up an entirely inappropriate and irrelevant issue as a sand-in-your-eyes distraction and an emotionally charged play for sympathy. No "reasonable person" in modern America, according to Shapiro's logic, could possibly see a Black man on trial for murdering two white people and a white racist cop as witness as having anything to do with race.

"Reasonable people" no longer see race at all. When police killed a young Black man in Queens leaving his bachelor party on the day he would have wed, the ensuing demonstrations against "racist cops" was described as playing the race card. When a group of Black students were expelled from a Decatur high school for a fight at a football game, and Reverend Jesse Jackson pointed out that there were no weapons and no injuries, and that a group of white girls in the suburbs received virtually no punishment for similarly outrageous behavior, he was charged with playing the race card. When *New York Times* columnist Bob Herbert points out the banal and accumulating daily humiliations suffered by youth of color at the hands of New York City cops and names it as a gathering time bomb, he's accused of flipping the race card. And as Barry Bonds surpassed Babe Ruth's—the good old Bambino's—home run record, and as the ongoing investigation into illegal drug use intensified and baseball fans booed him across the country, Malik Dohrn, who raises the question of racism as figuring into both fan and MLB reaction, is chided for playing the race card. It's the race card that's always the problem, since racism is a thing of the past.

Tim Wise offered a smart analysis of all this in a piece called "What Kind of Card Is Race?" Wise points out, for example, that "research indicates that people of color are actually reluctant to allege racism" for fear of being ignored, dismissed, or humiliated. "White denial has long trumped claims of racism," Wise continues, and "when it comes to playing a race card, it is more accurate to say that whites are the dealers with the loaded decks, shooting down any evidence of racism as little more than the fantasies of unhinged blacks, unwilling to take personal responsibility for their own problems in life."

There's a choice every person faces in America when she or he is faced with a racist slur or slight, an institutional obstacle, a policy, invisibility a tradition, the weight of history: Shut up or speak up. If you're Black and you shut up, you swallow hard or bite your lip or choke back tears or break into a sweat or tense your jaw or speed up your heart rate and raise your blood pressure—whatever—you absorb the blow.

If you choose to speak up, you take a terrible risk. There will surely be a reaction, a defense, a rationalization—no matter if the offense is small or monstrous. You'll be told you're delusional or hysterical or hyper-sensitive or too impatient or simply wrong: "You misunderstood"; "You over-reacted"; "You're imagining things." You might face legal action or even violence. For sure your experience, your interpretation, your perspective will be tossed aside as some form of special pleading—of course, you only say all of that because you're Black—we move on.

If you're white and you shut up you can blend into your welcoming crowd pretty easily. If you speak up you're a troublemaker or an idiot, you're a latte-sipping liberal or a politically correct puppet of some whacky ideology, a race traitor or a guilt-driven self-hater. These are all post-Civil Rights euphemisms: You love 'em.

***

It's possible to demonstrate that underneath every pose of innocence, everyone in America knows that race matters. We white people may protest that we ourselves harbor no feelings of prejudice or ill will, and insist that things are better and better for Black people—some will even argue that Blacks have the upper hand because of over compensation and affirmative action. We may only rarely consider—and usually under duress—all the little and large privileges that flow our way because of color, but when honest or when pressed, white people tend to fall back on whiteness.

Here's a parable that Andrew Hacker offers to white audiences:

You will be visited tonight by an official you have never met. He begins by telling you that he is extremely embarrassed. The organization he represents has made a mistake, something that hardly ever happens.

According to their records, he goes on, you were to have been born black: to another set of parents, far from where you were raised.

However, the rules being what they are, this error must be rectified, and as soon as possible. So at midnight tonight, you will become black. And this will mean not simply a darker skin, but the bodily and facial features associated with African ancestry. However, inside you will be the person you always were. Your knowledge and ideas will remain intact. But outwardly you will not be recognizable to anyone you now know.

Your visitor emphasizes that being born to the wrong parents was in no way your fault. Consequently, his organization is prepared to offer you some reasonable recompense. Would you, he asks, care to name a sum of money you might consider appropriate? He adds that his group is by no means poor. It can be quite generous when the circumstances warrant, as they seem to in your case. He finishes by saying that their records show you are scheduled to live another fifty years—as a black man or woman in America. How much financial recompense would you request?

When people play along, suspend disbelief, and assume it could happen, most respond that $50 million would not be out of line as compensation. Fifty million dollars. Without getting into the details, right there lies a powerful acknowledgement that white skin has a notable value— that to be African American would require protection—and, when pushed, white folks can even hang a giant price tag on it: $50 million.

TWO SYSTEMS OF YOUTH JUSTICE

Bernardine Dohrn

I shall create! If not a note, a hole.
If not an overture, a desecration.

—Gwendolyn Brooks

Those white things have taken all I had or dreamed, and broke my
heartstrings too. There is no bad luck in the world but white folks.
—Toni Morrison

Each Thanksgiving for the past decade, my son Zayd and I have gone to the Juvenile Temporary Detention Center, still known as the "Audy Home" (named after the founding warden), to serve Thanksgiving dinner to the some five hundred children incarcerated there. We, and other volunteers—largely the teachers and so-called "attendants" at the juvenile jail—are dressed in black suits and white shirts. We are assigned to a unit of the detention center—older boys, youngest boys, or girls—and ride the voluminous elevators up to the fourth or fifth floor to be admitted to a living unit.

It is a gloomy task: to provide cheer and comfort, in the form of a special Thanksgiving meal, to children who are locked up. No matter how chilly or sunny the day, no matter how generous or hateful the attendants, regardless of whether the children are vulnerable or tough—it is a paradoxical mission. We wait upon them, we offer second helpings (more gravy, corn pudding, cranberries?), we are kind. We leave, hours later, rushing home to our large families, excessive tables, and particular freedoms.

It has become ritual not because it helps anyone—certainly the children are not worse off if we don't show. Nor does it make us feel righteous, for it leaves a saddened, sickening, and helpless residue. Their incapacitation does not, I believe, make us safer. Probably we return because it is a bitter parable: a reminder of the banal, relentless mountain of cruelties against children deprived of their liberty. It is the other side of our freedoms and "rights": that invisible, watching world of those young people who are locked up. In their confinement, we are implicated, complicit, silent. They are children who most people choose, most days, not to notice.

There are some one hundred thousand children incarcerated on any given day in the U.S. Some are caged in dungeons—grey medieval fortresses that are reminders of eighteenth-century penitentiaries, such as the detention center in Atlanta where a child arrested and detained for truancy had committed suicide the year I visited. Some youth are confined at the cost of $100 a day and others, such as those once held by Sheriff Foti in New Orleans, were fed, clothed, and guarded on just $40 a day.

Hundreds of thousands of youngsters are incarcerated in juvenile justice facilities that are medieval snake pits, not only in Mississippi but in California and New Jersey, where parents are pressured to give up custody of their ill children in order to receive "treatment" that never comes. Children are given shots with the same needles, refused medical or dental care, held in facilities with mouse droppings and dead roaches; girls are confined in isolation cells without beds, toilets or clothing for status offenses like running away and curfew violations. Contemporary films like *The Magdalene Sisters,* *Evelyn,* and *Rabbit-Proof Fence* illustrate the brutal caging of girls in institutions determined to stamp out their sexuality, their culture, and their spirits

Our purpose in serving Thanksgiving food is to both keep these youth in our hearts on a day of family gatherings and to offer them a sort of treat with extra helpings and strawberry shortcake and whipped cream for dessert. The hours spent inside are filled with the surprises adolescents are likely to provide, but the experience is also sorrowful, being with youngsters who are deprived of their liberty on a day so redolent with family, food, and celebration. Whether we are assigned to the girls' units, or to the youngest boys', we are likely to find some children crying and some filled with sass. One year, we served turkey on a unique unit filled with plants and cactuses that were grown, pruned, and watered by the youngsters. This simple gesture transformed the dreary space, the waxed floors, and blaring TVs into a setting of calm, an oasis of tending and care. Occasionally, there is an Eastern European white girl among the unit of entirely African American and Latino kids. Calls to their parents on such special days are rationed, as if contact with their families were a form of contamination.

Each Thanksgiving, as we drive back through the city, we talk about the catalyst case that gave permission in a twinkling to unleash a new wave of hatred and fear against youth—certain youth. It happened one April night in 1989. Our own three boys were twelve, nine,, and eight. They cut their teeth on the swings, slides and sandboxes of Central Park playgrounds: Malik jogging around the reservoir with Bill; Zayd's birthday celebrated each April with picnics at the carousel; Chesa awe-struck watching West Indian cricket matches.

When the body of a twenty-eight-year-old jogger, a white investment banker, was found raped, bludgeoned—her left eye gouged, her skull bashed into her brain—and in a coma in the underbrush of Central Park, the telling became, like the river of terrible crimes before it, an international news story with epic legal and policy consequences. Why? That week alone, twenty-eight other women were assaulted and raped in New York City. These crimes of sexual violence against women are so heinous, so ubiquitous, and so damaging, yet they seem tolerated as inevitable or as background involving the poor. This woman, miraculously, survived. She subsequently married, had children, and wrote a book about her traumatic experiences. But why did her story take flight?

This is a tale about children—about those who are perceived as children, and those who are not. Five youngsters, children, were arrested and charged with gang rape and attempted murder within twenty-four hours. Antron McCray, Kevin Richardson, Yusef Salaam, Raymond Santana, and Kharey Wise—fourteen-, fifteen-, and sixteen-year-old high school students who had been in Central Park that lovely spring evening—became the tablet upon which America wrote its archetypical narrative. The youth were interrogated, and four confessed on videotape, two with their parents present; the fifth allegedly gave an "oral confession."

The immediate language of the reporting was unequivocal and it resonated:

> "*Wolf Pack's Prey*"; "*Packs of bloodthirsty teens from the tenements, bursting with boredom and rage, roam the streets, getting kicks from an evening of ultra-violence.*"

The liberal *Village Voice* columnist Pete Hamill wrote in the *New York Post*:

> "*They were coming downtown from a world of crack, welfare, guns, knives, indifference and ignorance. They were coming from a land of no fathers... They were coming from the anarchic province of the poor... And driven by a collective fury, brimming with the rippling energies of youth, their minds teeming with the violent images of the streets and the movies, they had only one goal: to smash, hurt, rob, stomp, rape. The enemies were rich. The enemies were white.*"

The *Post* used the slang "Wilding" and defined it as a Black and Latino youth fad straight from the violent raves of *A Clockwork Orange*.

After being interrogated by NYPD detectives and prosecutors over periods of fourteen to twenty-eight hours, Antron McCray's father (yes, he had a father who was present, a mechanic; his mother, a day care worker) threw a chair across the room because his son insisted on his innocence. The dad demanded that his son tell the police what they wanted to hear. Antron, age fifteen, confessed to holding the jogger's arms while others raped her and simulating sex "so everybody just know I did it." The other youngsters similarly confessed to kicking her, fondling her breasts, or beating her with a pipe. None admitted to having personally committed the rape but, one by one, each incriminated the others.

Almost immediately, all five adolescents repudiated their confessions. They were tried and convicted of rape, sodomy, sexual abuse, riot, assault—one of attempted murder— and sent to prison. The victim testified at the trials, but had no memory of the attack. There was *NO forensic evidence* linking any of them to the assault: no blood, no semen, no flesh, no DNA evidence. (The prosecution asserted that Richardson's clothing had hair Consistent with the jogger's; this was later discredited.) The blood-soaked victim, the semen found inside her and on her sock, produced no match to any of the five boys. But there were the videotaped confessions. Period.

It was Black and white, male and female: Wall Street v. Harlem, Law-Abiding Adults v. Barbaric Youth, Heroic Woman v. Feral Beasts, the Establishment v. Black Teens, Order v. Terror, Human v. Animal, Thoughtful v. Mindless.

The Central Park jogger case had immediate and rippling consequences far beyond the agonies of the youth accused. The death penalty was reinstated in New York state after Donald Trump—in full-page ads for which he paid $85,000—called for the death penalty for the five young defendants. "They should be forced to suffer.... "I want them to be afraid." The case became the catalyst for a decade of violent youth *superpredator* reporting, harsh sentencing statutes across the country, and widespread transferring of juvenile offenders into adult criminal court. The case became the poster child for a new wave of mobilized white popular fear of youth of color. Child advocates called the wave the *criminalization of youth*. It both escalated and transformed the landscape of child arrests, incarceration, stigmatization, and demonization—in the process reconfiguring youth (in) justice. It served as a catalyst for what would be known as the school-to-prison pipeline, especially for children of color.

But there would be another confession, thirteen years later. This confession came in a letter to the district attorney of Manhattan, Robert Morgenthau. It was written from New York state prison by Matias Reyes, a thirty-one-year-old serial rapist convicted for multiple rapes and a murder. His MO was gouging out the eyes of his rape victims. Reyes raped a woman on April 17, 1987, just two days before the Central Park jogger rape and assault—a rape crime that went unreported to the defense in the youths' trials in 1989. Reyes underwent a religious conversion in prison (where he briefly saw one of the defendants, young Kharey Wise) and wrote a letter confessing that he was the sole perpetrator of the Central Park jogger rape and assault. Reyes's confession was backed up by DNA evidence. Bedlam.

District Attorney Robert Morgenthau undertook a year-long investigation, pursuing prosecution and police theories that somehow the five convicted youth (now men) were connected to Reyes, or participated in the crime with him, or came along previously and assaulted her, or arrived subsequently and again raped or beat her. The police insisted on their original story. The two women prosecutors, Elizabeth Lederer and Linda Fairstein (Fairstein became a prominent sex crimes prosecutor for whom this was a career case), stuck to their version of the youths' guilt.

To the credit of Morgenthau's office, the fifty-eight-page report itemized the problems: "The gruesome details were often wildly inaccurate and inconsistent about who initiated the attack, who knocked the victim down, who undressed her, who struck her, who held her, who raped her, what weapons were used in the course of the assault." The conclusion was cogent and piercing: The verdicts should be set aside, based on the new confession, new DNA evidence, and "troubling discrepancies." The State Supreme Court agreed on December 19, 2003. The five young men had collectively served over forty years in prison and were listed on sex crime registries.

Antron McCray: Fifteen years old, ninth grade
Convicted of rape and assault
Sentenced: Five-ten years
Served: Six years

Kevin Richardson: Fourteen years old
Convicted of attempted murder, rape, sodomy, and robbery
Sentenced: Five-ten years
Served: Six years and six months

Salaam Yusef: Fifteen years old
Convicted of rape and assault
Sentenced: Five-ten years
Served: Six years and six months
(refused to express remorse)

Raymond Santana: Fourteen years old
Convicted of rape and assault
Sentenced: Five-ten years
Served: Eight years

Kharey Wise: Sixteen years old, second-grade reading level
Convicted of assault, sexual abuse, and riot
Sentenced: Five-fifteen years
Served: Eleven years and six months

How can their subsequent civil damage cases repair the loss of their childhoods, undo their notoriety, give back their years in prison? What would compensate their being treated as raging monsters rather than as precious adolescents? Would civil damages begin to relieve the consequences of their incarceration in adult prisons?

It is worth remembering that this paradigmatic case of juvenile violence turned out to be, as is the vast majority of violent crime in America, a case of adult violence. The five youngsters, none of whom had prior records of violence, were never described as children or as students—by the media, the prosecutors, the court. Age was not an element of their identities once they were characterized by white America as violent, as superpredators, as rapists. In contrast, when thirty white teens in Bensonhurst,

Brooklyn cornered sixteen-year-old Yusef Hawkin s and shot him to death, the defendants were referred to as "white young men" and "a gang of thirty white teens" by the New York and national media. There were no references to bloodthirsty teens, youth without fathers, Black enemies, ultra-violence, or coming from a world of indifference and ignorance. Mayor Koch referred to the murder of Yusef Hawkins, which took place during the trials of the five Central Park defendants, as an "enormous tragedy."

This classic case of the wrongful conviction of juveniles is not a typical case of children in conflict with the law. It is unlikely that most of the 1.2 million children petitioned into juvenile courts across the country each year are innocent of all wrongdoing. In fact, two of the five Central Park defendants were part of a group of youth arrested for harassing and assaulting joggers and cyclists earlier that fateful evening, up at 102nd Street and Central Park West. But scholars like Steven Drizin propose that wrongful convictions may also be prevalent in more routine cases and that juvenile defendants are at special risk of wrongful convictions. The five youth accused in the Central Park jogger case were not rapists, they did not attempt murder. They attended good schools and had attentive parents. And the youth consistently maintained their innocence in prison although their stance repeatedly cost them earlier parole releases.

Yusef Salaam, fifteen, at his September 1990 sentencing hearing told the court: "I look upon this legal lynching as a test by my God, Allah... Sooner or later, the truth will come out." Indeed, his arrest, interrogation, confession and trial carried echoes of the bitter legacy of lynching of thousands of young Black men. And for those historic crimes—in which African Americans were stripped, burned, castrated, beaten, *tortured* and hung, there was almost total impunity—no one was ever prosecuted or convicted. In the eyes of the media, the Central Park jogger youths were not only rapists, they were fools; the *New York Post* headline the day after Salaam's court statement about legal lynching read: *"SALAAM BALONEY."*

***

I teach a law school seminar on torture each year. It opens with the testimony of Chilean torture survivors and a class trip to the exhibit "Without Sanctuary: Photographs and Postcards of Lynching in America." It is an unbearable excursion, a crossing that confronts the viewer with the actual juxtaposition of slow, savage pain inflicted on the body of one person by another—and the celebratory ecstasy of a crowd of white men and women. Torture is not a word generally used to describe the homegrown North American practice of lynching. But the photographs do not lie.

The outstanding Chicago painter Kerry James Marshall captured the genteel bestiality of the lynch mob in his magnificent painting of three quintessentially innocent-looking Midwestern white women. His is a large painting, and the women are young, with bobbed hair, confidently and beatifically smiling at the camera, their pictures set sweetly in lockets. Moving through the gallery of Marshall's work, one wonders why this painting is hung in his exhibit of African American life. A closer look tells the story: The women's portraits are telescoped out from a large group posing in front of the tortured, mutilated, and lynched bodies of Thomas Shipp and Abram Smith in August 1930 in Marion, Indiana.

The six decades that followed the end of Reconstruction and the withdrawal of federal troops from the slave South was an era of terror and collective mass murder directed against the new citizens and former slaves—conducted through a complex interplay of both official policy and extra-legal violence. The patterns of legal complicity and vigilante/paramilitary violence would come to characterize the next century of African American subjugation and resistance, and influence contemporary criminal law, juvenile law, the prison enterprise, and law enforcement.

To the white population that celebrated lynchings with festivals and postcard souvenirs which sold by the thousands for 50¢, it was crime control. The terrible crime, the quick identification of a Black culprit, the certainty of law enforcement, the racialized frenzy of the media coverage, the identification of the alleged perpetrators as animals (wolf pack, beasts), as disease (vermin, plague, epidemic), as other than fully human—these footprints defined the era of de facto segregation and also moved North during the great Black migrations. Social control and punishment of the Black community became part of the fabric of Northern criminal justice: curfew and loitering laws, disorderly conduct prosecutions, police violence.

It is a bizarre irony that five Southern state legislatures have officially apologized for slavery in the opening years of the twenty-first century. Racism and sexual violence, the lethal blend of slavery and its aftermath, this story had been written on plantations in the slave South and in cities in the urban North, documented in souvenir photographs taken by white spectators and turned into postcards, thousands of lynchings, the Scottsboro trial, *Black Boy*, the murder of Emmett Till. In this context, the apologies and restitution take a long time. We have not yet begun to account for the Central Park jogger case and the tidal-wave acceptance of its slimy and violent archetypes.

***

In the wake of the jogger convictions and the disappearance of the young men into New York State's prison gulag, a trio of highly regarded criminologists, sociologists, and academics escalated their agitation about youth violence. John DiIulio, James Q. Wilson, and James Fox made themselves the Daniel Patrick Moynihans of the 1990s. (Moynihan wrote about the pathology and the matriarchy of the Black family in the 1960s.) DiIulio warned citizens that we were facing a rash of youth crime by kids who had absolutely no respect for human life. He projected a demographic crime bomb, where ever-growing numbers of hardened, remorseless juveniles would kill or maim on impulse, without any intelligible motive. He warned, writing in 1995, of a sharp, cataclysmic increase in youth crime and violence linked to the sharp increase in the number of super crime-prone young males. He claimed research and numbers. More boys begets more bad boys: By 2005, the number of fourteen to seventeen year olds will have risen 25 percent be predicted—for Blacks, 50 percent.

The provocative language of these academics drew upon and shadowed the old eugenics movement, where universities and biologists claimed to have scientific evidence linking African American physical characteristics with inferiority and criminal proclivities. Their rhetoric was inflammatory. They claimed to predict with confidence, in 1995, that an additional five hundred thousand boys by 2000 would mean at least thirty thousand more murderers, rapists, and muggers. They warned that each generation of crime-prone boys is "three times as dangerous" as the one before it. The use of numbers and claims to research created its own truth. The nightly media hype of violent youth crime seemed to verify the predictions. Oddly, and importantly, youth crime was plummeting as these scholars wrote. Across the board, youth crime—violent and nonviolent, murders and childish mayhem—declined precipitously from 1994 into the new century and millennium.

Other scholars, Franklin Zimring most decisively, dissected and destroyed their numbers, their research claims, their assumptions, their putative facts. But the icon of the "superpredator" was shaped and stamped on the public consciousness, stoked by media ratings, and seized upon by reactionary politicians, rabid prosecutors, willing politicians, and fearful communities. It led to a decade of the criminalization of youth. And the icon was all about race, power, crime, and white supremacy. "We're not just talking about teenagers," wrote John DiIulio:

> "We're talking about boys whose voices have yet to change. We're talking about elementary school youngsters who pack guns instead of lunches. We're talking about kids who have absolutely no respect for human life and no sense of the future. In short, we're talking big trouble that hasn't yet begun to crest... And make no mistake. While the trouble will be greatest in black inner-city neighborhoods, other places are also certain to have burgeoning youth-crime problems that will spill over into upscale central-city districts, inner-ring suburbs, and even the rural

heartland...All of the research indicates that Americans are sitting atop a demographic crime bomb. And all of those who are closest to the problem hear the bomb ticking."

"So long as their youthful energies hold out, they will do what comes 'naturally': murder, rape, rob, assault, burglarize, deal deadly drugs, and get high." "They," of course, is "them": African American children. "Growing up surrounded by deviant, delinquent, and criminal adults in abusive, violence-ridden, fatherless, godless and jobless settings... [They are] most likely to become criminally depraved when they are morally deprived."

DiIulio's notion of moral depravity or moral poverty in the Black community and his racist portrayal of the African American manchild rather speaks for itself. Writing as a pillar of white rectitude (no moral poverty among the privileged and the powerful whites), wrapped in the shroud of religion as the only answer (presumably Christianity), DeIulio saw "others" in the United States as breeders, drowning the white population in a sea of people of color. He forecast an impending tidal wave of tiny muggers, killers, and thieves, and urged law enforcement and the public to get ready.

Their predictions were wrong. Dead wrong. Too late, too little, DiIulio partially recanted. Juvenile (and adult) crime rates, including violent crime, declined from 1994 through 2005, across the board, reaching the lowest levels in thirty years. Crime rates and demographics are not congruent—to have any meaning populations must be looked at over time, backward as well as forward. Youth, as a proportion of the population as a whole, rises and falls without determining crime rates. The rates of youth violence increased in the late 1980s, as the youth population declined, and declined after 1993 as the youth population grew.

The racial demographics, the core of the argument that there was an impending "invasion of the barbarians," were not as the academic trio claimed: African American youth, as a proportion of the population of the U.S. as a whole, would just keep pace with the growth of the youth population. Latino youth constituted the growth story: In 1970, they constituted 5.7 percent of the youth population; by 2010, they would be 16.9 percent, a tripling in forty years. But population itself is simply not the big story on youth crime, and it is a notoriously unreliable predictor. So overall there would be no extreme youth population bulge, youth crime would decline across the period of the imagined demographic crime bomb. Yet African American youth would become and remain the icon of "remorseless, violent superpredators," and massive industries of control, caging, and crushing would thrive.

So the role of the professors was consequential. In the pandemonium of the 1990s, just after the end of the Cold War and before the so-called War on Terror, fear of our young seemed to fill the need for a declared "enemy," incarceration became a growth industry, and the juggernaut to criminalize youth was on.

***

Normal adolescent behavior was criminalized—particularly for African American youngsters. Youthful play was made a crime. Adolescent school conduct, such as talking back, tardiness, pushing and shoving, minor scuffles and fights, graffiti, name-calling and minor theft, was suddenly punished, not with school or family consequences but as criminal deeds. Misbehavior, once the terrain of teachers, vice principals, neighbors, coaches, families and parents, now resulted in police being called, children being shackled, arrests being made. A handful of high-profile school shootings (by white boys) resulted in a national hysteria about the allegedly growing Black youth population—not about white crime, nor about high-caliber, semiautomatic, cheap weaponry available to kids—and became a justification for further criminalizing African American children. Once there was a declared enemy, there had to be places to contain them.

The criminalization of youth facilitated the criminalization of young (adult) men of color. The U.S. can lay claim to the world's largest reported prison population. The number of (adult) prisoners rose substantially (from 789,610 to 1,252,830 in the years 1991-1998), while crime fell 22 percent. Prisons, for adults and for juveniles, was about something else in addition to crime: social control, assault on the Black family, removal of a significant sector of the labor force, response to de-industrialization, a source of new indentured labor, an invisible reign of terror. A full 81 percent of those sentenced to incarceration in state prisons in 2000 were there for nonviolent crimes (35 percent for drug offenses, 28 percent property crimes). By the beginning of the new millennium, one in every eight Black men in their twenties was in prison or jail, and an astounding one in every three Black men in their twenties (827,440) was under criminal supervision (prison, jail, probation or parole). Imagine the national emergency if these numbers were about Irish men or Jewish men. Imagine if it were true for all blue-eyed young men.

Imprisonment in both detention and correctional facilities skyrocketed, distorting state budgets, drawing on federal funding streams for prison construction, creating jobs and unions that then resist demobilization. Small towns across North America suddenly kept their young (white) children home because there were jobs as prison guards. Prison populations were counted in census data, inflating the revenue streams to these localities. Prisoners were, however, largely disenfranchised—denied the vote while incarcerated and often during parole and too often forever. Prisons were constructed far from the homes and families of inmates, even in the case of juvenile correctional facilities. Children and families suffer mutual exile—disconnected from visits and regular communication.

The false orchestration of a youth crime panic does not mean there was no problem. The sudden availability of cheap, high caliber, lethal handguns surely contributed to a sudden tripling of the juvenile homicide rate between 1986 and 1993. African American youth were the major victims of homicides and shootings (of the eight million new firearms manufactured each year around the world, more than half are purchased in the U.S.). New patterns of street drug trafficking and the export of industrial and entry-level jobs had a further impact on youth crime. The erosion of public schools, exclusion policies of zero tolerance, and unequal funding of education resulted in more teens out of school and out of work. Communities of color themselves wanted safety—for their children and for adults. They wanted gangs out of their neighborhoods, gangs controlled by and led by adults. But African American and Latino/a adults, in asking for greater community safety, did not intend for their children to be unequally or unfairly punished, to be subjected to escalated charges, to be caged, to disappear.

Few areas of contemporary life illustrate the systemic nature of white supremacy more than juvenile justice. The face of children in conflict with the law in major urban areas today is the face of children of color. As the purposes of juvenile justice shifted in the two previous decades from rehabilitation to punishment, the color of those children who are in the system changed. In the world's first juvenile court, Chicago's juvenile court of Cook County, a volunteer attorney waiting to be assigned a delinquency case asked me, "Where is the *white* juvenile court?" Between 2002 and 2004, African Americans were:

- 16 percent of youth.
- 28 percent of juvenile arrests.
- 30 percent of referrals to juvenile court.
- 37 percent of youth in detention (pre-trial).
- 34 percent of youth formally processed by the juvenile court.
- 35 percent of youth judicially waived to adult criminal court.
- 38 percent of youth in residential placement (locked institution/corrections).
- 58 percent of youth admitted to state adult prison.

When the poorly documented statistics of Latino/a, Asian American, and Native American youth are added, the cumulative inequality with white youth is further exacerbated. Youth of color constitute:

- 34 percent of the youth population.
- 62 percent of youth in detention.
- 66 percent of youth in public youth institutions.
- 75 percent of youth admissions to adult prisons.

Two Systems of Youth Justice

Overall, the incarceration of African American youth is four times that of white youth. African American youngsters are overrepresented in twenty-six of twenty-nine juvenile offense categories.

There are several possible explanations for such extreme racial disproportion in juvenile justice: African American children commit more crimes; the system reflects wholesale institutional bias; policing deployment and surveillance are concentrated in low-income, urban neighborhoods; other child institutions (schools, health care, recreation, the job market) fail African American youth, leaving the criminal/juvenile justice system as the last resort; the juvenile and criminal justice industry functions as a vehicle of social control of potentially disruptive and troubling populations—it is doing what it intends to do. These explanations are not mutually exclusive, nor are they comprehensive.

There is solid evidence that youth of different races and ethnicities commit crimes as adolescents at a similar rate (with the exception of the serious but relatively rare cases of murder). Self-reported offense rates among youth of different races are surprisingly similar, given the extreme disparities of who is in the nation's locked juvenile facilities and prisons. White, Black and Latino/a youth all report getting into fights, carrying weapons, marijuana use, entering buildings without permission, and petty theft at near identical rates. However, in what may surprise some, white youth report significantly higher involvement in serious drug behavior.

There is further strong evidence that, holding steady for the offense, prior history of arrests, and age, racial discrimination persists at startling levels at every stage of the juvenile justice system.

One way I think of it is that we have two systems of justice for children: one public, punishing, crushing, and humiliating for children and families of color and one private, protective, effective, and confidential for white and resourced children and families. In the U.S., these two systems of justice for children in conflict with the law are visibly and incontrovertibly defined by race and class.

To a surprising degree, most young males, regardless of skin color, break the law during their adolescence. Most are allowed to "grow out of it," to recover, to develop and mature. Shoplifting, drugs, property destruction, fighting, curfews, auto theft—it is a rare boychild growing up in this culture who does not violate the law.

Our three sons were never arrested, but their friends were arrested for all the typical youth crimes, except the rare crime of murder: drug possession or sale, major theft, robbery, auto theft, sexual assault, larceny (shoplifting), criminal destruction of property, disorderly conduct. But these children with parents of some wealth are rarely confronted by the police, and if they are, they are driven home to parents who may seek a private solution. They will not go to juvenile or criminal court.

The few who do will plead guilty to an offense that will be expunged from their records. White and privileged youth may be placed in a hospital, a psychiatric unit, given therapy and meds, or enrolled in a drug treatment program. They may be sent to private school or military school or to relatives in another state. They may pay a fine or restitution and do community service. These private solutions are generally effective and should be available to all children.

The well-known remedies for adolescents who are getting into trouble is to remove them from the epicenter of the problem (other kids in trouble), to surround them with care and constraints, and to let them age out of it. The goal is to keep open as many doors as possible, and to keep the youngsters out of stigmatizing harm without a public record.

To understand the vast channeling of young children of color into the prison pipeline, a further factor that must be looked at is the so-called "War on Drugs." It is well known that white youth engage in the same or slightly more use and sale of illegal drugs and alcohol as Black youth. White youth between twelve – seventeen years of age are one-third more likely to have sold drugs than African American youth. White kids use both cocaine and heroin in significantly greater rates than African American youngsters. The youngsters locked up in the Juvenile Temporary Detention Center of Cook County ingest approximately the same illegal drugs and alcohol as do those in the entering class at Harvard.

Yet the consequences of boyish misbehavior expose the "white discount" —the other race card, if you will. Even when Black and white youth are arrested for the same drug offense, 75 percent of the arrested African American youth result in a formal juvenile court case, compared to 51 percent for white youth. White adolescents were 69 percent of the drug cases petitioned to court but only 58 percent of the cases transferred to adult criminal court; Black youth were 29 percent of the drug cases petitioned but 41 percent of those transferred to adult criminal court. Transfer to adult court has savage consequences, including mandatory adult sentencing, an adult criminal record, and greater exposure to violence.

The analysis of the prison industrial complex by Angela Davis became a catalyst for two decades of organizing and agitating about racism, incarceration, disenfranchisement, and the pervasive role of the gulag that characterizes every state landscape and budget. New generations of young activists have come of age and consciousness through their work with prisoners and against snake-pit prison conditions. By the time of the first Critical Resistance Conference in Berkeley in 1998, there was an extraordinary level of grassroots political resistance and organizing against the U.S. prison system, both from within and without. I spoke at that remarkable conference about the caging of children of color and about how some children are designated as delinquent, criminal, and superpredators, while others are deemed troubled, alienated, or mentally ill. The gathering exposed what had previously been invisible: the wide and deep level of organizing to support prisoners, the rank racism of incarceration (involving Native American children, Latino/a youth, and specific Asian populations), the gulag's decisive role in the economy, intolerable conditions of confinement, and the effort to silence and bury political prisoners. Since that moment a decade ago, organizing and activism about the imprisonment of youth have produced another generation of fresh activists and organizers.

***

The conditions of confinement for incarcerated children, whether detention (pre-trial) or corrections (post-conviction), range from gloomy to hideous. The rare exceptional model, like the Missouri youth corrections system or Washington, D.C.'s Department of Youth Rehabilitation Services only throws into sharp relief the degrading, monotonous, and humiliating conditions of most regimented youth prisons where the staff (with some exceptions) and the supervisors seem to be playing war games on confined children. These youth prisons have high-security razor wire and technological gear and video cameras. The children are shackled, chained, surveilled, punished with isolation, pepper spray and restraints. They are lined up, searched, and restrained, subjected to violence for every form of difference: gender, sexual identity, ethnicity, size, health, disability, mental health diagnoses. Teachers, doctors, visiting parents, attorney consultations, art, music, literature and recreation are rarely in evidence, let alone the heralded treatment, rehabilitation, or preparation for reentry and reintegration back into society. Juvenile correctional facilities are sites of endemic scandal, abuse, and violence against the children.

A fresh example is Texas Youth Commission. But before Texas, we could go to any state into what are variously called juvenile reformatories, youth care centers, juvenile training schools, boot camps, youth correctional facilities, or privately run, so-called "residential treatment centers." Georgia, Maryland, Colorado, California, New York—all have had recent scandals and documented reports about the violence, humiliation, and neglect that characterize their caging of kids. Texas convicts and incarcerates some 4,700 children between the ages of ten and twenty-one in their public correctional "schools." On April 2, 2004, a retired TYC official e-mailed the governor's office, documenting agency hires of sex offenders and asking for whistle-blower protection. An immediate Texas Ranger investigation resulted in a two hundred twenty-nine-page report, documenting graphic findings at the West Texas State School in Pyote. End of response.

Over a year later, an assistant supervisor and a principal left "in lieu of resignation." It was not until February 18, 2007, when *The Dallas Morning News* and *The Texas Observer* broke the scandal, that evidence of systemic physical violence and sexual assault and the coverup at the highest levels of state government came to light. Heads have rolled, two indictments were filed, the TYC was put under the control of a Special Master, and it was "discovered" that 111 adult TYC employees had felony arrests or convictions, 437 had misdemeanors. Some 800 children were released. After review of the sentences of 1,027 young "inmates" whose sentences were "extended" beyond their release date, 226 additional youth were released on parole. The cleanup and quiet resignations proceed with fresh scandals of unspeakable treatment of youth behind bars in Texas. The right to liberty of the young adolescents who survived under this system, the beatings and violations imposed on them, their mandated nighttime appearances in locked closets and offices with staff—these were invisible to all, even though it was well known or could have been known.

Meet Shaquanda Cotton, a fifteen-year-old African American girl who was arrested, tried, and convicted for pushing a hall monitor in her school in Paris, Texas. Shaquanda was tried and convicted, sent to TYC for an indeterminate sentence of up to seven years. Although eligible for release for good behavior, her sentence was extended in prison because she refused to admit her guilt, and because she was found with contraband in her cell—an extra pair of socks. Were it not for the widening TYC scandal, her case would have remained anonymous.

Like most other girls in the juvenile justice system designed for males, Shaquanda is confined for minor misbehavior, subject to disproportionate charges and incarceration as an African American girl, and additionally punished for defiance. Young women are only 25 percent of youth arrested and more than half of their arrests are for either status offenses (such as truancy, running away from home, curfew violations, or gendered offenses such as being unruly or incorrigible) or for larceny (shoplifting). However, the girls who are incarcerated have extensive histories as child victims of rape, sexual assault, sexual abuse and intimate partner or family physical violence. Their sexual behavior and sexual identities are scrutinized and punished, while their experiences of violation and violence are ignored or discounted and re-inflicted.

The Texas Youth Commission story is rarely described in its racial dimensions. But in Texas, the residential custody rates (per 100,000) of children by race tell a story:

Whites:	194
African Americans:	771
Latinos:	327
Native Americans:	138

Asian/Pacific Islanders: 18

In fairness to the South, similar conditions were exposed in the South Dakota Training School at Plankuiton when the Youth Law Center sued the state for a wrongful death in the 1990s. There, the "overrepresentation" of youth of color was beyond extreme:

Whites:	310
African Americans:	3,199
Latinos:	1,499
Native Americans:	1,575
Asian/Pacific Islanders:	873

More devastating than these conditions of juvenile correctional facilities are the circumstances of children confined in adult prisons. Equally shocking and even more harmful are the consequences of children being incarcerated with adults, in adult prisons. Children of color are also much more likely than white youth to be incarcerated in adult prison. Twenty-six out of every 100,000 African American youth are serving time in adult prison while for white youth the rate is only 2.2 per 100,000. On a state-by-state basis, these disparities are magnified.

One can only conclude that white youth do not break the law, or that there is a secret, privileged passageway into another system when they do.

The parallel overcrowding and misuse of pre-trial juvenile detention has been well documented and the subject of a national campaign by the Juvenile Detention Alternatives Initiative (JDAI) of the Annie E. Casey Foundation and the W. Haywood Burns Institute. In this unprecedented effort to reduce both juvenile detention populations and the disproportionate detention of African Americans and other youth of color, it has become clear that there are effective techniques for monitoring, for using more objective criteria for detention, and for creating alternatives to detention to assure that the youth will appear at trial and do not re-offend.

James Bell, director of the Burns Institute, argues that "a key component of reducing racial disparities is the use of effective, culturally appropriate neighborhood programming that primarily serves communities of color." These efforts have engaged thousands of community members, youth activists, and juvenile justice personnel and resulted in numerous sustained reductions of detention populations in Chicago, Portland, Santa Cruz, and smaller jurisdictions. The excitement of JDAI and Burns is their assumptions that caging kids is bad, most often unnecessary poor policy, destructive, and expensive, and that the explosion of detaining youngsters falls most heavily on youth of color. Quite simply, James Bell says, "No child's race or place of residence should unfairly determine their life outcomes."

***

Fast forward twenty years from the Central Park jogger case to the infamous case of the Jena 6. We can leapfrog over the intermediate roll call of iconic, notorious juvenile crime cases: Yummy Sandifer, Nathanial Abrahmson, Lionnel Tate, Kip Kinkle, Nathanial Brazil, Eric Harris, Dylan Klebold, the two tiny boys accused of murdering fourteen-year-old Ryan Harris, Lee Boyd Malvo. Cumulatively they resulted in harsh, "adultified" social and legal policies: 250,000 children each year tried as adults (240,000 of them because of a lower age of adult, state criminal jurisdiction), mandatory sentencing/blended sentencing/extended juvenile jurisdiction; life without possibility of parole sentencing for 2,373 juvenile offenders in the U.S.; incarceration; in adult prisons and jails; more detention, more incarceration, longer incarceration, juvenile sex offender registries; an explosion of girl arrests; zero tolerance rather than tolerance; the construction of the school to prison pipeline; gang terrorism laws, gang databases; and the deportation of immigrant children, to name a few.

The arrest of six African American students in Jena, Louisiana, on charges of attempted murder and conspiracy illustrates in dramatic form what has become the common practice across the U.S. the arrest of Black students with escalated charges for school misbehavior, the failure to charge white students for similar behavior, and the trial and sentencing of students of color in adult criminal court. And yet, because the mobilization and organizing to bring justice to the Jena 6 reaches national proportions, I dare to hope that the Jena 6 case also illustrates an innovative movement for equal justice for children, a social force that represents a newly strengthened coalition, a justice movement that demands equal treatment for all children.

The core facts are not disputed. In August 2006, an African American student asked the principal during a Jena High School assembly if he could sit under an oak tree outside the school known as a "white tree" because only white students gathered there. He was told he could, and he and several friends went to the tree. The next day, someone hung several nooses from the tree, conjuring up the hundred-year history of lynching. School officials identified three white students as the perpetrators and the principal recommended school expulsion. He was overruled by a school superintendent who imposed only suspensions. Student fights and provocations in and outside the school escalated through the fall, and in

December 2006, a white student, Justin Barker, was hit and briefly knocked unconscious by a Black student and kicked while down. Justin was hospitalized, treated for cuts and bruises, and released within hours. Police then arrested six Black students, aged fourteen to eighteen, and the local prosecutor, Reed Walters, charged them with attempted second degree murder and conspiracy. Those charged in adult criminal court were subject to sentences of up to seventy-five years in prison.

In June, an all, white jury convicted Mychal Bell, sixteen years old at the time of the assault, of reduced charges of aggravated second degree battery, agreeing with the prosecutor that Bell's tennis shoes were "dangerous weapons." Bell faced the possibility of up to twenty-two years in prison. His court-appointed attorney (himself African American) put in no evidence, called no witnesses, and failed to challenge the racial composition of the jury. Bell served ten months as the case gathered national attention. In the face of an unprecedented campaign waged by parents, color of justice organizers, a single independent black radio station announcer (Michael Baisden), and students at the historically black colleges, the Jena 6 case became known through the Internet and the mass media. President Bush was asked about the Black Jena 6 students at a press conference. A national demonstration of fifteen thousand people converged on tiny Jena (pop. 3,000), sparked by ordinary people. A defensive *New York Times* op-ed by District Attorney Reed Walters was unconvincing. Mychal Bell's charges have been overturned, he was remanded to juvenile court, rather than adult criminal court, for retrial. Days before the retrial, on December 3, 2007, Bell pled guilty to a reduced sentence of eighteen months in a juvenile facility with credit for time served. The other defendants are awaiting trial.

In response, a notable white backlash was made visible, with nooses appearing across the country as a revived symbol of white supremacy.

Historian Adam Green notes that the Black parents of the Jena 6 have not asked that the white students who hung the nooses be criminally prosecuted, or that what happened to their children should happen to the white students. They simply want for their children the mild rebuke and decriminalized response that the white students received. The Jena 6 case signals a new hope: mobilizing people of color and their allies, in communities, to insist that their youth be treated fairly, equally and with full human rights, and to challenge the systematic deployment of youngsters into the destructive machinery of the dual oxymorons—the juvenile justice and criminal justice systems.

In an act of bizarre denial by the adults involved, the city of Jena cut down the oak tree.

***

On the occasion of the 100th anniversary of the Emancipation Proclamation, James Baldwin wrote a letter to his young nephew. "Now my dear namesake," he wrote, "these innocent and well meaning people, your countrymen, have caused you to be born under conditions not very far removed from those described for us by Charles Dickens in the London of more than one hundred years ago...By a terrible law, a terrible paradox, those innocents who believed that your imprisonment made them safe are losing their grip of reality."

So what has been accomplished in the two decades between the Central Park jogger case and the Jena 6? My partial list of partial victories includes:

- The emergence of bold movements of formerly incarcerated youth, speaking up for themselves and their peers, such as the Center for Young Women's Development in San Francisco, the Youth Justice Coalition in Los Angeles, and the Community Justice Network for Youth of the Burns Institute.

The Center for Young Women's Development is run and led entirely by young women who have been incarcerated and/or been street workers. CYWD has created girls-run empowerment programs, where young women from every housing project, from every gang turf, from every group home and jail cell around San Francisco are creating transformative changes for themselves, their families, and communities. Marlene Sanchez, the director, says:

> "Having come to The Center for Young Women's Development nearly ten years ago seeking refuge and self-determination, I experienced the breadth, power, and promise of The Center's amazing work. I am one of the hundreds of young sisters that CYWD has trained, employed, and loved—and there is no stopping us now!"

- The formation and mobilization of the National Juvenile Defender Center, creating a field of zealous legal practice on behalf of children and adolescents.

- *Roper v. Simmons*, a Supreme Court victory abolishing the execution of juvenile offenders in the U.S. as a violation of the Eighth Amendment's prohibition against cruel and unusual punishment, and holding that children are "categorically less culpable" than adults.

- The practice and spread of the Juvenile Detention Alternatives Initiative (JDAI) by the Annie E. Casey Foundation, reducing juvenile detention across more than one hundred jurisdictions.

- The exposure of widespread false confessions by children and adolescents due to coercive interrogations by police authorities. Steven Drizin has won legal victories overturning juvenile convictions based on false confessions, and conducted research showing that 33 percent of the 125 documented cases of false confessions involve juveniles.

- The recognition of human rights standards across the field of juvenile justice, bolstered by the discussion of international law by the U.S. Supreme Court in *Roper v. Simmons*, the case that abolished the execution of juvenile offenders.

- The Burns Institute model of reducing discriminatory arrest, prosecution, detention, and incarceration of African American youth and children of color, mobilizing system professionals and communities to identify, transform, and monitor unequal practices.

- The campaigns against the discriminatory treatment of girls in juvenile justice, particularly African American girls and young women of color, and the development of gender-specific efforts to address their real needs.

- The rollback of discriminatory drug laws in Illinois that transferred African American youth to adult criminal court; Passage of legislation raising the age of juvenile court jurisdiction to eighteen years of age in Connecticut.

- The impact of Families and Friends of Louisiana's Incarcerated Children (FFLIC), a parent-led, grassroots advocacy force that shut down the scandalous for-profit Tallulah juvenile prison and sparked passage of an enlightened juvenile justice statute;

- The development of balanced and restorative justice models as an alternative to juvenile court processing and as sentencing options, such as Community Justice for Youth Institute, peer juries, and circles.

- Documentation and advocacy for LGBT youth who suffer extreme violence and abusive treatment in the justice system; Brilliant work with gang kids and former gang members, especially across California: Homies Unidos, Tia Chucha, Homeboys Industries.

- The renewed engagement of professionals and communities in the once isolated and taboo world of justice for the child. Such involvement includes doctors, teachers, brain imaging researchers, developmental psychologists, child poverty and child health activists, parents, and youth themselves.

• Grassroots organizations across the country, like Books Not Bars, Friends of Island Academy, and the Southwest Youth Coalition. And tons of too often unheralded local work by heroic probation officers, judges, prosecutors, teachers, reporters, public defenders, social workers, law students, and parents.

What are our major challenges? First, the larger context of child poverty and racial discrimination underlies the workings of justice in the wealthiest country in human history. A change in that set of priorities would transform the work of fighting for justice for children in conflict with the law. Second, juvenile justice is the child part of America's addiction to incarceration. Over 2.1 million people in prison or jail on a given day is both a framework that cannot be sustained and a sorrowful expression of the racial/class divide. So within that uneasy framework, those fighting white supremacy and for equal justice have a unique role to play. The major challenges are:

1. To release the vast majority of children behind bars to safe, effective, community alternatives to detention and incarceration.

2. To immediately abolish the incarceration of children with adults and to roll back the transfer of children into adult criminal court and the legal transformation of children—some children—into adults.

3. To utilize the tools of balanced and restorative justice to keep youngsters *out* of the juvenile and criminal justice systems, appropriately sanctioned in communities with the tools, institutions, and support to develop their strengths and their passions in ways that tap into their brilliance.

4. To give children their right to zealous, competent counsel   once they are in conflict with the law and their liberty and futures are in jeopardy.

Now is the time. As the great poet Gwendolyn Brooks wrote:

> Seize the little moment
> Be it gash or gold
> For it will not come again
> In this identical disguise.

SCHOOL AND SOCIETY

Bill Ayers

When you control a man's thinking you do not have to worry about his actions. You do not have to tell him to stand here or go yonder. He will find his "proper place" and will stay in it. You do not need to send him to the back door. He will go without being told. In fact, if there is no back door, he will cut one for his special benefit. His education makes it necessary.

—Carter G. Woodson

On October 26, 1992, the U.S. Congress designated Monroe Elementary School, one of the segregated Black schools in Topeka, Kansas, a National Historic Site because of its significance in the famous case of *Brown v. Board of Education*. The National Archives include several documents from the case in its digital classroom. Monroe Elementary is a living museum.

Brown v. Board of Education, the 1954 Supreme Court decision that overturned the "separate but equal" doctrine and heralded the legal termination of racially segregated schools, has become an icon in the popular story America tells itself about its flawless goodness and its inevitable upward trajectory. America the Beautiful, *Brown* as icon. The whole country seems as devoted to *Brown*, myth or symbol, as it is dedicated to Superman's motto: "Truth, Justice, and the American Way."

Brown occurred in the wake of World War II, in the wash of that reenergized sense of freedom. The decision followed incessant and increasingly intense demands by African Americans that the country live up to the promise of the Fourteenth Amendment. And, importantly, *Brown* coincided with clear white interests that had nothing to do with Black well-being: avoiding a revolution led and defined by subjugated African Americans; transforming the feudal South and integrating it into a repositioned capitalist juggernaut; removing a blatant and embarrassing fact of American life that was being effectively wielded against the U.S. in the escalating Cold War. White power needed *Brown*—but only a bit of *Brown*.

Brown was the result of relentless action and activism from below, and we see a long line that continues up through the present. Whenever I read an account that begins with something like, "As a result of *Brown*, America experienced a wave of activism for justice...," I want to offer an amendment: "As a result of a wave of activism for justice, America got *Brown*..." In any case, today, more than fifty years later, it's important to note that the promise of *Brown* was not simply about ending segregation in public schools. The promise, rather, rested on a profoundly democratic aspiration—that all individuals will receive equal education and opportunity, and that each will be afforded full dignity and equal respect. The most radical possibilities of *Brown* are that the country might recognize Black people's full humanity, their complete membership in the nation. Ralph Ellison wrote at the time that "the court has found in our favor and recognized our human psychological complexity and citizenship and another battle of the Civil War has been won." Another battle won, perhaps, but not necessarily the last.

The language of *Brown* includes the language of justice. It repudiates racial segregation and says—correctly—that separate is inherently unequal. It affirms the full humanity of African Americans. It endorses core principles of democracy. It cries out for equality.

To take *Brown* to heart would require a hard look at the racial reality we inhabit—a system with institutions operating at every level to construct a false concept of white superiority and Black inferiority, and to deny full participation in social and political and economic life to Black people. The hard look would hopefully lead to an iron commitment, then, to smash the institution of white supremacy. No such luck—yet.

Brown embodies a fundamental, even a fatal, flaw that also runs deep in the American racial narrative. The argument in the case turns on the specific harm suffered by Black children and the feelings of inferiority that are a result of segregation, rather than the despicable, immoral, and destructive system of white supremacy itself. Black people—not racism—were the acknowledged concern; Black pathology, however, not white privilege became the focus of action.

And so *Brown*, the widely celebrated and lofty statement of principle, was followed immediately by its lesser-known brother, the betrayer and assassin, *Brown II. Brown II* was the implementation, or remedy phase, of the decision, and here again—consistent with the long tradition of all things racial—the remedy fit neither the crime nor the injury. In fact *Brown II* gave the local school districts, the parties defeated in *Brown*, the power and responsibility to construct the solution—to desegregate their schools *"with all deliberate speed."* The fox—far from being banished from the hen house—was given the only set of keys.

The Supreme Court had never in history issued an order to implement a constitutional right that was so damnably vague. The Court made clear, according to Lew Steel, a civil rights lawyer, that it "would protect the interests of white America in the maintenance of stable institutions" and that it "considered the potential damage to white Americans resulting from the diminution of privilege as more critical than continued damage to the underprivileged."

"With all deliberate speed" turned out to mean "never." The activity in the courts over the decades following *Brown* went decidedly South: Racially isolated Black communities were denied the right to draw students from adjoining white suburbs, children were denied the right to equal school funding, the concept of "neighborhood school" was reinforced and reified even if the result was resegregation. On and on. On June 28, 2007, the Supreme Court virtually reversed *Brown* and ruled against *voluntary* desegregation plans in Seattle and Louisville in which race was only one of several factors used to maintain a diverse student body in public schools. More than half a century after *Brown*, school segregation is alive and well, more firmly entrenched than ever, and each year schools are more racially divided. *Brown* is all but dead.

As usual, white supremacy is hiding in plain sight. The most dissembling hypocrites argue that anyone who sees race is a racist, that race-conscious integration is the equivalent of Black-hating segregation—because both are based on skin color. This is an invented and wholly fictitious symmetry that removes from the equation the problem of power. Who decides? Who controls? Who is left powerless? The difficulty in America is not and has never been race consciousness *per se*; the problem has always been white supremacy *in fact*. Anything that undermines white supremacy and fights for inclusion and equality sides with humanity; anything that excludes, segregates, subordinates is on the side of oppression and exploitation. And so, using the lofty language of *Brown*, ordinary white supremacists continue to herd Black children into unnatural, chronically underfunded, and inferior schools, build ever higher walls, and lock the gates. Savage inequalities.

Monroe Elementary—that iconic temple in Topeka elevated as a National Historic Site—may as well be turned from a museum into a mausoleum: Here is one more place where African American aspirations and struggles for decent and equal education were laid to rest.

***

When Rudyard Kipling, Great Britain's celebrated imperial poet, wrote his famous poem "The White Man's Burden" in 1899—written in solidarity with his white brethren in response to the U.S. takeover of the Philippines from Spain—he was popularizing a view that, beyond conquest, theft, stolen labor, and wealth, empire was at its heart a project of righteousness, that old and convenient mission into the wilderness to help the savages. Further, the beneficent, well-meaning whites must understand that the sullen, half-devil heathens will never fully comprehend or appreciate their sacrifices and that white folks would just have to man-up and recognize that only other whites would ever really understand the good they'd done:

> Take up the White Man's burden—
> Send forth the best ye breed—
> Go bind your sons to exile
> To serve your captives' need;
> To wait in heavy harness,
> On fluttered folk and wild—
> Your new-caught, sullen peoples,
> Half-devil and half-child.

On and on, for six more stanzas, each a catalogue of the generosity and beneficence and thankless efforts of the whites. This was the popular view, and even those who opposed imperialism rarely challenged those foundational white supremacist assumptions. Racial purification was the order of the day. Africans were seen as a separate species, living fossils, and a link between humans and apes. Lathrop Stoddard authored two influential texts, *The Revolt Against Civilization: The Menace of the Underman* and *The Rising Tide of Color: Against White World Supremacy* with an introduction by Madison Grant, head of the Bronx Zoo and the American Zoological Society. Stoddard argued that "it is this prodigious spawning of inferiors which must at all costs be prevented if society is to be saved from disruption and dissolution. Race cleansing is apparently the only thing that can stop it. Therefore, race cleansing must be our first concern."

Eugenics was both accepted science—the systematic study of racial hierarchy favoring "Nordic superiority"—and a popular movement justifying white supremacy. Eugenics ideology explained racial and class inequities in terms of innate ability and heredity, it encouraged white workers to see their solidarity with wealthy whites and not with Black workers, and this explanation elided comfortably with traditional assumptions among white people concerning their own superiority. It also carried the gloss of modern science—forward-looking and irrefutable—and so it was a brilliant and convenient marriage of tradition and modernity.

Invented in the U.S., eugenics developed in collaboration with American wealth and power, and was exported to, among other destinations, Germany, where Hitler enacted its clearest organized expression in the Holocaust. The *Official Handbook for Schooling of Hitler Youth*, published in 1937, acknowledged eugenics as progenitor and defined race as "a collection of individuals differentiated from every other group ... by its unique combination of bodily characteristics and soul attributes and continually reproduces its own kind." What distinguished the Nordic race? "It is uncommonly gifted mentally. It is outstanding for truthfulness and energy."

Eugenics introduces a central paradox: A nation founded on the ideal that "all are created equal" became obsessed—and the obsession is still with us—with the drive to find a scientific basis for human inequality. The authors of that founding principle could not and did not believe that there were no differences among human beings; rather they encoded a moral principle—the solidarity of humanity, *equality*—as an end to aspire to, as well as a means of dealing with the challenges of human difference. They were stating that despite differences, in the arena of law and politics we must be treated as equals; further, they argued, there is some core essence of personhood that must be acknowledged in every human being. Of course slavery sat outside the door, a dagger at the heart of the new democracy.

The eugenics movement was another dagger—extraordinarily active in promoting segregation, restrictive immigration policies, forced sterilization and regulation of reproduction, marriage restriction, and institutionalization in the land of "all are created equal." And it was wildly successful. Involuntary sterilization laws designed to weed out "defective strains," including the "feeble-minded," epileptics, paupers, alcoholics, delinquents, prison inmates, and the sexually deviant, among others, were passed in more than thirty states and affected a majority of Americans into the 1970s. California led the nation with 20,000 sterilizations, and North Carolina, third with 8,000, performed 80 percent of its sterilizations from 1945 - 1974. Harry Laughlin, who was a leading proponent and was honored by the German government in the 1930s as they modeled their own eugenic sterilization laws after those in the U.S., defined "socially inadequate classes" as:

> (1) Feeble-minded (including the mentally backward). (2) Insane (including the neurotic and psychopathic). (3) Criminalistic (including the delinquent and wayward). (4) Epileptic. (5) Inebriate (including drug habitués). (6) Diseased (including tuberculous, the syphilitic, the leprous, and others with chronic, infectious segregated diseases). (7) Blind (including those with greatly impaired vision).(8) Deaf (including those with greatly impaired hearing). (9) Crippled (including the deformed and ruptured). (10) Dependent (including orphans, old folks, soldiers and sailors in homes and institutions).

Eugenics fingerprints are all over the Progressive Era, when a range of activists campaigned for a wide array of reforms, each of which could comfortably embrace a eugenics goal. Here is Margaret Sanger, properly hailed by feminists for her early work on women's right to birth control:

> Everywhere we see poverty and large families going hand in hand. Those least fit to carry on the race are increasing most rapidly. People who cannot support their own offspring are encouraged by Church and State to produce large families. Many of the children thus begotten are diseased or feeble-minded; many become criminals. The burden of supporting these unwanted types has to be borne by the healthy elements of the nation. Funds that should be used to raise the standard of our civilization are diverted to the maintenance of those who should have never been born.

Immigration reform ran along a parallel track. A headline from the *Boston Sunday Herald*, June 26, 1921, announced:

DANGER THAT WORLD SCUM WILL DEMORALIZE AMERICA
If We Don't Do Something About Immigration
We Shall Have a Mongrelized America

In the first half of the twentieth century, close to four hundred colleges and universities offered courses in eugenics, including Harvard and Columbia, Cornell and Brown, Northwestern and Wisconsin. These courses were based on "the science of improvement of the human germ plasm through better breeding." High school textbooks—87 percent of science texts offered eugenics as a topic—presented the science of eugenics as straightforward and sensible. And all of it helped to prop up popular mass campaigns against immigration, for sterilization and institutionalization, and in favor of marriage as a procreational responsibility toward "fitter families."

Compulsory schooling would make all youngsters visible and sortable, training them to take their suitable and destined place in society. Categorization of individuals and groups, whatever the rhetoric, justifies and normalizes existing relations, and it always has. Teachers were pressed into the service of testing—Intelligence Quotient tests were a popular new rage—and child observation, and were often given checklists to separate the strong from the weak, the gifted from the feeble-minded.

Superior persons were of intense interest. In a 1929 article Leta Hollingworth, a renowned researcher and professor at Teachers College, wrote about the "gifted child":

> The great majority of the gifted originate in families where the fathers are professional men or business executives, including proprietors;
>
> Very few gifted children originate from fathers in semi-skilled manual trades or in unskilled labor; Gifted children existing within the period since mental tests have been available have very few siblings, the average being about one brother or sister each.

Horace Mann Bond, an historian and theorist and the father of civil rights activist and NAACP leader Julian Bond, contested all of this. In 1927, he wrote:

> [E]ver since the "measurement of minds" became a popular field in which to pursue investigations, the testing of Negro children has easily ranked as a major indoor sport among psychologists... The rules of the game are simple and seem to be standardized throughout the country with but few exceptions. First one must have a White examiner; a group of Negro children; a test standardized for White children tested by

> *White examiners; and just a few pre-conceived notions regarding the nature of "intelligence" and the degree to which Negro children are endowed, if at all... and the fact that the social status of negro children need not be considered as an extra allowance for scores different from Whites...*

> *[I]f Negro children make lower scores than White, they are inferior, they were born that way and though we had a sneaking suspicion that this was the act all along, we are now able to fortify our prejudices with a vast array of statistical tables, bewildering vistas of curves and ranges and distributions and the other cabalistic phrases with which we clothe the sacred profession of psychology from the view of the profane public.*

Strict racial segregation was assumed, and in the wake of the 1954 *Brown* decision White Citizens' Councils were formed to prevent—what else?—the "mongrelization" of the white race.

Our system of compulsory education came to life in the cauldron of eugenics and the crucible of white supremacy, and American schools have never adequately faced up to that living heritage. So while it's true that we no longer talk of "miscegenation" or "imbeciles," and we are likely to look upon forced sterilization and race-based marriage laws as archaic, any sense of forward progress we might grant ourselves ought to be tempered by relooking at our own obsessions with "standards" and "accountability," test scores and grades, and rigid hierarchies of human value. White supremacy can change its spots while remaining durable and dominant.

It's not a huge step forward to *A Nation at Risk* and *Goals 2000*, the whole new era of "standards" and accountability. We're still in the business of sorting based on some socially constructed scheme that makes sense mostly to those who construct it. Instead of "morons" and "idiots," we talk of "at-risk youth," and we all know who that is. In place of "superior stock," we are in search of the "gifted and talented." Through it all, the quest for perfection prevails, and the basic assumption that there are "advanced" and "slow" kids—their "condition" a result of their "backgrounds"—is generally accepted and widely institutionalized.

***

The dominant narrative in contemporary school reform is once again focused on exclusion and disadvantage, race and class, Black and white. "Across the U.S.," the National Governor's Association declared in 2005, "a gap in academic achievement persists between minority and disadvantaged students and their white counterparts."

186

This is the commonly referenced and popularly understood "racial achievement gap," and it drives education policy at every level. Once again, whether heart-felt or self-satisfied, the narrative never mentions the monster in the room: the system of white supremacy and its complex, intimate relatives: class gender, and ethnicity.

It's true, of course, that standardized test scores reveal a difference between Black and white test-takers: (26 points in one area of comparison)—fourth-grade reading, 20 points in another, 23 in a third.

But the significance of those differences is wildly disputed. Some argue—as Charles Murray and Richard Herrnstein did in their popular and incendiary book *The Bell Curve*—that genetic differences account for the gap, and there's little that can be done to lift up the poor inferior Black folks. An alternate theory—popular since the 1960s—holds that Blacks are not inherently inferior to whites but merely culturally deprived, and that fixing the "massive pathologies" in the family and community will require social engineering on a grand scale. Another analysis points to class and poverty, noting a larger number of African Americans in professions or business leaving the precincts of the poor.

Each of these explanations has its large and devoted following. The first, while difficult for many whites to endorse publicly, carries the reflected power of eugenics and the certainty that what they'd always secretly suspected—that whites are indeed superior beings—is true. The second has the advantage of pretending to give a bit more than a pig's eye for the well-being of Black people while disturbing none of the pillars of white privilege. The third is often cited as proof that the prejudices of the past are dying or dead. All of these theories can live comfortably beneath the obsessive focus on the so-called achievement gap.

Gloria Ladson-Billings upends all of this with an elegant reversal: There is no achievement *gap*, she argues, merely a glancing reflection of something deeper and more fundamental—America has a profound education *debt*. The educational inequities that began with the attempted annihilation of Native peoples and the enslavement of Africans, the conquest of a continent and the importation of both free labor and serfs, has transformed into apartheid education, something anemic, inferior, inadequate, and oppressive for millions of young people. Over decades and then centuries the debt has accumulated and has passed from generation to generation, and it continues to grow and pile up. Jonathan Kozol has documented the way the debt—far from being ameliorated—grows year by year based on spending: Chicago serves 86 percent Black and Latina/o students and spends around $8,000 per pupil per year while, a few miles away in the Tony suburb of Highland Park, 90 percent white, the school district spends $17,000 per student; New York City, 72 percent Black and

Latina/o, spends around $12,000 per pupil annually, while suburban Manhasset, 91 percent white, spends over $22,000. The highest poverty districts receive the fewest resources.

Ladson-Billings imagines what could be done if the political powers took the "achievement gap" seriously: Immediate reassignment of the best teachers in the country to schools for African American and Latina/o poor children, rich curricula and access to global knowledge guaranteed places for those students in state and regional colleges and universities, smaller classes, a Marshall Plan-type effort to rebuild school infrastructure.

Ladson-Billings argues that the U.S. also owes a moral debt to African Americans, a debt that "reflects the disparity between what we know is right and what we actually do." Debt demands payment; injury cries out for repair.

***

The syndicated columnist Derrick Z. Jackson wrote a piece for *The Boston Globe* entitled "If You Think the MCAS Test is Relevant, Try This Exam." Jackson had published questions from the tenth-grade history Massachusetts' Comprehensive Assessment System history exam in an earlier column and criticized them as being "grossly Eurocentric and of questionable relevance." Many readers sent letters objecting to this assessment, arguing that while the Edict of Nantes and the Treaty of Tordesillas may seem obscure, these kinds of things "are not trivia—they are part of the framework within which we try to evaluate our own nation's attempts to shape the world."

Jackson responds that to understand "how our nation shaped itself, you have other questions" to attend to, questions not included in the MCAS or any other state standardized test. Here's Jackson's test, published on June 30, 2000, in the *Globe*:

> *(1) According to Goree Island's slave museum, the number of stolen Africans is the equivalent of emptying out the current metropolitan areas of:*
>> *(a) Milwaukee*
>> *(b) Tokyo*
>> *(c) Los Angeles*
>> *(d) New York, Los Angeles, Chicago, Washington, San Francisco and Philadelphia combined*
>
> *(2) According to most histories, the number of stolen Africans who actually made it alive to the Americas is the equivalent of:*
>> *(a) New York, Los Angeles, Chicago, Washington,*

San Francisco and Philadelphia combined
(b) New York, Los Angeles and Chicago combined
(c) Los Angeles and Chicago combined
(d) Just San Francisco and Philadelphia

(3) The conservative value of slave labor to the American economy, when it was analyzed in 1983, is nearly the equivalent of the 1999 spending budget for:
(a) Wisconsin
(b) The Rolling Stones Tour
(c) The New York Yankees
(d) The United States

(4) The World War II generation will bequeath $8 trillion to its children. In the years 1929 to 1969, wages lost by African Americans to discrimination were:
(a) nothing, because we are now a color-blind society
(b) $1.6 billion
(c) Irrelevant because Michael Jordan owns part of
the Washington Wizards and Magic Johnson owns part of the
Los Angeles Lakers
(d) $1.6 trillion, nearly equal to the 1999 federal
budget of $1.7 trillion

(5) One result of post-slavery discrimination is that the average white baby boomer and the average black baby boomer will respectively inherit:
(a) $50,000.00 and $42,000.00
(b) $80,000.00 and $50,000.00
(c) $20,000.00 and $15,000.00
(d) $65,000.00 and $8,000.00

(6) Under "40 Acres and a Mule," about 40,000 newly freed slaves were given Southern coastal land that had been abandoned by unpardoned Confederate families. These black people held the land for two years before angry white people stole it through beatings, torture and legal chicanery. During those two years, the black occupants were known for:
(a) being lazy and shiftless
(b) being top local athletes
(c) wanting back the good old days, where you could
depend on a bowl of gruel and a watermelon from massa
(d) fine crops and self-governance

(7) New England is far from cotton fields and sugar plantations. Thus it is interesting that Brown University:
>   *(a) created a chair in honor of abolitionist John Brown*
>   *(b) named its music department after James Brown*
>   *(c) named its graduate school of business after Ron Brown*
>   *(d) was founded by the Browns of Rhode Island*
>   *who profited from the triangular slave trade*

(8) In Lowell, Mass., in 1835, politicians, law enforcement, lawyers, doctors and shopkeepers signed petitions to:
>   *(a) call for the end of slavery*
>   *(b) volunteer to go south for a Freedom Summer to*
>   *understand the plight of the slaves*
>   *(c) build a new Fenway Park for the Red Sox*
>   *(d) oppose abolition because the textile mills*
>   *depended on slave-picked cotton*

(9) African Americans fought in every U.S. war, hoping their participation would result in equality. After the Civil War, World War I and World War II, black sacrifice for America and the world was rewarded with:
>   *(a) full voting rights*
>   *(b) free tickets to Jack Johnson and Joe Louis fights*
>   *(c) free coupons for watermelon*
>   *(d) lynchings and white race riots*

By the way, the answer is (d) on all questions.

Jackson's quiz points up the fact that any of us can be sharp in some ways and dull in others, literate on some dimensions and illiterate on others. There are many intellectually gifted people who are at the same time ethically challenged and socially retarded. To be an educated person one would have to have her eyes open, her mind engaged, and her heart connected to humanity.

Any community that fails to educate its young is entering into a murder/suicide pact: We'll kill you, and then we'll kill ourselves. Any society that fails to invest in its children will be consumed by its children. That's a natural law.

School policy is always enacted in a larger political and economic policy context. What is described by the powerful as a "school reform plan" is quite often in fact a corporate or financial scheme. In Chicago, for example, what is sold to the public as a "choice" plan, or a policy to close "failing," "underutilized," or "underperforming" schools, turns out to be at bottom about real estate development. Schools are shut down, "receiver schools" explode, and the whole exercise results in mass out-migration from neighborhoods and the in-migration of more prosperous home buyers. Better schools are being built in Chicago neighborhoods today, but they're built for the families who are coming, not the ones who are leaving.

If we allow ourselves to remain unaware of this larger reality, we are like the ancient Greeks who felt themselves constantly disrupted and derailed by capricious gods hurling lightning bolts at their unsuspecting heads. The difference is that the invisible controlling force is not capricious, nor is it the result of some dark conspiracy—it's public policy, hiding in plain sight, and it's imposed on people who are not paying attention and who, therefore, have no say.

The current assault on public education serves a larger political and economic agenda that reifies "the market" as a magical force that is always efficient, productive, and fair, and demonizes anything "public" as inefficient and lazy and backward. The result is a restricted public space and an eclipse of the public citizen accompanied by a massive transfer of public wealth into private hands: the creation of greater structural and resource deficits combined with even more pronounced democratic deficits. The state is weakened in relation to social well-being and the common good, and at the same time massively strengthened in regard to control, surveillance, and military power. The state government's role becomes almost exclusively to protect markets where they exist, and to create markets where they don't exist. This is why we see today all manner of "public-private partnerships" involving dismantling traditionally public functions— schools, public housing, social security, prisons, public safety—in favor of profit-making providers. And this also explains why poor African American neighborhoods are the targets of these efforts: The powerful consider these communities "soft spots" for the larger effort to privatize everything. From this barbaric perspective, Hurricane Katrina, far from being a catastrophe, can be seen as a godsend: It washed away all the people with their complex and idiosyncratic needs and capacities and desires, leaving a "blank space" for the powerful to experiment and build.

The assault on public education takes the form of a radical narrowing of the meaning of education: Schools are to produce workers not multidimensional thinkers, actors, or citizens. An unhealthy and obsessive interest in a single measure of cognitive capacity to stand for the universe of educational achievement, combined with the elevation of "zero tolerance" as the sound bite expression of learning to live together, is the result.

The triumph of a fierce and relentless market fundamentalism is everywhere apparent, on the street, of course, but penetrating our homes as well, our families, our places of worship—our vaunted private lives—while forcing a reimagined and redefined public space, encompassing everything from health care to criminal justice, from waste management to elections, from safety to the distribution of water. In this bizarrely misshapen world, hierarchy rules, competition of every kind is always good, profit an undisputed virtue, efficiency and standardization a given, advertising a fine art, individual consumption the pinnacle of participation. The current iteration of the school wars mirrors all this—the marketeers are in full eruption, leading the retreat from the dream of a robust, diverse, and well-funded public educational system in the hands of the many (the reality includes, of course, significant exclusions) toward a system of private schools for the benefit of a few. The Edison schools are an egregious example—steeped in the rhetoric of freedom and the market, these proudly for-profit McSchools produce nothing and sell nothing, relying instead on a neat shell game whose chief accomplishment seems to be to transfer public monies to private hands under the banner of "free choice." The dismantling of mass education is under way.

In less than full-blown mode the skirmishes are widespread, and so are the markers: vast resources directed to the simplistic task of sorting youngsters into camps of winners and losers; intolerant school cultures that reward obedience and conformity while punishing initiative and courage; a curriculum that is fragmented, alienating, and irrelevant; layers of supervision and regulation that reduce the role of the teacher to that of a clerk or a functionary and constitute a dagger in the intellectual and ethical heart of teaching.

To question the tenets of the marketeers, to wonder if our schools, for example, or our children are being well served by any of this, is the essential duty of a teacher who is committed to ethical action.

There is, in fact, a need to rethink in fundamental terms the whole purpose and larger meaning of school in light of the end of work as we know it. We witness massive displacement, with all manner of attendant pauperization and alienation. What will this mean for human survival or happiness and well-being for all? What are our choices? Schooling as job training and career preparation is an anachronism, and yet that reductive goal is preached repeatedly from the White House to the statehouse. Schools need to radically reconsider and restructure in a way that connects to the reality of the modern world. Martin Luther King, Jr., had a sense of this forty years ago: "The work which improves the conditions of mankind, the work which extends knowledge and increases power and enriches literature and elevates thought is not done to secure a living. It is not the task of slaves, driven to their task either by the lash of a master or by animal necessities. It is the work of men who perform it for their own sake... In a ... society where want is abolished, work of this sort could be enormously increased." While schools are established to re-create the norms and values of the larger society, they are also sites of contention, reflecting, for example, the dynamic motion of society and the long-term struggles and conflicts between democratic impulses and oppressive relationships. To justify or recommend a society's schools, one must be able to somehow warrant the society that those schools serve. The "failure" of Black schools in apartheid South Africa was, after all, no failure at all. It fit at least some of the overarching needs and goals of South African society. However, South Africa's schools were also a key source of the liberation movement, the place where liberating ideas were learned and sometimes even practiced. The sustained struggle of South African militants arose from the schools, and schools were both site and seedbed for the liberation struggle.

A similar argument can be made here at home—the failure of some schools and some children in Chicago, for example, is not due to a failure of the system. That is, if one acknowledges (even tentatively) that our society, too, is one of privilege and oppression, inequality, class divisions, and racial and gender stratifications, then one might view the schools as a whole as doing an adequate job both of sorting youngsters for various roles in society and convincing them that they, and they alone, deserve their various privileges and failures. Indeed, sorting students—curtailing choices, narrowing options—may be the single most brutal accomplishment of schools, even if it runs counter to the ideal of education as a process that opens possibilities, provides opportunities to challenge and change fate, and empowers people to control their own lives. Nowhere is this contradiction more visible than in the experience of poor and Black children and youth in American schools.

All of this needs to be countered and resisted by teachers in alliance with families and communities. *Rethinking Schools*, an urban educational journal, articulates the principles of school reform at the level of policy:

> *(1) Public schools are responsible to the community, not to the marketplace, they argue. Education reform must be grounded in the democratic vision that all of society is responsible for educating the next generation...*

> *(2) Schools must be actively multicultural and anti-racist, promoting social justice for all.*

> *(3) Curriculum must be geared to learning for life and the needs of a multicultural democracy.*

> *(4) All children and all schools must receive adequate resources.*

> *(5) Reform must center on the classroom and the needs of children. The first criteria of reform is that it will improve teaching and learning*

for children in classrooms, particularly low-income students and students who have been marginalized because of race, ethnicity, or language. Standards should be geared toward high-quality and rigorous academics for all children, not on setting up systems of rewards and punishments that perpetuate existing social inequalities.

(6) Good teachers are essential to good schools.

(7) Reform must involve collaboration among educators, parents, and the community.

(8) We must revitalize our urban communities, not just our schools. Joblessness, poverty, substance abuse, and sub-standard housing affect our schools, and massive and ongoing intervention is necessary to address these conditions. Schools can also be centers for community support and renewal by serving the entire community with a variety of recreational, educational, cultural, job training, and social service programs. Working together, schools, labor unions, community groups, religious congregations, and civic leaders can boldly address problems that are too large for any one group to solve on their own.

Rethinking Schools sums up as well reform in the realm of classroom practice:

(1) Grounded in the lives of our students, they write. Curriculum should be based on respect for students and rooted in their lives, needs, and experiences and should help students examine how their lives are connected with the broader society.

(2) Critical. Students should learn to "talk back" to the world. Curriculum and instruction should help students pose critical questions about society, examining popular culture, social structures, government actions, and school life, and should move outside the classroom to connect with real world problems.

(3) Multicultural, anti-racist, pro-justice. A social justice curriculum includes the lives and perspectives of everyone in society, especially people who are marginalized. It should engage students in a critique of the roots of inequality.

(4) Participatory, experiential. Students should experience concepts

first-hand, e.g., through projects, experiments, and role plays, and should have opportunities for democratic participation by questioning, challenging, making decisions and collectively solving problems.

(5) Hopeful, joyful, kind, visionary. Classrooms should make children feel emotionally and physically safe, significant and cared about, modeling the just and democratic society we envision.

(6) Activist. Children should come to see themselves as truth-tellers and change-makers. Teachers should encourage children to act on their consciences and should give students historical and contemporary examples of people from all cultures who act to make a difference and struggle for justice.

(7) Academically rigorous. Children should develop the tools to change the world and to maneuver in the one that exists. By speaking directly to the alienation so many students feel, teachers aim to inspire and motivate all students to levels of academic performance far greater than those measured by standardized tests or grades.

(8) Culturally and linguistically sensitive. As schools become increasingly diverse, teachers must listen to and learn from students and their families, and teachers need to call on culturally diverse colleagues and community resources for insights into the communities they serve.

***

In any culture defined by an ideology of materialist acquisition, happiness is always tied to notions of wealth and success. The prevailing wisdom tells us that this is just the way things are: "Human nature is selfish"; "Human beings are motivated by self-interest"; "It's a dog-eat-dog world." Or so it seems. But we might pause here and note, as this bit of common sense becomes a controlling metaphor, that Aristotle, for one, found the "common sense" of self-interest to be nonsensical. He argued that our human nature drives us to fulfill our unique capacity for excellence and virtue. The good life is by no means one of material wealth or social and political power, but is rather shaped by the effort to become more fully human. For Aristotle, the path to deeper, more realized humanness is an arduous one—one develops virtues by practicing them, exercising them, trying them out: One becomes brave by acting bravely, compassionate by acting compassionately.

Other thinkers, too, have expressed a view of human nature dramatically different from the wealth/success paradigm. For Martin Luther King, Jr., for example, the leading human virtue was love—practical love, gritty, complex, and difficult love. Human fulfillment comes from loving others, he said, acting out of love for others, practicing love, promoting love and fulfillment in our fellow humans, even when it is most difficult to do. "It is not enough for us to talk about love," he said. "There is another side called justice... Justice is love correcting that which revolts against love." Building the social conditions that make love possible, and then make virtue and justice and excellence more likely, became King's main task. No one can thrive during a genocide; no one can thrive at war; no one can thrive while starving. This is practical ethics—if you want to be good, you are more likely to get there if you work toward a good society. Ethics and moral commitment, then, must include an engagement with the material conditions of life. That is, an ethics of feeling is inadequate; there must also be an ethics of acting, of building peace and justice, of feeding the hungry and healing the sick, of feeling the weight of the world. This kind of ethics asks us to reach beyond self-interest, beyond charity or service in search of new forms of associative living. We think in terms of reciprocity, solidarity, and sharing the joys and the difficulties and the wealth of life.

Joining with others is in part an exercise in reaching beyond the boundaries of home, neighborhood, state, or nation. For most Americans, particularly privileged Americans, some form of exile, some traveling outside the boundaries of the easy and the familiar, is an essential condition to freedom, to full membership in the human community, even if it wins you few hometown friends. Transgressing privilege, not being entirely at home in our homes, is a step toward humanizing ourselves, expanding our horizons, becoming moral.

Teachers who want to educate students fully will necessarily choose to take the side of human liberation and enlightenment. This means committing to seeing the world as it is and then to becoming truth-tellers and risk-takers with their students. It means committing yourself to your students and also to their families and communities. It means arming yourself to participate. I want to at least try to confront the lies, to act on what the known demands. This is the only hope for my students and for myself.

Teaching about the everyday dishonesty we breathe in might help us live more fully and more freely—it may allow us all to move beyond the myths and the imposed cognitive dissonance: "This is the greatest country on earth"; "We are a peaceful nation"; "We're living a post-Civil Rights dream"; on and on. Telling the truth can help us regain some sense of balance and dignity, some sense of an authentic identity as whole people within a multiplicity of other persons, perhaps a sense of community-in-the-making.

"How is it," Edward Said asks, "that the premises on which Western support for Israel is based are still maintained even though the reality, the facts, cannot possibly bear these premises out?" This is a risk-taking question. In a notable 1984 essay, "Permission to Narrate," Said attempts an honest answer to his own complex question: "Facts," he writes, "do not at all speak for themselves, but require a socially acceptable narrative to absorb, sustain, and circulate them." A thinking person has to seek the truth, uncover the facts, but also critically examine the narratives that circulate the facts.

Think, for example, of newspaper headlines that, while the facts and the content may be upsetting, are nonetheless instantly absorbed because they fit easily into a script already written, that is, they conform to a socially accepted narrative: "Toddler Left Unattended in South Side Apartment Bitten by Rat"; "Eight City High Schools Labeled 'Failing'"; "Two Teens Charged with Playground Shooting."

The *Chicago Tribune* ran a front-page feature in its "Perspective" section on November 11, 2007, with a full-color painting of the African continent torn in two, and a pair of light-skinned hands trying to mend the tear. The headline read: "Even with the best intentions... Money and love only go so far amid Africa's complexity." The opening lines: "Go to an exotic developing nation. Be charmed by throngs of beaming children... Build a school, or a clinic, or a library. Feel like a hero. Then watch it fall apart, as things so famously do in places like Africa." Places like Africa? The story offers a sympathetic gloss to the failures of the Peace Corps, U.S. aid, and beneficent celebrity donors.

The facts in the Africa piece and each of the others are supported by a familiar and, therefore, comfortable story. The story absorbs the facts, sustains them, and circulates them repeatedly, far and wide. In a sense these stories are already written, resting comfortably in the back of a computer somewhere, awaiting only this or that predictable event as an authenticating detail, at which point they explode instantly onto the front pages.

Imagine the disequilibrium that would accompany a headline that organized the same facts in the service of a different narrative: "Centuries of Brutal Colonialism Continue in the Guise of Charity with Predictable Results"; "Failure of City to Eradicate Vermin Claims Another Victim"; or "City Bureaucracy Delays Child-Care Benefit; Unattended Boy Sustains Rat Bite"; "Chronic Underfunding of Urban Schools Reaps Predictable Results"; "Easy Access to Assault Weapons Puts Guns in Kids' Hands."

Every narrative is, of course, incomplete, each a kind of distortion. Reality is always messier, always more complicated, always more idiosyncratic than any particular story can honestly contain. A single insistent narrative by its nature lies.

Perhaps that's why courtrooms are ultimately dissatisfying—sometimes profoundly, often mildly: The struggle is always to fit the available facts into a credible narrative for judge or jury, and one of the narratives must necessarily triumph over the other. And in newsrooms, too, there seems to be little room for nuance, none at all for two contradictory narratives existing side by side. And perhaps that's what makes classrooms at their best such infinitely wondrous places: Not only are all the master narratives and triumphalist stories—as well as all manner of orthodoxy—challenged and laid low, but whatever emerges as the new truth is then questioned, reflected upon, seen as inadequate in itself. Teachers can always find ways to make classrooms into sites of curiosity, investigation, skepticism, agnosticism—places where the truth is sought, enlightenment expected, liberation a possibility. It's not always easy, but it is always a necessary aspiration.

***

In *Beloved*, Toni Morrison's searing novel of slavery, freedom, and the complexities of a mother's love, a character named Schoolteacher comes to Sweet Home with his efficient, scientific interest in captured Africans and makes life unbearable for the people there. Schoolteacher is cold, sadistic, brutal—a disturbing, jarring person for those of us who want to think of teachers as thinking and compassionate people. He is all about control and management and maintaining the status quo. He and others like him are significant props in an entire system of dehumanization, oppression, exploitation.

Toward the end of Amin Maalouf's dazzling *Samarkand*, a historical novel of the life of Omar Khayyam and the journey of the *Rubaiyat*, Howard Baskerville, a British schoolteacher in the city of Tabriz in old Persia at the time of the first democratic revolution, explains an incident in which he was observed weeping in the marketplace: "Crying is not a recipe for anything," he begins. "Nor is it a skill. It is simply a naked, naive and pathetic gesture." But, he goes on, crying is nonetheless important. When the people saw him crying they figured that he "had thrown off the sovereign indifference of a foreigner," and at that moment they could come to Baskerville "to tell me confidentially that crying serves no purpose and that Persia does not need any extra mourners and that the best I could do would be to provide the children of Tabriz with an adequate education." "If they had not seen me crying," Baskerville concludes, "they would never have let me tell the pupils that this Shah was rotten and that the religious chiefs of Tabriz were hardly any better."

Morrison and Maalouf show us that teaching occurs in contexts, and that pedagogy and technique are not the wellsprings of moral choice. Teaching can be colonial or anti-colonial, entangling or liberating. Teaching becomes ethical practice when it is guided by an unshakable commitment to encouraging human beings to reach the full measure of their humanity, and a willingness to join together to stretch toward a future fit for all—a place of peace and justice.

In *A Lesson Before Dying*, Ernest Gaines creates a riveting portrait of a teacher locked in struggle with a resistant student, wrestling as well with his own doubts and fears about himself, and straining against the outrages of white supremacy. Grant Wiggins has returned with considerable ambivalence to teach in the plantation school of his childhood. He feels trapped and longs to escape to a place where he might breathe more freely, grow more fully, achieve something special.

The story begins in a courtroom with Grant's elderly Tante Lou and her lifelong friend, Miss Emma, sitting stoic and still near the front. Emma's godson, Jefferson, had been an unwitting participant in a failed liquor store stickup—his two companions and the store owner are dead—and, as the sole survivor, he is convicted of murder. The public defender, pleading for Jefferson's life, plays to the all-white jury with zeal:

> *"Gentlemen of the jury, look at this-this-this boy. I almost said man, but I can't say man... I would call it a boy and a fool. A fool is not aware of right and wrong...*

> *"Do you see a man sitting here?... Look at the shape of the skull, his face as flat as the palm of my hand—look deeply into those eyes. Do you see a modicum of intelligence?... A cornered animal to strike quickly out of fear, a trait that he can do—but to plan?... No, gentlemen, this skull here holds no plans... A thing to hold the handle of a plow, a thing to load your bales of cotton... That is what you see here, but you do not see anything capable of planning a robbery or a murder. He does not even know the size of his clothes or his shoes... Mention the names of Keats, Byron, Scott, and see whether the eyes will show one moment of recognition. Ask him to describe a rose... Gentlemen of the jury, this man planned a robbery? Oh, pardon me, pardon me, I surely did not mean to insult your intelligence by saying 'man'...*

> *"What justice would there be to take this life? Justice gentlemen? Why I would just as soon put a hog in the electric chair as this."*

But the lawyer's pleas are no good. Jefferson is sentenced to death. He has only a few weeks, perhaps a couple of months, to live. As devastating as the sentence is, it is that last comment from the public defender—that comparison of Jefferson to a hog—that cuts most deeply. "Called him a hog," says Miss Emma. And she turns to Grant Wiggins: "I don't want them to kill no hog." She wants Grant to visit Jefferson, to teach him to be a man before he dies.

Wiggins resists, shaken by the challenge and the context: How do you teach someone to be a man? How do you teach someone else things you are uncertain of yourself?

Miss Emma and Tante Lou, along with their preacher, insist that Grant join them in their visits to Jefferson, although the sheriff surely does not want Grant there because, as he says, "I think the only thing you can do is just aggravate him, trying to put something in his head against his will. And I'd rather see a contented hog go to that chair than an aggravated hog." Jefferson himself is wracked with hopelessness; he is uncooperative, resistant: "It don't matter... Nothing don't matter," he says, as he refuses to eat unless his food is put on the floor, like slops for a hog.

Grant begins by simply visiting Jefferson, being there, speaking sometimes, but mostly just sitting in silence. Witnessing. He brings Jefferson some small things: peanuts and pecans from his students, a small radio, a little notebook and a pencil. He encourages Jefferson to think of questions and write down his thoughts. This monologue begins with Grant encouraging Jefferson to be kind to his grandmother, to eat some of the gumbo she has brought:

> "I could never be a hero. I teach, but I don't like teaching. I teach because it is the only thing that an educated black man can do in the south today. I don't like it; I hate it... I want to live for myself and for my woman and for nobody else.
>
> That is not a hero, a hero does for others... I am not that kind of person, but I want you to be. You could give something to her, to me, to those children in the quarter... The white people out there are saying that you don't have it—that you're a hog, not a man. But I know they are wrong. You have the potentials. We all have, no matter who we are...
>
> I want to show them the difference between what they think you are and what you can be. To them, you're nothing but another nigger—no dignity, no heart, no love for your people. You can prove them wrong. You can do more than I can ever do. I have always done what they wanted me to do, teach reading, writing, and arithmetic. Nothing else—nothing about loving and caring. They never thought we were capable of learning those things. 'Teach these niggers how to print their names and how to figure on their fingers'. And I went along, but hating myself all the time for doing so...
>
> White people believe that they're better than anyone else on earth—and that's a myth. The last thing they want is to see a black man stand, and think, and show that common humanity that is in us all. It would destroy their myth...

All we are, Jefferson, all of us on this earth, [is just] a piece of drifting wood, until we—each of us, individually—decide to be something else. I am still that piece of drifting wood... but you can be better. Because we need you to be and want you to be..."

Teachers can appreciate the irony of teaching what we ourselves neither fully know nor understand, of learning more than we teach. We resonate to the notion of teaching the condemned. We recognize the resistant student, the student who refuses to learn. And we can uncover moments of intense self-reflection, consciousness shifts, and personal growth brought on by our attempts to teach, our listening, our embracing students' lives, our witnessing their voyages.

Many teachers know what it means to teach against the grain, against oppression, opposition, and obstinacy. Against glib, common-sense assumptions. Against white supremacy and a whole history of evil. When the sheriff compares education to agitation, and the teacher to an organizer "trying to put something in his head against his will," one is reminded of Frederick Douglass's captor and owner exploding in anger when he discovers that his wife has taught the young Douglass to read: "It will unfit him to be a slave."

In the end, Jefferson stands up for himself, and while he cannot escape death, he transcends the dehumanization forced onto him. He stands up, and the entire system that put him in this dreadful spot is exposed for anyone willing to see. It's a terrible moment of loss, and a wondrous moment of triumph. It's a lesson before dying.

***

Education of course lives an excruciating paradox precisely because of its association with and location in schools. Education is about opening doors, opening minds, opening possibilities. Education is unconditional—it asks nothing in return. Education is surprising and unruly and disorderly. Education unleashes the unpredictable, frees the mind, opens to the possible.

When the drumbeat of our daily lives is all about controlling the crowd, moving the mob, conveying disembodied bits of information to inert things propped at desks before us, students can easily become the enemy, the obstacle. The need, then, to remind ourselves of the meaning of teaching at its best becomes intense, and the desire to fight for ourselves and our students becomes imperative; there is, after all, no basis for education in a democracy outside of a faith in the enduring capacity for growth in ordinary people and a faith that ordinary people—unpredictable, unmanageable, unlikely to fit into any neatly prescribed slots in our increasingly bureaucratized and regimented society—can, if they choose, change the world.

Hannah Arendt reminds us that "education is the point at which we decide whether we love the world enough to assume responsibility for it and by the same token save it from that ruin which, except for renewal, except for the coming of the new and the young, would be inevitable. And education, too, is where we decide whether we love our children enough not to expel them from our world and leave them to their own devices, nor to strike from their hands their chance of undertaking something new, something unforeseen by us, but to prepare them in advance for the task of renewing a common world."

In a time when the universe of political discourse is receding, disappearing, teachers need to wonder how to continue to speak the unhearable. How can the unspoken be heard? How does self-censorship perpetuate the silence? The tension between aspiration and possibility is acute, and the question of what is to be done a daily challenge.

It's essential that we "tell no lies and claim no easy victories," as Amilcar Cabral cautioned. There is often no simple solution, no single right way to oppose injustice, to mobilize for a better way. We must remain skeptics and agnostics, even as we stir ourselves to act on behalf of what the known demands of us. We must resist becoming credulous in the face of official, authoritative knowledge, or despairing about the possibility of people to act. We must live out the teacher's credo: You can change your life. Wherever you've been, whatever you've done, you're still a work-in-progress. You can change the world.

***

Myles Horton, who died in January 1990 at the age of eighty-four, founded the Highlander Folk School in Tennessee in 1932. Highlander was a free space in a decidedly and distinctively oppressive world. It was a place where labor organizers, civil rights activists, anti-poverty workers, and environmental educators, and others could assemble, pose problems, and work to develop their own solutions. Myles claimed his job was "to provide opportunities for people to grow, not to make them grow because no one can do that... My job as a gardener or as an educator is to know that the potential is there and that it will unfold. People have a potential for growth; it's inside, it's in the seed..."

For many years Highlander was the only place in the South where white and African American citizens could live and work together, something illegal and unthinkable in that strictly segregated society. Highlander, Myles once claimed, held the record for sustained civil disobedience, breaking the Tennessee Jim Crow laws every day for over forty years, until the segregation laws were finally repealed.

The list of students at Highlander over the years is a roll call of social activists: Ella Baker, Bob Moses, James Lawton, Rosa Parks, Eleanor Roosevelt, Pete Seeger, Charlie Cobb, Bernice Reagon, James Foreman, Woody Guthrie, Martin Luther King, Jr., Andrew Young, Fannie Lou Hamer, Stokely Carmichael, Rap Brown, John Lewis. People gathered at Highlander with a purpose: to define their problems, to name the obstacles in their work, to gather the necessary conceptual, human, and material resources to continue, and to return home with a plan for forward progress. The school was under constant attack from white supremacists, anti-labor groups, and the government.

We saw Myles in Minnesota near the end of his life and reminisced for an evening about the early struggles at Highlander. As we sorted through a box of photos we came upon a picture of King sitting in a circle of people in a workshop at Highlander that was made famous by the Ku Klux Klan because they paid to have it reproduced on billboards throughout the South with the heading: "King at Communist Training School." Myles laughed as he held a photograph of a highway billboard with the King photo and told us about a time when he drove to a rally with some young people, passing one and then another of the notorious signs. Finally, as another loomed ahead, one of the youngsters turned to Myles and said, "That's the dumbest advertisement I've ever seen; it doesn't even give you the phone number."

When Myles was asked how he managed to keep going, how he maintained his spirit and his vision, he said,

> "I think about two things: I think about all the wonderful people who've come to Highlander, who've suffered and struggled and won, who had to change themselves in order to change the world. And I think how lucky I was to be part of that great human drama, the struggle for a better world. And then I think about my little house in the Smoky Mountains, and how I like to walk out on the ridge at night and look up at the Milky Way and realize that I'm just a little speck of dust in the cosmos. I like to think about how tiny I am and how big we can be. That keeps me going."

Amen.

Myles felt he could learn from many sources, but that in the end he was responsible to himself and his own ideals. "I have to be the final arbiter of my beliefs and my actions," he said, "and I can't fall back and justify it by saying, I'm a Marxist, I'm a Christian, I'm a technological expert, I'm an educator." Perhaps this kind of stubborn individualism helps explain why he worked with a wide range of people who shared a broad vision of what they thought would be a better world, and yet he never joined a party: "I understood the need for organizations, but I was always afraid of what they did to people... [O]rganizations... end up in structures and structures become permanent and most of them outlive their usefulness."

At Highlander Folk School the purpose of education was to make people more powerful, more capable in their work and their lives. Myles Horton embraced what he called a "two-eyed" approach to teaching: one eye on things as they are, the other on things as they could be. Myles thought people had a lot of latent power and that his job was to capitalize on people's strengths, to mobilize that power. It's a demanding challenge because people often don't know that they have the solutions and often act in ways that are contrary to solving their own problems. The alternative, he thought, was patronization or worse. Horton built a learning environment where people could explore, share, risk, make decisions, and construct answers—a place where people became stronger. It was a school where experience counted most, a place that opposed passivity and obedience, and valued imagination and initiative. Experience, imagination, and initiative were the raw materials of learning, but reflection was necessary for growth. "An experience you don't learn from," Horton said, "is just a happening."

Traveling the mountains of Eastern Tennessee is a trip into an indefinite time. The road cuts deep into the green hills, swings up past a white frame house where an ancient woman sits sewing in a rocker on the porch. Nearby a farmer and a boy work a field. Down a steep grade and around another sharp bend looms a prodigious automobile graveyard, hulk upon hulk of rusting bodies in a strange monument to modern times. Beyond this, a larger-than-life smiling Dolly Parton points south to Dollywood. And everywhere the characteristic haze rising from every hill and hollow, giving the place its name: the Smokey Mountains. We'd come for a memorial tribute to Myles's life. We told our stories and then set out to collect the stories of others:

Maxine Waller:

> *Myles taught me to say, "Hell, no. I don't like the world the way it is and I'm going to change it." I hope I can get a lot of people to spend a lot of sleepless nights; I haven't slept so well myself.*

> *Myles started out in the church, and he found out that that's where God's work wasn't being done. Highlander's been called a lot of things, but I call it God's work. Myles Horton was a man of God and he did God's work. All my life I've slept with the Bible. Now I sleep with the Bible and The Long Haul.*

> *Myles taught that all people are smart and all people can do anything if*

they apply themselves correctly. But you've got to do the work, and then you're responsible for it.

Highlander ain't perfect. Highlander's life, and life is never perfect.

Bernard LaFayette:

We came to Highlander in the early 1960s on a retreat from the non-violent battles in Nashville. It was a place to get away, to think, and to connect with ourselves.

We had become convicts: convicted and jailed by the courts, and convicted by our own principles. Our convictions drove us, and they were unescapable.

In one workshop I attended Myles asked "Why shouldn't white folks have a right to eat by themselves?" We were flabbergasted and I got up and had a fuss with him. I had never heard the concept of a devil's advocate. Myles caused me to think critically about why I was doing what I was doing. He taught me that you must doubt your first impression, to think about what you think.

Where do we go from here? What we must do is to give birth to Highlanders all over the country. We must transplant Highlander.

Rosa Parks:

Myles was asked once how he managed to get Black and white people to eat together in the strictly segregated South. His response was simple and straight-forward: "All I did was put the food on the table and ring the bell."

I miss Myles very much.

Juliett Merrifield:

Participatory research is a way of documenting people's knowledge of their own situations, a way to reclaim and validate knowledge.

It also is a way of linking knowledge of a situation with conduct. It is action-oriented. It is different from telling people what is good for them.

It is beyond information, although that's a part of it. It has to do with being critical, with naming obstacles, and with understanding possible actions.

It has to do with community building.

Myles said that we have lots of facts, and lots and lots of information. The question is which facts and which information matter, what is the significance of it all, and what are you going to do about it?

Sarah Jane Petit:
Myles was the first white man I ever met I didn't hate. He was a gentle man, a big man, a real human man. Before I met him I hated all white folks, but I came to see that there were a few good ones. So now I mostly aim to harass white folks, but not the Myles-type whites.

Myles believed in sticking to something once he started it. He was, he said, a person "for the long haul." He founded Highlander in 1932 as an adult education center focused on social change, and he was still at it when he died at Highlander fifty-eight years later. Early on he decided to set out on a life's work that was big enough to contain his considerable energy, vision, and experience. Once started, he said, he didn't want to have to stop and start over. Highlander was a place where students and teachers could live, work, and study together, developing through their own experiences a sense of how to participate in a changing world. It was harassed and attacked burned down by racists and rebuilt, but Highlander has remained a center of social action and change for over seventy years now, responding to the needs and demands of gathering generations of social activists.

Myles had a holistic view of education. "The universe is one," he said, and he resisted chopping life into discreet bits of information, subject matter, or courses. It was all one. He had an intense belief in the innate goodness and potential wisdom of ordinary people, and he believed that people needed opportunities to make the decisions that impacted their lives. "I look at people with two eyes," he said. "One eye focuses on who the person is, and the other looks at who that person might become."

TRUDGE TOWARD FREEDOM, CRAWL TOWARD LOVE

Let us realize that the arc of the moral universe is long, but it bends toward justice.

—Martin Luther King, Jr.

But primarily for us all, it is necessary to teach by living and speaking those truths which we believe and know beyond understanding. Because in this way alone we can survive, by taking part in a process of life that is creative and continuing, that is growth.

—Audre Lorde

If we are convinced that all history is past, that we are somehow *not* moving inside a living, constantly constructed history, if we think that all the "historic moments" happened before we got here—and, incidentally, had any of us been around for one of them, Abolition, say, women's suffrage, or the fight for the eight-hour day, we're equally convinced that not only would we have been on the side of the angels, but we'd have been gutsy and agitating heroes—we not only have a distorted view of the past, but, more important, we are blinded to our own moment, to all the inherent dangers and all the yeasty possibilities that present themselves right here, right now. We experience the time being as somehow a point of arrival, the only possible outcome, and we are rendered powerless, then, to imagine another world, or to act on behalf of what could be, but is not yet. We get it wrong about *then*, but, worse, we get it wrong about *now*.

In reality, during the days of slavery most U.S. citizens took it as normal and unchangeable—just the natural order of things. It took acts of imagination and courage and focused effort to break with that heavy, ubiquitous taken-for-granted. Those who spoke up *for* Abolition found that they were also speaking up *against* the government and the law, tradition and the *status quo*, the teachings of their churches and in most cases, of their families and their friends as well. A few did, and then more, and eventually the idea of slavery as a normal, natural state was undermined and overcome. And, of course, we're all Abolitionists now, and we might be inclined to flatter ourselves by thinking we'd have also been Abolitionists when it actually mattered.

And so, today, what are the injustices and imbalances, the unnecessary sufferings, the pain and the harm that we simply cannot see? What form does white supremacy take now? Fifty years from now, what glaring atrocity of today might we recognize as totally unacceptable? Can we shake off our blindness and open our eyes?

It's important here to make a distinction between personal virtue—be honest, do your work, show up on time—and social or community ethics. Personal virtue is an undisputed good in almost every society, but we would be hard-pressed to say a slave owner who paid his bills and was kind to his wife was an ethical person. We need to worry about how we behave collectively, how our society behaves, how the contexts of politics and economics, for example, interact with what we hold to be good. Most of us, after all, most of the time follow the conventions of our cultures—most Spartans act like Spartans, most Athenians like Athenians, and most Americans like Americans. To be a person of moral character in an unjust social order requires us to work to change society. The only place for a just person in a slave state, as Thoreau argued when it mattered, is in prison.

Trudge Toward Freedom Crawl Toward Love

We focus on the unique and endlessly cruel forms of white supremacy and racism in the U.S., but there are global dimensions to race, class, and gender that increasingly impinge on every discussion. Malcolm X saw the urgency: "The newly awakened people all over the world pose a problem for what is known as Western interests, which is imperialism, racism, and all these other negative isms or vulturistic isms." And Edward Said noted: "The web of racism, cultural stereotypes, political imperialism, dehumanizing ideology holding in the Arab or the Muslim is very strong indeed, and it is this web which every Palestinian has come to feel as his uniquely punishing destiny." Said's pathbreaking *Orientalism* opened the door for studies, art, and discourse reclaiming and rediscovering histories from below, upending the imperial Western narrative, rejecting the observation of the "other" as backward, degenerate, and unequal. The subsequent explosion of gender perspectives, indigenous rights, critical race theory, and ethnic studies, for example—the voice of the landless, the exile, the displaced, and the migrant—all contribute to a complex and layered excavation and re-construction of what has gone before, and what is now, at home and across the earth. The domestic discourse of race/gender/class is continually extended and enriched, while the insights, songs, and language of the Black Freedom Movement have gone global and been embraced by people from Soweto to Bolivia to Beijing.

Most people in the U.S. are mis-educated and conditioned to think of ourselves as the center of the world—in reality the U.S. population is 4.8 percent of the world's people, even as U.S. corporate, financial, and military power controls 60 percent of the world's wealth. This is the very definition of instability: It is constituent of violence, for this rampant level of U.S. corporate and market control must be maintained by military bases to protect the extraction of wealth, collaboration with local thieves, the promotion of local war, and tolerance of famine, and genocide. One result is massive displacement of people, forced migration, emigration for survival. This de-stabilization of local wisdom, leadership, a sense of place, and self-defined needs can be seen in the "shock and awe" occupation of Iraq and Afghanistan, as well as in the post-Katrina privatized "rebuilding" of the Gulf coast and continuing displacement of people of color.

A major challenge is to find those points of convergence between our struggles within the U.S. and the global dispossessed, to find the unity of unnecessary suffering, to connect the two Gulfs, to reject the walls. The fence on the Mexican/U.S. border, the gated community, the Israeli wall cutting through the West Bank, the prison landscape—all seem to characterize the moment, all attempting to separate the desperately poor from those who strive to stay relatively rich. "The precondition for thinking politically on a global scale," writes John Berger, "is to see the unity of the unnecessary suffering taking place."

The ongoing task is to acknowledge both the unique aspects of U.S. history and the role of racism, while connecting the crises and struggles here with those most oppressed across the globe—those who have also been largely marginalized and subjugated by race and class and gender. While the history of slavery is specific to the U.S., slavery and the slave trade defined all of the Americas, as well as Africa and Europe. The urgency is "to universalize the crisis, to give greater human scope to what a particular race or nation suffered, to associate that experience with the suffering of others," as Edward Said wrote.

What is to be done? The answers change every day, and yet they remain in principle the same. We shake ourselves awake, open our eyes and our minds, and name the obstacles to our freedom, to our humanity. We link up and unite with others to the extent possible. We fight the obstacles: U.S. war and expansion in Iraq, for example, or Israel's insistence on its right to annihilate the Palestinian people; the caging and disenfranchisement of Black men; the U.S. use of indefinite detention, "rendition," torture, and extrajudicial killings since 9/11; the militarization of our borders, the low-intensity war against immigrants; savaging of the planet's integrity and the environmental burden foisted on Black and Latino communities; the violent assault on women's reproductive freedom, sexuality, economic equality, and independence; persistent child poverty; job loss; the hateful demonizing of gays and lesbians and queers. In a world of so much injustice, it's not hard to find something important to do, some appropriate place to dive into the wreckage.

There's so much to do, the problems loom so large, and it's easy to feel shut-down or overwhelmed: "I can't do everything," we repeat, and it's true. But can we do anything, anything at all? In a darkened auditorium, if someone lights a candle anywhere it challenges the darkness everywhere. Light one candle.

We might find some hope in the growth of opposition to war and expansionism worldwide. Or from the growing reparations and prison abolition movements. Or from the economic and social transformations underway in Latin America. Or from the world and U.S. social forums as a manifestation of globalization from below. Or from the vibrant organizing and activism of young people against all forms of racism and injustice.

But mainly we find hope in this self-evident truth: The future is unknown, and, more important, it is entirely unknowable. History is always in-the-making, and we are—each one of us—works-in-progress; what we do or fail to do will inevitably make a difference. Nothing is predetermined, and we are acting largely in the dark with our limited consciousness and our contingent capacities. This can be cause for despair if your mood be solemn, but it can, as well, open to a field of possibility. It can call us to get busy.

Trudge Toward Freedom Crawl Toward Love

We've watched with horror and anger and oppositions as the country has been marched step by step toward a more certain and definitive authoritarianism since 9/11. "The state of emergency in which we live," wrote Walter Benjamin, "is not the exception but the rule." It's not the whole story, to be sure—but it is, without a doubt, a bright thread that is both recognizable and knowable:

- Empire resurrected in the name of a renewed and powerful patriotic and jingoistic nationalism.

- War without end.

- Identification of opaque enemies as a unifying cause.

- Unprecedented and unapologetic military expansion and militarism.

- Rampant supremacy.

- Sexism intact and unyielding and organized campaigns to violate the fundamental rights of women and girls.

- Mass incarceration and disenfranchisement.

- Intertwining of religion and government.

- Unprecedented concentration of wealth.

- Overwhelming greed putting planetary survival in question, and abdication of responsibility for environmental catastrophe.

- The shredding of constitutional and human rights, and the hollowing out of democracy.

- Corporate power unchecked.

- The creation of popular movements based on bigotry, intolerance, and the threat of violence, and the scapegoating of targeted vulnerable groups.

- Fraudulent elections.

- Disdain for the arts and for intellectual life.

And on and on.

What is our response? What should it be? As Nina Simone might lament: "Why can't you see it? / Why can't you feel it? / I don't know, / I don't know."

A young African American soldier is taken to Walter Reed Army Medical Center missing her legs and her face. Shall I make a reservation for dinner and a show? A young Black man is shot in the back by the Chicago police. Shall I take that vacation in Jamaica? Two more prisoners commit suicide at Guantanamo. Shall I get that new car I'd been wanting? Four million Iraquis are refugees or internally displaced because of the U.S. invasion. Shall I send a contribution to one of the rascals revving up his or her political ambitions?

We're reminded that privilege is always anesthetizing, and that the privileged and relatively privileged are necessarily blind to our own blind spots. It's of course an effort for white people to see the obstacles placed in the paths of African Americans, for men to see the injuries visited upon women, for the relatively comfortable to comprehend the daily life of low-wage workers, for the able-bodied to feel the dislocation and banal discrimination experienced by the disabled, or for straight people to experience the pain of children routinely beaten and taunted and marginalized in our schools, of teachers asked to deny their identities, of parents pushed around in unfriendly settings, of human beings asked to hide their closest loved ones. The ideal of social justice must include full and mutual recognition: Seeing the human faces and hearing the human voices of outrage and injury, of aspiration and dignity.

Bertolt Brecht, who knew something about the dark times, asked this question in his poem "Motto": "In dark times, will there also be singing?" And his answer: "Yes, there will be singing. / About the dark times." Our work here and now is in part to sing the dark times. It is essential for us to begin with a particularly precious ideal—the belief that every human being is of incalculable value, each the one and only who will ever trod the earth, and that our work as teachers and citizens and artists and activists living in a democracy must be geared to helping every human being reach a fuller measure of his or her humanity. This ideal invites people on a journey to become more thoughtful and more capable, more powerful and courageous, more exquisitely alive in their projects and their pursuits. An unyielding belief in the unity and dignity of humanity—always revolutionary, and never more so than today—is never quite finished, never easily or finally summed up, and yet it is central to achieving a just society. Neither a commodity with readily recognized features nor a product for consumption, the democratic ideal is an aspiration to be continually nourished, engaged, and exercised, a dynamic, expansive experiment that must be achieved over and over again by every individual and each successive generation if it is to live at all.

Trudge Toward Freedom Crawl Toward Love

Rosa Luxemburg, the Polish revolutionary jailed for publicly opposing World War I in Germany, wrote to a friend from prison, urging her, she said, to be a *mensch*, a Yiddish word loosely translated as a person who does good in the world. A *mensch*, she elaborated, is someone who loves his or her own life enough to celebrate each sunrise and sunset, to admire the shape of the clouds, to enjoy well-prepared and healthy food, to invest in friends and loved ones. But a *mensch* must also be willing to put his or her shoulder on history's great wheel when required. To love only one's own life is to sink into narcissism; to love only the collective is to strip life of its complex three-dimensionality. So, a joyous and passionate embrace of the life we're each given combined with an eagerness to oppose suffering and injustice—somehow both are necessary.

We were schooled long ago—a lesson taught to us by the Vietnamese, the South African resistance, and the Cubans—to make a sharp distinction between the American people and the U.S. government. When a delegation of student activists met with a delegation from North and South Viet Nam in 1968, the participants spent a week exchanging stories of our families along with analyses of the war and the world. Madame Pham Than Van and Bernardine exchanged rings, Madame Van's made from the metal of a U.S. B-52 bomber plane that had been brought down.

These small acts of solidarity are repeated across the world as people are angry about the U.S. government and corporate interests but open to the humanizing possibilities of the U.S. people. The script is not yet finished. We've tried for decades—even in our most desperate days—to find some balance between participating wholeheartedly in the daily joys and challenges life brings—raising our children, teaching our students, taking long, surprising walks through the city at night—and at the same time trying to be wide awake, aware of everything, engaged in society and the world, and willing to participate fully in whatever the known demands. When we don't know what to do, we can at least know how to live; while we'll never be at peace with empire and occupation, conquest and white supremacy, we can at least be at peace with ourselves.

There is in fact no promised land in this struggle for justice—there is instead an aching persistent tension between reality and possibility. What are we working for? What are we working against? We want to work against oppression and subjugation, for example, and against exploitation, unfairness, and unkindness, and we want others to join in that commitment. We want to work toward freedom, for enlightenment and awareness, wide-awakeness, protection of the weak, cooperation, generosity, compassion, and love.

"Insane generosity," Albert Camus writes in *The Rebel*, "is the generosity of rebellion." It may be that man is mortal, "but let us die resisting; and if our lot is complete annihilation, let us not behave in such a way that it seems justice!" Camus speaks of a generosity that consistently refuses injustice, that is determined to allow nothing to pass, and that makes no calculations as to what it offers. "Real generosity toward the future," Camus concludes, "lies in giving all to the present." Giving it all, here and now, the only time we've got after all.

***

Let's talk about race, about transformation and change, about justice and peace.

We approach this moment with a kind of aberrant and zany hope and with a battered but still abiding faith in King's vision of a moral universe whose arc—while long—bends toward justice. In spite of the lateness of the hour and the awkwardness of all available venues, in spite of all the natural and inevitable misunderstandings, we want to spark and participate in a courageous conversation, a dialogue of questioning and struggle: Who are we? Why are we here? What are the impediments to justice, to enlightenment, to liberation? What is the particular responsibility of those in the belly of the beast in the task of dismantling the structures of white supremacy? How can we resist the logic of empire, conquest, occupation, and construct a new framework of love and peace and sustainability? How can we even pose the questions, recognizing we have to learn than to teach? Where can we hope to find happiness, togetherness, openness, loveliness, and peace?

We remind ourselves that in every authentic discussion, deliberation, or dialogue there are mistakes and struggles—we open to the heartfelt and the emotional—and yet, it is the disequilibrium of dialogue that leads to exploration, discovery, and change. Dialogue is improvisational and unrehearsed, and must be undertaken with the serious intention of engaging—we speak with the possibility of being heard; we listen with the possibility of being changed. Our conviction, then, must be tempered with agnosticism and a sense of the contingent—we commit to questioning, exploring, inquiring, paying attention, going deeper. But it is not enough to put ourselves forward and assert our perspectives; we must also allow for the possibility of being ourselves transformed. We might see this, then, as a profoundly pedagogical moment—we might all risk learning something new.

We have a large framed broadside on a wall in our house in the style of an old grainy wanted poster or an announcement of a public auction: stolen, it cries out in oversized letters, and then, in a slightly smaller font, millions of people, trillions in wealth. The list that follows is cramped together to fit: land, timber, gold, oil, tin, bauxite, diamonds, uranium, rubber, ivory, coffee, lead, phosphate, manganese, cotton, cocoa, iron, cobalt, zinc, fish, on and on. Another crowded list names the thieves: the United States, Great

Britain, Portugal, the Netherlands, France, Belgium, Germany, and all the rest, as well as the corporate grants from Standard Oil and Shell to United States Steel and Lipton Tea. At the bottom of the poster there are demands for repair and payback in the form of money, technology, infrastructure, and trade. The poster refers, of course, to Africa. Repair the harm. Pay back the debt. Reparations.

Reparations for the crime of slavery was widely recognized and supported after the Civil War as both just and practical. Providing land and the means of production to former slaves was not only the ethical thing to do, it was a potentially effective plan to incorporate a large, formerly excluded and exploited group into the social and economic life of the country. Of course, it never happened. Reconstruction was dismantled, a campaign of terror was launched, and the slave system was reconstituted as a feudal stronghold recapitulating the wrongs of slavery under a new legal framework.

But the dream never died, and calls for reparations have echoed down the generations: Marcus Garvey, Mary Church Terrell, Harry Haywood,Esalanda Goode Robeson, Louise Thompson Patterson, James Foreman, Randall Robinson. Malcolm X noted that the son who inherits a wealthy estate from his father must assume the debt along with the benefits. The only reason the present generation of white Americans is in its position of incredible economic strength, he said, is that the fathers of the whites worked the fathers and mothers of African Americans for centuries with no pay. So, he said, pay up. Or, as Le Roi Jones put it more abruptly in the mouth of one of his protagonists in *Dutchman*: "Up against the wall M/F, we come for what's ours."

Reparations is as relevant today as ever, and although the form it might take is debatable, the justness of it is irrefutable. Wherever a case of social effects can be plotted by race, reparations is both justified and necessary: jobs and income, for example, access to decent health care, adequate housing, equal schools, safe neighborhoods, transportation, cultural institutions, and more. The demand is to invest the socially produced wealth to repair the socially produced harm.

A program and a campaign against white supremacy must find a way to connect the dots historically as well as to make the links socially, culturally, and economically. We came to see that the problems of today are the living embodiment of the crimes of the past, and that solutions for now require a serious revisiting and rethinking of how we got here. And we see that racism is linked to imperialism is linked to economic hardship is linked to sexism and scapegoating is linked to global warming and the systematic undermining of democracy and so on. If we can't find the connections, we can't organize for a comprehensive answer and we won't be able to build a movement or a series of linked movements for fundamental change.

Reparations in excess of a Marshall Plan-type investment in Black communities is a start. Abolition of the death penalty and then of prisons as the center of our social sense of justice is a start. Ending the wars in Afghanistan and Iraq, and then demilitarizing our schools and our society is a start. And all of it carried forward by an open and public mobilization and conversation about how we want to live in a democracy as full and free and equal.

***

Gwendolyn Brooks was one of our dazzling truth-tellers. Winner of a Pulitzer Prize in 1949 and later Poet Laureate of Illinois, she never left her bustling and bracing neighborhood and, perhaps more important, never left the commitments and concerns that animated her intelligence and her heart: the lives of the children and families, indeed, the lives of all the ordinary people of Chicago's south side.

Gwendolyn Brooks understood the disruptive role the arts can play: "Does man love art?" she asks to begin one of her poems. Her answer: "Man visits art but cringes. Art hurts. Art urges voyages." Brooks's bracing and generous imagination allowed voyages and dreams, a constantly expanding sense of human possibility. In contrast, a useful definition of a bigot is a person with a stunted or withered imagination. When in danger—and we are surely in danger now—our best defense might be to fire up and liberate our most radical imaginations.

What might we hope for? The destruction of white supremacy? The end of empire? An end to exploitation? Living together in peace and harmony? Rebuilding our cities and our society on principles of balance and fairness? Surely we can work for justice, nourish a spirit of solidarity and fight to build community, we can try to temper our outrage with generosity and strive to live with our values explicitly guiding our daily actions. Audre Lorde said, "Poetry is not only dream and vision; it is the skeleton architecture of our lives. It lays the foundation for a future of change, a bridge across our fears of what has never been before." At its best, art urges voyages that we undertake with a necessary sense of urgency at this precise moment.

In 1967, at the age of fifty, with the flames of freedom in the air and an exuberant sense of change sweeping throughout the whole world, Gwendolyn Brooks—with several books of poetry, a novel, and that Pulitzer Prize under her belt—wrote of the grand rebirth of consciousness during those early days of the Black Arts Movement:

> *I who have 'gone the gamut' from an almost angry rejection of my dark skin by some of my brainwashed brothers and sisters to a surprised queenhood in the new black sun—am qualified to enter at least the kindergarten of new consciousness now.*

Trudge Toward Freedom Crawl Toward Love

New consciousness and trudge-toward-progress. I have hopes for myself.

"New consciousness and trudge-toward-progress"—we're reminded that we can become, all of us, seekers in a dynamic and uncertain world. It's the urgency of youth that can set the pace and the tone of what is to come, of what is to be done, and still, in the grace and fullness of age we might learn to follow along, to enter at least the kindergarten of the new. Having hopes for our students and our young colleagues in their quest to bury white supremacy and its progeny in favor of building a more just and peaceful and sustainable and balanced world, having ethical ambitions for our children and our grandchildren, we have, as well, hopes for ourselves.

NOTE
November, 2008

Commentators, media people, and especially politicians fell all over themselves proclaiming that the 2008 election had, "nothing at all to do with race." And yet every event, every speech and comment, every debate and appearance had race written all over it. Stephen Colbert, the brilliant satirist, hit it on the head when he asked a Republican operative, "How many euphemisms have you come up with so far so that you won't have to use the word 'Black?'" Everyone laughed good-naturedly.

It turns out that they and everyone else had plenty. When Hillary Clinton spoke of "hard-working Americans workers" everyone knew who she meant, but just in case they missed it she added, "white workers." All the talk of Senator Obama's exotic background, all the references to him as "unknown," "untested," a "stranger," or a "symbolic candidate," or "alien," a "wildcard," or an "elitist," which one Georgia congressman admitted meant "uppity," all the creepiness packed into the ominous "what do we really know about this man?" and all the questioning of his patriotism, the obsession with what went on in his church but not any of the other candidates' clergy or places of worship—all of it feeds a specific narrative: he's not a real American, he's not reliable, he's the quintessential mystery man. This is white code talk for "he's not one of us." The invisible race talk is about "blue collar," or "working class," or "mainstream," or "smalltown," or "hockey mom," by which we are meant to think "white." The discourse is all about race, us and them, understood by everyone in the U.S. even when the words African American, Black, or white are not spoken. Anyone who dared to point to these proxies and to call them what they are was immediately accused of being a racist, and, of course, of playing the ever-useful race card.

In this carnival atmosphere throbbed the omnipresent and not so clandestine campaign drumbeats that the Senator is a secret Muslim, that because his father was a Muslim, the son is forever a Muslim—assuming somehow that being a Muslim is bad; forget being married to the same woman for nineteen years with two remarkable daughters, a family constructed within Protestant churches. If you're Black, you cannot be a real Christian.

Then there is the lethal mix of gender, race and class. In the wake of Obama's primary win in the heartland (white) state of Iowa, the Clinton campaign escalated. Gloria Steinem's Op Ed in the New York *Times* on primary eve in New Hampshire, "Women are Never Front-Runners," laid down the gauntlet: asserting a hierarchy of oppression, claiming that it was women who were the most despised, vilified and unfairly treated by the media and by history—compared to the (supposed) deference to Black men. "Why," she wrote, "is the sex barrier not taken as seriously as the racial one?" Forget that this question obliterates Black and Latina and Asian American and Native American and Arab women. Forget that it ignores the intersections of race/gender/ethnicity and class. What might have been a complex analysis of the breakthroughs of discriminatory barriers became instead an assertion of superior victim status on the part of white, powerful women. Steinem's intervention made a dichotomy of race and gender, as if half of African Americans are not women, and half of women are not women of color. Intending to highlight the real river of misogynist venom unleashed against Clinton, it posed and perpetuated racial division rather than intersection and unity—which were the popularly recognized hallmarks of the Obama campaign.

And in New Hampshire, in the face of Hillary Clinton's express emotional response, she became aggrieved—as Princeton Professor Melissa Harris-Lacewell notes—"discernible, understandable and recognizable to these (white women) voters in her moment of anxiety and stress."

Hillary and Bill Clinton seized on this framing of feminism as a white women's concern with escalated race talk. Hillary proclaimed on Fox News, "I don't think any of us want to inject race or gender in this campaign." The Clintons resort to the "Southern strategy" in South Carolina and the border states, their dismissive references to Reverend Jesse Jackson's historic campaigns of 1984 and 1988 as purely race-based rather than a unique coalition that included white workers, farmers and professionals, and their flagrant appeal to white voters' identity as "workers" and "women"—give white people any reason to vote against him without saying he's Black—followed a too familiar and dismal road of racial discourse that appeals to white supremacy, fear and anxiety. In fact, the prolonged Democratic primary served to chart the Rovian path the Republicans would later hone and utilize in the general election against Obama. Combined with their brazen strategies of voter suppression, the defense of the color line remained at the core of the McCain/Palin media attack machine. Fabricated issues such as "character," values, and patriotism dominated their discourse, appeals were floated to white voters' racial resentments and fears, and the deliberate marketing of the Republican Party (our kids used to call them Repulsicans) as the bastion of white peoples' interests spread across the land.

On March 18, 2008, Barack Obama delivered a major speech in Philadelphia, Pennsylvania on race and identity designed to redeem his campaign momentum in the wake of relentless, replaying videos multiplying and racing around the media of Reverend Jeremiah Wright, Obama's pastor, a distinguished theologian and major intellectual of the United Church of Christ. Using a technique honed by the far right over thirty years, the media seized upon and de-contextualized a sentence from Wright's decades as pastor, replaying it endlessly as anti-white, unpatriotic, and—apparently most dangerous of all—delivered by an angry Black man. For three months, Wright's lifetime work was characterized as "ranting", "raving," "divisive" - and liberals joined the party, referring to him as that "loony preacher", spewing "bigoted and paranoid rantings." In reality Reverend Wright's sermons were no more incendiary than everyday conversations when white people aren't looking or listening, or than Dr. Martin Luther King's sermons a generation before, but the real King has been largely written out of history, replaced by a saint of racial unity—- this explains in part why the US Commission of Fine Arts demanded that a commissioned statue of King be redesigned to soften the edges and reverse the posture that they said was "too confrontational."

In contrast Senator McCain's active association with the Reverends Hagee, Parsley, and Robertson and the remarks by the Rev. Jerry Falwell following the terror attacks of 9/11 remained unmemorable and apparently unremarkable. Hagee's political preaching remained in the realm of the acceptable, including his assertions that AIDS is an incurable plague, God's curse against a disobedient nation, until an audio clip surfaced in which he preached that what Hitler did in the Holocaust was God's plan to drive Europe's Jews back to the land of Israel. Only then, did McCain disassociate himself from his insidious religious flock.

Senator Obama's masterful Philadelphia speech was called, "A More Perfect Union." It tapped a deep longing to be free from the racialized straightjacket of anxiety, fear, and separation. The comedian Jon Stewart got it right when he said, "He treated the

American public as if we were adults!" Obama managed to frame the discussion of racial justice in terms of broad American unity.

As soon as Barack Obama began winning primary battles, Michelle Obama, the Senator's brilliant, accomplished, strong, opinionated wife, mother of Malia and Sasha, became a target for the far right-wing haters. Brazen commentators mixed up a bitter brew of misogyny and racism, and sloshed it generously throughout the blogosphere: she's anti-American; she's a disgruntled and hectoring Black nationalist seething with unresolved racial rage; she's Reverend Wright but with estrogen and even more testosterone; she's a ball-breaker who wears the pants in the family. Maureen Dowd referred to the attacks as "Round Two of the sulfurous national game of 'Kill the witch.'"

Demonizing Michelle Obama began in earnest when, in February 2008, she said that because of her husband's campaign, hope was sweeping the nation, and that, "For the first time in my adult life, I am really proud of my country." Those 15 words were played over and over in a stuttering loop of outrage on right-wing cable, and stood as absolute proof that she (and he) came up fatally short in the "real American" department. In this narrative, uncritical pride-in-country is assumed to be a given, the default of all the good people; anyone who can separate affection for people, a land, an ideal from the actions of a state or a government is a *de facto* traitor. There's absolutely no room here for refusal or resistance, for criticism, skepticism, doubt, complexity, nuance, or even thought. Citizenship equals obedience. Right-wing gas-bag Bill O'Reilly's first reaction to Michelle Obama's proud-of-my-country comment was to say , "I don't want to go on a lynching party against Michelle Obama unless there's evidence, hard facts, that say this is how the woman really feels." Interestingly, almost no one remembers her joy in the expanding and participatory electorate she was seeing, in contrast to her relatively mild critique—after all the "first time" never stopped repeating; and almost no one recalls O'Reilly's racialized threat of personal violence—it conveniently disappeared from the media discourse without a trace.

Fox News called her "Obama's baby mama," derogatory slang for the unwed mother of a man's children, a clear racist stereotype, and later apologized. The *National Review* featured her on its cover as a scowling "Mrs. Grievance," and referred to Trinity United Church of Christ as a "new-segregationist ghetto of Afro-centric liberation theology." Always Black people who have to answer—an unstated assumption: John and Cindy McCain's church (like George Bush's and Ronald Reagan's) are models of "post-racial," integrated America. Take a look. It's like the famous question: "Why are all the Black kids sitting together in the cafeteria?" The white kids never explain why *they* sit together.

On the night Barack Obama claimed the nomination, he walked on stage with Michelle and she turned and gave him a pound or a dap, a playful and affectionate little fist bump. It flew around the internet like topsy—reviewed, debated, photoshopped, commented upon—until E.D. Hill called it a "terrorist fist jab" on Fox News and that proved to be one step too far—Hill was ridiculed and scorned and eventually apologized. Simultaneously, of course, it was seized upon and imitated by new waves of young admirers.

But Michelle Obama had become an established, larger-than-life target for racial and gender animus on conservative blogs. Where were the (white) feminists to defend her and decry the rot? And the liberals seemingly can't help themselves either—the *New York Times* ran a positive puff piece on her in which they noted that compared to her husband, "Michelle Obama's image is less mutable. She is a black American, a descendent of slaves and a product of Chicago's historically black South Side. She tends to burn hot where he banks cool, and that too can make her an inviting proxy for attack." So much racialized and racist craziness packed into three short sentences.

The liberal blog, the *Daily Kos*, ran a cartoon of Michell Obama, a caricature of a sexed-up Black woman in distress, her hands bound by thick rope hung over a tree branch, Klansmen advancing from the distance. The text read: "Fear Mongering and Race-Baiting/Our New Hi Tech/Southern Strategy." On June 21, 2008, the *New Yorker* magazine cover was a cartoon of Barack and Michelle Obama in the Oval Office, he in Muslim robes and turban, she in tight dress, angry face and overflowing Afro, bandoliers crisscrossing her chest and rifle at the ready, offering her husband the now famous fist jab as an American flag burns in the fireplace. Again, it was a slate upon which people would inscribe their own meanings, their own senses of humor and dread and despair and hope. Many read the cover as ironic and silly, a satirical reference to the right-wing mobilization of hate and fear. Others saw it as despicably racist. Historian Barbara Ransby picked up on one more attack on the legacy of the Black Freedom Movement: whether you think the cartoon works as satire or not, she argued, one possible reading is that to be a Black revolutionary or a radical woman in the tradition of, say, Angela Davis, is absolutely beyond the pale, outside any reasonable discourse, marginal to what any thinking person could imagine is possible.

Apparently there was something that the so-called "undecided voter" – that illusory white working class or white small-town woman or unemployed poor white male – should not tolerate about candidate Obama. Was it his opposition to the war against Iraq? His position on health care or tax cuts for the rich? Or was it a clinging to the illusion of a "superior" identity, the not-so-clandestine "Bradley effect?" Perhaps gender trumped race so that the caricatured, beer-drinking, macho, blue collar tough guy became eager, suddenly, to vote for a woman for President or Vice-President because he had become an ally of women's rights and gender equality.

Is it a racial matter that the African American candidate for President cannot ever be publicly angry, much like Jackie Robinson just sixty years earlier? When Robinson broke the baseball color line in 1948, it's worth remembering that while he was a great ballplayer, he was not considered the greatest athlete from the Negro leagues. But he had a certain temperament, a grace and calm, a capacity to absorb hate and to focus on what he wanted to accomplish in a whirlwind of insults, threats, humiliations, and ignorance. Jackie Robinson paid a heavy price, no doubt, but there he was, standing tall, for all to see.

It is worthy of note that the Obama campaign indeed offered a new paradigm, activated young people under thirty who have not heretofore exercised the franchise, and illustrated that substantial numbers of white people and Latino people and Asian-American people would indeed vote for a Black man. The very definition of "Obama's white problem" led to his intentional design and execution of a—as much as possible—non-racialized campaign. The Obama campaign itself quietly refered to "white validators"—those white politicians and campaign activists whose assignment was to reassure white voters. They were supporters of Senator Obama, and their unspoken message is, "Look!, it doesn't hurt; If I can do it, so can you!" Yet within the context of careful denial and the cultivation of the myth of being a post-racial society, the Obama campaign inspired and mined a deeper longing for humanizing racial unity—even racial unity based on justice. There is change in the air—evidence that the population has travelled some distance—as well as the familiar stench of a racist history.

There was much speculation in the media and among the commentators and bloviaters that Obama's candidacy represented the triumph of post-racial America and the end of Black politics. This fantasy got front-page play for months and months in the spring of 2008, and on August 10 the New York *Times* Magazine ran a lengthy cover story called, "Is Obama the End of Black Politics?" in which the author argued that the rising generation of post-civil rights Black politicians—epitomized by Obama and Corey Booker of Newark, for example, but not by their generational cohort Ray Nagin of New Orleans—is spelling the end of a uniquely Black politics, and the end as well of white supremacy. This, of course assumes, falsely we think, that Black politics equals electoral politics, and that a community's leaders are always elected leaders. Gary Younge wrote in the *Nation* magazine that, "The emergence of this cohort [of new African-American politicians] has filled the commentariat with joy—not just because of what they are: bright, polite and, where skin tone is concerned, mostly light—but because of what they are not. They have been hailed not just as a development in black American politics but as a repudiation of black American politics; not just as different from Jesse Jackson but the epitome of the anti-Jesse."

The end-of-white-supremacy narrative further assumes that the creation of a significant and more economically well-off group of African-Americans over the last half century represents the condition of African Americans in general. It's true that a new Black "middle class" has constituted itself, but it's also true that Black poverty ranges between 20–25 percent and is still twice that of whites. The class profile of African-Americans trends downward, and in the last 30 years, while the median income for African-American women rose dramatically, it fell for African-American men. Economic chaos and collapse will not be experienced equally across America, and the suffering will be disproportionately experienced by the poor, by women and children, and by people of color.

Another fiction in the end-of-race story is that racial injustice is exclusively a matter of overt apartheid and legal discrimination. Affirmative action for white people over many generations, as we argue in this book, has built up an enormous Black/white gap in terms of wealth, access, and cultural capital. Discrimination still exists, especially in employment, education, health care, and housing, but perhaps more insidious is the privilege that is stitched deep within the social fabric. But the fiction of a largely color-blind society and the relegation of racial discrimination to the deep, deep past mean that discussion of real racial disparities may be cast entirely off the table.

When Obama was asked during the heat of the primary battle with Senator Clinton who he thought Martin Luther King Jr. would support, he responded: Reverend King wouldn't support or endorse any of us, because he'd be in the streets building a movement for justice, and holding our feet to the fire. Exactly right.

Lyndon Johnson, the most effective politician of his generation, was never involved in the Black Freedom Movement, although he did pass far-reaching legislation in response to a robust and in many ways revolutionary movement in the streets. Franklin Delano Roosevelt was not a labor leader, and yet he presided over critical social and pro-labor legislation in a time of radical labor mobilization in shops and factories across the land. And Abraham Lincoln was not a member of an abolitionist political party, but reality forced upon him the freeing of an enslaved people. Each of these three responded to grassroots movements for social justice on the ground.

And it's to movements on the ground that we must turn as we think beyond this election or the next, and consider the problems and possibilities of building a future of peace and love and harmony. We may not be able to will a movement into being, but neither can we sit idly waiting for a social movement to spring full grown, as from the head of Zeus. We have to agitate for democracy and egalitarianism, press harder for human rights, learn to build a new society through our collective self-transformations and our limited everyday struggles. We must seek ways to live sustainably, to stop the addiction to consumption and development and military power, to become real actors and authentic subjects in our own history.

At the turn of the last century Eugene Debs told a group of workers in Chicago, "I would not lead you into the Promised Land if I could, because if I could lead you in, someone else would lead you out." We must figure out how to become our own leaders, how to become the people we've been waiting for.

***

AN ECLECTIC READER

Here are a few pieces that we refer to in our own race course and our own learning. Neither a bibliography nor a page of references, neither neat nor linear nor in any sense complete, we will call it simply "An Eclectic Reader":

Al-Amin, I. J. (1994). *Revolution by the Book: (The Rap Is Live)*. Beltsville, MD: Writers' Inc.

Alexander, E. (2005). *American Sublime*. St. Paul, MN: Graywolf Press.

— (2004). *The Black Interior: Essays by Elizabeth Alexander*. St. Paul, MN: Graywolf Press.

Alkalimait, A. (Ed.). (1990). *Perspectives on Black Liberation and Social Revolution*. Chicago: Twenty-first Century Books and Publications.

Allen, J., Als, H., Lewis, J., & Litwack, L. F. (2004). *Without Sanctuary: Lynching Photography in America*. Santa Fe, NM: Twin Palms Publishers.

Anderson, Carol. 2003. *Eyes Off the Prize: The United Nations and the African American Struggle for Human Rights, 1944-1955*. Cambridge, UK: Cambridge University Press.

Arsenault, R. (2006). *Freedom Riders: 1961 and the Struggle for Racial Justice*. New York: Oxford University Press.

Avey, E. (1906). *The Capture and Execution of John Brown*. New York: Thomas Y. Crowell.

Baldwin, J. (1998). *Baldwin: Collected Essays*. New York: The Library of America.

— (1962). *The Fire Next Time*. New York: The Modern Library.

— (1952). *Go Tell It on the Mountain*. New York: Dial Press.

Banks, R. (1998). *Cloudsplitter*. New York: HarperCollins.

Baraka, I. A. (1969). *Raise Race Rays Raze: Essays since 1965*. New York: Vintage Books.

Bates, D. (1986). *The Long Shadow of Little Rock.* Fayetteville, AR: University of Arkansas Press.

Bell, D. (1992). *Faces at the Bottom of the Well: The Permanence of Racism.* New York: Basic Books.

Bell, D. (2004). *Silent Covenants: Brown v. Board of Education and the Unfulfilled Hopes for Racial Reform.* New York: Oxford University Press.

— (2007). "Shadow Boxing with the Apocalypse." Youth Law Center Newsletter.

Bensman, D. (2000). *Central Park East and Its Graduates: "Learning by Heart."* New York: Teachers College Press.

Berger, J. (2007). *Hold Everything Dear: Dispatches on Survival and Resistance.* New York: Pantheon Books.

Berger, M. (1999). *White Lies: Race and the Myths of Whiteness.* New York: Farrar, Strauss and Giroux.

Bhaba, H., & Mitchell, W. J. T. (Eds.). (2005). *Edward Said: Continuing the Conversation.* Chicago: The University of Chicago Press.

Boggs, J., & Boggs, G. L. (1974). *Revolution and Evolution in the Twentieth Century.* New York: Monthly Review Press.

— (1963). *The American Revolution: Pages from a Negro Worker's Notebook.* New York: Monthly Review Press.

— (1970). *Racism and the Class Struggle: Further Pages from a Black Worker's Notebook.* New York: Monthly Review Press.

Branch, T. (2006). *At Canaan's Edge: America in the King Years 1965-68.* New York: Simon & Schuster.

—. (1998). *Pillar of Fire: America in the King Years 1963-65.* New York: Simon & Schuster.

—. (1988). *Parting the Waters: America in the King Years 1954-63.* New York: Simon & Schuster.

Brooks, G. (1994). *Blacks.* Chicago: Third World Press.

Brown, C. S. (2002). *Refusing Racism: White Allies and the Struggle for Civil Rights.* New York: Teachers College Press.

Brown, E. (2002). *The Condemnation of Little B.* Boston: Beacon Press.

Brown, J. F. (1998). *Betty Shabazz: A Sisterfriend's Tribute in Words and Pictures.* New York: Simon & Schuster.

Brown, R. (2000). *Half a Heart.* New York: Farrar, Straus and Giroux.

Carmichael, S. (1965). *Stokely Speaks: Black Power Back to Pan-Africanism.* New York: Vintage Books.

Carmichael, S., & Hamilton, C. V. (1967). *Black Power: The Politics of Liberation in America.* New York: Vintage Books.

Carmichael, S., & Thelwell, E. M. (2003). *Ready for Revolution: The Life and Struggles of Stokely Carmichael (Kwame Toure).* New York: Scribner.

Cary, L. (2005). *Free! Great Escapes from Slavery on the Underground Railroad.* Philadelphia: New City Community Press.

Casella, R. (2001). *"Being Down": Challenging Violence in Urban School.* New York: Teachers College Press.

Chang, J., & Herc, D. J. K. (2005). *Can't Stop Won't Stop: A History of the Hip-Hop Generation.* New York: St. Martin's Press.

Chinweizu. (1975). *The West and the Rest of Us: White Predators, Black Slavers and the African Elite.* New York: Vintage Books.

Clark, K. B. (1965). *Dark Ghetto: Dilemmas of Social Power.* New York: Harper & Row.

Clark, R. X. (1973). *The Brothers of Attica.* New York: Links Books.

Cleage, P. (1987). *Deals with the Devil: And Other Reasons to Riot.* New York: Ballantine Books.

Cole, D. (1999). *No Equal Justice: Race and Class in the Criminal Justice System.* New York: The New Press.

Conley, D. (2000). *Honky*. New York: Vintage Books.

Coval, K. (2005). *Slingshots (A Hip-Hop Poetica)*. Channahon, IL: EM Press.

Davis, A. Y. (2005). *Abolition Democracy: Beyond Empire, Prisons, and Torture*. New York: Seven Stories Press.

—. (2003). *Are Prisons Obsolete?* New York: Seven Stories Press.

—. (1984). *Women, Culture, & Politics*. New York: Vintage Books.

—. (1981). *Women, Race & Class*. New York: Vintage Books.

Dellums, R. V., & Halterman, H. L. (2000). *Lying Down with the Lions: A Public Life from the Streets of Oakland to the Halls of Power*. Boston: Beacon Press.

Delpit, L. (1995). *Other People's Children: Cultural Conflict in the Classroom*. New York: The New Press.

—, & Dowdy, J. K. (2002). *The Skin That We Speak: Thoughts on Language and Culture in the Classroom*. New York: The New Press.

Douglass, F. (1945). *Frederick Douglass: Selections from His Writings* (F. S. Foner, Ed.). New York: International Publishers.

Drizin, Steven A, and Richard A Leo. 2004. *"The Problem of False Confessions in the Post-DNA World."* North Carolina Law Review. 82 (3): 891-1007.

Duberman, M. B. (1988). *Paul Robeson*. New York: Alfred A. Knopf.

Du Bois, W. E. B. (1935). *Black Reconstruction in America 1860-1880*. New York: The Free Press.

— (2002). *Du Bois on Education* (E. F. Provenzo, Jr., Ed.). Walnut Creek, CA: AltaMira Press.

—. (1971). *A W. E. B. Du Bois Reader* (A. G. Paschal, Ed.). New York: Collier Books.

—. (1968). *Du Bois: Writings*. New York: The Library of America.

—. (1909). *John Brown*. New York: International Publishers.

—. (1889). *The Philadelphia Negro: A Social Study*. New York: Schocken Books. Elevand, M. (Ed.). (2007). *The Spoken Word Revolution: Redux*. Naperville, IL: Sourcebooks MediaFusion.

— (Ed.). (2003). *The Spoken Word Revolution: Slam, Hip Hop & the Poetry of a New Generation*. Naperville, IL: Sourcebooks MediaFusion.

Ellison, R. (1947). *Invisible Man*. New York: Vintage International.

Espada, M., & Perez-Bustillo, C. (1990). *Rebellion Is the Circle of a Lover's Hands = Rebelión Es El Giro De Manos Del Amante*. Willimantic, CT: Curbstone Press.

Fine, M., Weis, L., Powell, L. C., & Wong, L. M. (1997). *Off-White: Readings on Race, Power and Society*. New York: Routledge.

Finnegan, W. (1999). *Cold New World: Growing Up in a Harder Country*. New York: Random House.

Forman, J. (1994). *High Tide of Black Resistance' and Other Political and Literary Writings*. Seattle, WA: Open Hand Publishing.

Fosl, C. (2002). *Subversive Southerner: Anne Braden and the Struggle for Racial Justice in the Cold War South*. New York: Palgrave Macmillan.

Foster, M. (1997). *Black Teachers on Teaching*. New York: The New Press.

Foster, W. Z. (1954). *The Negro People in American History*. New York: International Publishers.

Fraser, S. (Ed.). (1995). *The Bell Curve Wars: Race, Intelligence, and the Future of America*. New York: Basic Books.

Fried, A. (1978). *John Brown's Journey: Notes and Reflections on His America and Mine*. Garden City, NY: Anchor Press/Doubleday.

Galdean, E. (2006). *Voices of Time*. New York: Metropolitan Books.

Giovanni, N. (1970). *Black Feeling, Black Talk, Black Judgement*. New York: William Morrow & Company.

Gitlin, T. and Hollander, N. (1970) *Uptown: Poor Whites in Chicago.* New York: Harper and Row.

Gooding-Williams, R. (2006). *Look, a Negro! Philosophical Essays on Race, Culture and Politics.* New York: Routledge.

Greenlee, S. (1969). *The Spook Who Sat by the Door.* Detroit, MI: Wayne State University Press.

Guskin, J., & Wilson, D. L. (2007). *The Politics of Immigration: Questions and Answers.* New York: Monthly Review Press.

Hacker, A. (1992). *Two Nations: Black and White, Separate, Hostile, Unequal.* New York: Charles Scribner's Sons.

Haley, A. (1974). *Roots.* Garden City, NY: Doubleday & Company.

— (1965). *The Autobiography of Malcolm X.* New York: Ballantine Books.

Hall, H. (2006). *Mentoring Young Men of Color: Meeting the Needs of African American and Latino Students.* Lanham, MD: Rowman & Littlefield Education.

Hampton, H., & Fayer, S. (1990). *Voices of Freedom: An Oral History of the Civil Rights Movement from the 1950s Through the 1980s.* New York: Bantam Books.

Hancock, L. (2003). *Wolf Pack: The Press and the Central Park Jogger.* Columbia Journalism Review, at http://cjarchives.org/issues/2003/i/rapist-hancock.

Haskins, J. (1969). *Diary of a Harlem Schoolteacher.* Briarcliff Manor, NY: Scarborough Books.

Haywood, H. (1976). *Negro Liberation.* Chicago: Liberator Press.

He, M. F. (2003). *A River Forever Flowing: Cross-cultural Lives and Identities in the Multicultural Landscape.* Greenwich, CT: Information Age Publishing.

Henry, A. (1998). *Taking Back Control: African Canadian Women Teachers' Lives and Practice.* Albany, NY: State University of New York Press.

Hilliard, A. G. (1982). *Strengths: African-American Children and Families*. New York: The City College Workshop Center.

Holt, L. (1965). *An Act of Conscience*. Boston: Beacon Press

Holt, T. C. (2000). *The Problem of Race in the 21st Century*. Cambridge: MA: Harvard University Press.

Hooker, J. R. (1967). *Black Revolutionary: George Padmore's Path from Communism to Pan-Africanism*. New York: Praeger Publishers.

hooks, b. (2003). *Teaching Community: A Pedagogy of Hope*. New York: Routledge.

—. (2000). *Where We Stand: Class Matters*. New York: Routledge.

—. (1995). *Art on My Mind: Visual Politics*. New York: The New Press.

—. (1992). *Black Looks: Race and Representation*. Boston: South End Press.

Hooper, L. (2007). *Art of Work: The Art and Life of Haki R. Madhubuti*. Chicago: Third World Press.

Hurston, Z. N. (1937). *Their Eyes Were Watching God*. Urbana, Il: University of Illinois Press.

Jackson, G. (1970). *Soledad Brother: The Prison Letters of George Jackson*. New York: Bantam Books.

Jackson, T. F. (2007). *From Civil Rights to Human Rights: Martin Luther King, Jr., and the Struggle for Economic Justice*. Philadelphia: University of Pennsylvania Press.

James, J. (1996). *Resisting State Violence: Radicalism, Gender, and Race in U.S. culture*. Minneapolis, MN: University of Minnesota Press.

Jelloun, T. B. (1999). *Racism Explained to My Daughter*. New York: The New Press.

Jennings, R. (2006). *Malcolm X and the Poetics of Haki Madhubuti*. Jefferson, NC: McFarland & Company.

Johnson, J. W. (1927). *The Autobiography of an Ex-Coloured Man*. New York: Vintage Books.

Jones, L. (1964). *Dutchman and The Slave: Two Plays by LeRoi Jones.* New York: William Morrow and Company.

Jordan, J. (2005). *Directed by Desire: The Collected Poems of June Jordan* (J. H. Levi & S. Miles, Eds.). Port Townsend, WA: Copper Canyon Press.

Jordan, W. D. (1974). *The White Man's Burden: Historical Origins of Racism in the United States.* New York: Oxford University Press.

Kelley, R. D. G. (2002). *Freedom Dreams: The Black Radical Imagination.* Boston: Beacon Books.

Kincaid, J. (1978). *At the Bottom of the River.* New York: Penguin.

Kohl, H. (2005). *She Would Not Be Moved: How We Tell the Story of Rosa Parks and the Montgomery Bus Boycott.* New York: The New Press.

Kunjufu, J. (1985). *Countering the Conspiracy to Destroy Black Boys.* Chicago: African-American Images.

Ladson-Billings, G. (2005). *Beyond the Big House: African American Educators on Teacher Education.* New York: Teachers College Press.

— (1994). *The Dreamkeepers: Successful Teachers of African-American Children.* San Francisco: Jossey-Bass.

Landsman, J. (2001). *A White Teacher Talks About Race.* Lanham, MD: The Scarecrow Press.

Lanker, B. (1989). *I Dream a World: Portraits of Black Women Who Changed America.* New York: Stewart, Tabori & Chang.

LeBlanc, A. N. (2003). *Random Family: Love, Drugs, Trouble and Coming of Age in the Bronx.* New York: Scribner.

Lebowitz, M. A. (2006). *Build it Now: Socialism for the Twenty-first Century.* New York: Monthly Review Press.

Lee, D. L. (1971). *Directionscore: Selected and New Poems.* Detroit, MI: Broadside Press.

Lewis, A. (2003). *Race in the Schoolyard: Negotiating the Color Line in Classrooms and Communities.* Piscataway, NJ: Rutgers University Press.

Lewis, M. C. (1988). *Herstory: Black Female Rites of Passage.* Chicago: African-American Images.

Liebow, E. (1967). *Tally's Corner: A Study of Negro Streetcorner Men.* Boston: Little, Brown and Company.

Lorde, A. (1984). *Sister Outsider: Essays and Speeches.* Berkeley, CA: Crossing Press.

— (1982). *Zami: A New Spelling of My Name.* Freedom, CA: The Crossing Press.

Lowe, J. (1995). *Conversations with Ernest Gaines.* Jackson, MS: University of Mississippi Press.

Lynch, A. (1993). *Nightmare Overhanging Darkly: Essays on Black Culture and Resistance.* Chicago: Third World Press.

MacLeod, J. (1995). *Ain't No Makin' it: Aspirations and Attainment in a Low-Income Neighborhood.* Boulder, CO: Westview Press.

Madhubuti, H. R. (2005). *YellowBlack: The First Twenty-one Years of a Poet's Life.* Chicago: Third World Press.

—. (1996). *Groundwork: New and Selected Poems of Don L. Lee / Haki R. Madhubuti from 1966-1996.* Chicago: Third World Press.

Malouf, D. (1993). *Remembering Babylon.* New York: Pantheon Books.

Mansbach, A. (2005). *Angry Black White Boy.* New York: Three Rivers Press.

Marable, M. (2002). *The Great Wells of Democracy: The Meaning of Race in American life.* New York: Basic Books.

Marable, M. (1983). *How Capitalism Underdeveloped Black America.* Boston: South End Press.

Markowitz, G., & Rosner, D. (1996). *Children, Race, and Power: Kenneth and Mamie Clark's Northside Center.* Charlottesville, VA: University Press of Virginia.

McLaughlin, M. W., Irby, M. A., & Langman, J. (1994). *Urban Sanctuaries:*

Neighborhood Organizations in the Lives and Futures of Inner-City Youth. San Francisco: Jossey-Bass.

Mead, M., & Baldwin, J. (1971). *A Rap on Race.* New York: Dell Publishing.

Medoff, P., & Sklar, H. (1994). *Streets of Hope: The Rise and Fall of an Urban Neighborhood.* Boston: South End Press.

Meier, D. (1995). *The Power of Their Ideas: Lessons for America from A Small School in Harlem.* Boston: Beacon Press.

Melendez, M. (2003). *We Took the Streets: Fighting for Latino Rights with the Young Lords.* New York: St. Martin's Press.

Michie, G. (1999). *Holler If You Hear Me: The Education of a Teacher and His Students.* New York: Teachers College Press.

Mills, C. M. (1997). *The Racial Contract.* Ithaca, NY: Cornell University Press.

Minter, W. Honey, G., and Cobb, Jr. C (2008). *No Easy Victories.* New York. Africa World Press.

Moody, A. (1968). *Coming of Age in Mississippi.* New York: Dell Publishing.

Moore, M. (2001). *Stupid White Men ... and Other Sorry Excuses for the State of the Nation.* New York: ReganBooks.

Morrison, T. (1992). *Playing in the Dark: Whiteness and the Literary Imagination.* Cambridge, MA: Harvard University Press.

Mull, M., & Rucker, A. (1985). *The History of White People in America.* New York: Perigree Books.

Muller, L., & Blueprint Collective (Ed.). (1995). *June Jordan's Poetry for the People: A Revolutionary Blueprint.* New York: Routledge.

Muwakkil, S. et. al. (2007). *Harold! Photographs from the Harold Washington Years.*

National Advisory Commission on Civil Disorders. (1968). *The Kerner Report.* New York: Bantam Books.

National Park Service. (1973). *John Brown's Raid.* Washington, D.C.: U.S. Department of the Interior.

Nelson, T. (1962). *People with Strength: The Story of Monroe, N.C.* New York: People to Aid the Monroe Defendants.

Nudelman, F. (2004). *John Brown's Body: Slavery, Violence, and the Culture of War.* Chapel Hill, NC: The University of North Carolina Press.

Orfield, G. (1983). *Public School Desegregation in the United States, 1968-1980.* Washington, DC: Joint Center for Political Studies.

Paley, V. G. (1979). *White Teacher.* Cambridge, MA: Harvard University Press.

Parks, R., & Haskins, J. (1992). *Rosa Parks: My Story.* New York: Dial Books.

Parsons, L. (2004). *Freedom, Equality, and Solidarity: Writings and Speeches, 1878-1937* (G. Ahrens, Ed.). Chicago: Charles H. Kerr.

Payne, C. M. (2007). *I've Got the Light of Freedom: The Organizing Tradition and the Mississippi Freedom Struggle.* Berkeley, CA: University of California Press.

Perlstein, D. H. (2004). *Justice, Justice: School Politics and the Eclipse of Liberalism.* New York: Peter Lang.

Perry, M. (2000). *Walking the Color Line: The Art and Practice of Anti-Racist Teaching.* New York: Teachers College Press.

Perry, T., Steele, C., & Hilliard III, A. (2003). *Young, Gifted, and Black.* Boston: Beacon Press.

Peshkin, A. (1991). *The Color of Strangers, the Color of Friends: The Play of Ethnicity in School and Community.* Chicago: The University of Chicago Press.

Polakow, V. (Ed.). (2000). *The Public Assault on America's Children: Poverty, Violence, and Juvenile Injustice.* New York: Teachers College Press.

Ransby, B. (2003). *Ella Baker and the Black Freedom Movement: A Radical Democratic Vision.* Chapel Hill, NC: The University of North Carolina Press.

Rathbone, C. (1998). *On the Outside Looking In: A year in an Inner-City High School.* New York: Atlantic Monthly Press.

Rattansi, A. (2007). *Racism: A Very Short Introduction.* Oxford, England: Oxford University Press.

Reporting Civil Rights part one: American Journalism 1941-1963. (2003). New York: The Library of America.

Reporting Civil Rights Part Two: American journalism 1963-1973. (2003). New York: The Library of America.

Richie, B. E. (1996). *Compelled to Crime: The Gender Entrapment of Battered Black Women.* New York: Routledge.

Robinson, C. C. (2007). *From the Classroom to the Corner: Female Dropouts' Reflections on Their School Years.* New York: Peter Lang.

Robinson, R. (2001). *The Debt: What America Owes to Blacks.* New York: Plume.

Roderick, T. (2001). *A School of Our Own: Parents, Power, and Community at the East Harlem Block Schools.* New York: Teachers College Press.

Roediger, D. R. (Ed.). (1998). *Black on White: Black Writers on What It Means to Be White.* New York: Schocken Books.

— (1991). *The Wages of Whiteness: Race and the Making of the American Working Class.* London: Verso.

Rooney, J. (1995). *Organizing the South Bronx.* Albany, NY: State University of New York Press.

Rothenberg, P. S. (1992). *Race, Class, and Gender in the United States: An Integrated Study* (2nd ed.). New York: St. Martin's Press.

Ruchames, L. (1969). *John Brown: The Making of a Revolutionary.* New York: Grosset & Dunlap.

Said, E. W. (1979). *Orientalism.* New York: Vintage Books.

Schaffner, L. (2006). *Girls in Trouble with the Law.* New Brunswick: Rutgers University Press.

Senna, D. (1998). *Caucasia.* New York: Riverhead Books.

Shakur, A. (1987). *Assata: An Autobiography.* Westport, CT: Lawrence Hill & Company.

Shames, S. (2006). *The Black Panthers.* New York: Aperture Foundation.

Shields, D. (1999). *Black Planet: Facing Race During an NBA Season.* Lincoln, NE: University of Nebraska Press.

Silberman, C. E. (1970). *Crisis in the Classroom: The Remaking of American Education.* New York: Random House.

Singleton, G. E., & Linton, C. (2006). *Courageous Conversations About Race: A Field Guide for Achieving Equity in Schools.* Thousand Oaks, CA: Corwin Press.

Skelton, A., & Batley, M. (2006). *Charting Progress, Mapping the Future: Restorative Justice in South Africa.* Pretoria, South Africa: Restorative Justice Centre.

Smead, H. (1986). *Blood Justice: The Lynching of Mack Charles Parker.* New York: Oxford University Press.

Smith, A. D. (1993). *Fires in the Mirror: Crown Heights, Brooklyn and Other Identities.* New York: Anchor Books.

Smith, M. M. (2006). *How Race is Made: Slavery, Segregation, and the Senses.* Chapel Hill, NC: The University of North Carolina Press.

Sontag, S. (2007). *At the Same Time: Essays and Speeches.* Picador.

Spofford, T. (1988). *Lynch Street: The May 1970 Slayings at Jackson State College.* Kent, OH: The Kent State University Press.

Sutherland, E. (Ed.). (1965). *Letters from Mississippi.* New York: Signet Books.

Tatum, B. (2007). *Can We Talk About Race? And Other Conversations in an Era of School Resegregation.* Boston: Beacon Press.

Taulbert, C. L. (1989). *Once Upon a Time When We Were Colored.* Tulsa, OK: Council Oaks Books.

Taylor, C. (Ed.). (1973). *Vietnam and Black America: An Anthology of Protest and Resistance.* Garden City, NY: Anchor Books.

Troutt, D. D. (2007). *After the Storm: Black Intellectuals Explore the Meaning of Hurricane Katrina.* New York: The New Press.

Turner, L., & Alan, J. (1986). *Frantz Fanon, Soweto and American Black Thought.* Chicago: News and Letters.

Valenzuela, A. (1999). *Subtractive Schooling: U.S.-Mexican Youth and the Politics of Caring.* Albany, NY: State University of New York Press.

Watkins, W. H. (2001). *The White Architects of Black Education: Ideology and Power in America, 1865-1954.* New York: Teachers College Press.

—, Lewis, J. H., & Chou, V. (Eds.). (2001). *Race and Education: The Roles of History and Society in Educating African American Students.* Boston: Allyn & Bacon.

Weinberg, E. (1981). *Portrait of a People: A Personal Photographic Record of the South African Liberation Struggle.* London: International Defence and Aid Fund for Southern Africa.

Weis, L., & Fine, M. (Eds.). (2000). *Construction Sites: Excavating Race, Class, and Gender Among Urban Youth.* New York: Teachers College Press.

West, C. (2004). *Democracy Matters: Winning the Fight Against Imperialism.* New York: The Penguin Press.

— (1994). *Race Matters.* New York: Vintage Books.

Whittemore, K., & Marzorati, G. (1993). *Voices in Black and White: Writitngs on Race in America from Harper's Magazine.* New York: Franklin Square Press.

Wieder, A. (2003). *Voices from the Cape Town Classrooms: Oral Histories of Teachers Who Fought Apartheid.* New York: Peter Lang.

Wilkinson, J. H., III. (1979). *From Brown to Bakke: The Supreme Court and School Integration, 1954-1978.* New York: Oxford University Press.

Williams, G. H. (1996). *Life on the Color Line: The True Story of a White Boy Who Discovered He Was Black.* New York: Plume.

Williams, J. F., & Harris, C. F. (1970). *Amistad 1: Writings on Black History and Culture.* New York: Vintage Books.

Williams, P. J. (1991). *The Alchemy of Race and Rights: Diary of a Law Professor.* Cambridge, MA: Harvard University Press.

Williams, T., & Kornblum, W. (1994). *The Uptown Kids: Struggle and Hope in the Projects.* New York: Grosset/Putnam.

Wimsatt, W. U. (1994). *Bomb the Suburbs: Graffiti, Race, Freight-hopping, and the Search for Hip-Hop's Moral Center.* Chicago: The Subway and Elevated Press of Chicago.

Winfield, A. G. (2007). *Eugenics and Education in America: Institutionalized Racism and the Implications of History, Ideology, and Memory.* New York: Peter Lang.

Wise, T. (2005). *White Like Me: Reflections on Race from a Privileged Son.* Brooklyn, NY: Soft Skull Press.

Wolf, L. C. (1978). *Reflections on Identity and Ethnicity in a Pluralist Society.* New York: Bank Street College of Education Publications.

Wright, R. (1937). *Black Boy.* New York: Harper & Row.

X, M. (1989). *Malcolm X: The Last Speeches* (B. Perry, Ed.). New York: Pathfinder Press.

—. (1970). *Malcolm X on Afro-American History.* New York: Pathfinder Press.

Yates, M. D. (2007). *More Unequal: Aspects of Class in the United States.* New York: Monthly Review Press.

Yeshitela, O. (1983). *Stolen Black Labor: The Political Economy of Domestic Colonialism.* Oakland, CA: Burning Spear Publications.

Zimring, F. E. (1998). *American Youth Violence.* New York, NY: Oxford University Press.

Zinn, H. (1964). *Student Nonviolent Coordinating Committee: The New Abolitionists.* Boston: Beacon Press.

ACKNOWLEDGMENTS

Age is a curious thing, paradoxical and contradictory—time for us seems to be both accelerating and slowing down, simultaneously elastic and finite: things reverse themselves unexpectedly; we suddenly plunge ahead; we surprisingly hold on. We wake up each day to another paradox: we've never been older than we are at this exact moment, *and* we'll never be this young again.

One thing is abundantly clear: We are encircled in a vast community without which we would be nothing.

Thanks to Zayd Dohrn, Malik Dohrn, Chesa Boudin, and Rachel DeWoskin for taking the time to read and comment on the manuscript, for editorial assistance and incisive criticism. Mostly, thanks for being our inspiration and our hope, at once our sail and our anchor.

Thanks to Rick Ayers, James Bell, Martha Biondi, Rick Feldman, Paige James, Prexy Nesbitt, Barbara Ransby, and Eleanor Stein for reading (Eleanor twice!) early versions and helping us to think and re-think, shape and re-shape this work. None of it was easy and we recognize the loving effort undertaken in already busy and productive lives. We note as well the value of fighting through complex and consequential ideas. (Thanks, Barb!) What remains in these pages is, of course, our responsibility alone.

Thanks to Mona Khalidi and Rashid Khalidi, Jeff Jones and Eleanor Stein, Harriett Beinfield and Efrem Korngold—extended family for decades now—for helping organize the physical and intellectual and emotional space for us to write, to think, to act; and to Florence Garcia, who helped us care for our parents for eight years, and in the process became family.

Thanks to Isabel Nunez for her invaluable assistance, to her sister Irma Nunez for wondrous copyediting, to Toni Curtis for keeping us on course, and to Diana Ruiz, as always, for her insights and assistance, her steady effort, and her vital presence along the way.

And, finally, thanks to the good and wise people at Third World Press: Haki Madhubuti for convincing us it could be done, Bennett Johnson for brilliant storytelling, energy, and guidance, Solomohn Ennis for taking it up and carrying it on, Relana Johnson for the cover design, and Cathy Compton for marketing and publicity.